THE
HAGLEY WOOD
MURDER

THE HAGLEY WOOD MURDER

NAZI SPIES AND WITCHCRAFT IN WARTIME BRITAIN

M. J. TROW

PEN & SWORD
TRUE CRIME

First published in Great Britain in 2023 by
Pen & Sword True Crime
An imprint of
Pen & Sword Books Ltd
Yorkshire - Philadelphia

Copyright © M.J. Trow, 2023

ISBN 978 1 39906 645 7

The right of M. J. Trow to be identified as the Author of this work has been asserted by him in accordance with the Copyright, Designs and Patents Act 1988.

A CIP catalogue record for this book is available from the British Library.

All rights reserved. No part of this book may be reproduced or transmitted in any form or by any means, electronic or mechanical, including photocopying, recording or by any information storage and retrieval system, without permission from the Publisher in writing.

Typeset in INDIA by IMPEC eSolutions
Printed and bound in England by CPI (UK) Ltd.

Pen & Sword Books Ltd. incorporates the Imprints of Pen & Sword Archaeology, Atlas, Aviation, Battleground, Discovery, Family History, History, Maritime, Military, Naval, Politics, Railways, Select, Transport, True Crime, Fiction, Frontline Books, Leo Cooper, Praetorian Press, Seaforth Publishing, Wharncliffe and White Owl.

For a complete list of Pen & Sword titles please contact

PEN & SWORD BOOKS LIMITED
47 Church Street, Barnsley, South Yorkshire, S70 2AS, England
E-mail: enquiries@pen-and-sword.co.uk
Website: www.pen-and-sword.co.uk

or

PEN AND SWORD BOOKS
1950 Lawrence Rd, Havertown, PA 19083, USA
E-mail: uspen-and-sword@casematepublishers.com
Website: www.penandswordbooks.com

Contents

Acknowledgements vi
Introduction vii

Chapter 1   The Wych Elm   1
Chapter 2   There Was a War On   7
Chapter 3   The Thin Blue Line   16
Chapter 4   Old Bones   24
Chapter 5   The Victim From Another World   34
Chapter 6   The Writing on the Wall   48
Chapter 7   All the Bellas in the World   61
Chapter 8   Bloody Foreigners   68
Chapter 9   The Children of the Moon   77
Chapter 10   Anna and the Flying Dutchman   86
Chapter 11   The Spies Who Came in From the Cold   94
Chapter 12   *Aktion Hess*   106
Chapter 13   'If I were a Blackbird' and the sillier stories   120
Chapter 14   Lord of the Gallows   134
Chapter 15   The Shadow of Meon Hill   147
Chapter 16   The Fantasy Historian   155
Chapter 17   Case Closed   162
Chapter 18   The Raggedy Rawney   168
Chapter 19   The Last Days of Bella   180

Bibliography 187
Notes 190
Index 193

Acknowledgements

No book is ever written without help from other people and this is perhaps especially true of this one. I had been fascinated by this case ever since picking up a copy of Donald McCormick's *Murder By Witchcraft* in a second-hand bookshop many years ago. The case is tortuous but my researches were made simpler by being able to go to the right people to find out the little bits of nitty gritty to fill in the gaps. So, my thanks go to David Maidment, who knows everything there is to know about trains and to Helen McArthur, Community Hub Officer of the Central Library, Middlesbrough who had the very book I needed on her shelves. The staff at the Worcester Archive were helpful and interested and my thanks also go to them.

I would like to say a special thank you to Heather Williams for giving me the chance to write the first full length book on the Hagley Wood case. I would, as always, like to thank my editor Gaynor Haliday, for her sensitive work on my words and for her very positive feedback.

I always thank my wife, Carol, for all the work she does when a book is in production, but she needs special thanks this time. She has been talking this case over with me for over fifty years and knows it as well as anyone. She helped me with note taking at the Archive, with the complexities of wartime underwear and even knitted a section of a jumper, to see how it would look in the real world. So, once again, I say it; thank you.

M.J. Trow
Vectis
Date

Introduction

Some years ago, I attended a crime writers' conference at which a panel of experts debated the idea that 'murder was the only game in town'. Other crimes, like fraud, larceny, blackmail, even grisly ones like grievous bodily harm and rape, do not have the same impact on society.

Murder is also one of the very few human activities that can horrify and delight us. Crime fiction promises delight; true crime gives us horror. We all curl up with a good book or snuggle down in front of the telly and watch Hercule Poirot, Jane Marple, Sherlock Homes and a host of lesser-known fictional detectives go through their paces. We love nothing better than seeing them arrive at a satisfying conclusion and say to our nearest and dearest – 'Of course!' with a click of our fingers. Or, 'I knew it was him by page five/after the second ad break.' or, more honestly, 'Well, I didn't see that coming.'

But true crime is not like that. Some people are repelled by it. They don't read books like this one, or watch TV documentaries because they find them too upsetting. Other people cannot actually tell the difference between crime fiction and crime fact.

And that has been the problem I encountered in writing *The Hagley Wood Murder: Nazi Spies and Witchcraft in Wartime Britain*. I expected a case, cold, it is true, because of the passage of the years, but one in which the facts are spelt out and we can draw various conclusions. What I found instead was a confused mish-mash of 'faction', what one historian has called 'mythistory', in which ever more farcical and far-fetched ideas are allowed to proliferate because someone, somewhere, did not do their job properly.

As you will read in the pages ahead, four teenaged boys found human remains inside a wych elm in Hagley Wood, Worcestershire in April 1943. There was a war on which meant that newsprint was in limited supply and the details which today would be all over the media, were dealt with scantily. Journalists, however, are journalists, who know what sells papers and they 'juiced up' the story of the wych elm to grip their readers. They indulged, as the media still does, in fictions because they had so few facts to go on. Today, because of that, we cannot be sure which of the four boys actually found the body. Nor, because it was destroyed by the police to remove the remains in the first place, do we know exactly where the tree was. Nothing daunted, newspapers photographed another tree labelled 'Body Found Here', the first of many fictions that appear.

There was an inquest, as there had to be, in Stourbridge, but there are no newspaper accounts of that inquest, the first and most important part of any murder enquiry. Worcestershire CID then began their enquiries. The effect of the war on constabularies was huge. Hagley Wood lies at the edge of a large and militarily important industrial conurbation centring on Birmingham, the target of serious and sustained bombing raids. 'Careless talk costs lives' and the police had to deal with a whole raft of new, paranoid legislation designed to keep Britain safe. It meant that coppers, from the bobby on the beat to the chief constable, were busy as never before and could not give their all to the investigation in Hagley Wood.

What they did – a basic error of humanity – was to latch on to something which was only tangentially relevant. Within months of the body being found, a series of writings appeared on the walls of buildings all over the Midlands – 'Who put Bella in the wych elm?' The police wasted hundreds of man hours trying to discover the author/s of these daubings and failed. Would a solution to this have led to detection of the killer? Almost certainly not, but the police pursued it anyway.

The forensics disappointed. There were various tell-tale pieces of evidence – the dead woman's dentition, her clothes, her shoes – but these led nowhere and the wrong conclusions were drawn. Bella became the established name for the dead woman, although it was certainly *not* her name, so even that is fiction.

As the case settled into the past and police and press turned to other issues and other problems, no new leads were forthcoming and Bella became part of the folklore of the industrial Midlands.

Then, fiction kicked in again. What could explain the most bizarre body disposal method in the history of true crime? It had to be the supernatural, very much in vogue in the 1950s and in the realms of witchcraft, *nothing* is real. So much hokum has been written about what is actually an historical and social phenomenon, that a reader has to tread *very* warily to separate fact from nonsense. Larger than life figures, like the 'beast' Aleister Crowley and the 'wizard' Gerald Gardner, both of whom would probably be sectioned today, took centre stage. Ask anyone with a nodding acquaintance with the Bella case and they will say, 'She was a witch, wasn't she?' That angle appeals to our darkest fears – and again, we are in the realms of fiction. What scared us in the darkness of our nursery years? 'Ghoulies and ghosties and long leggedy beasties and things that go bump in the night.' We shudder; Bella was part of all that.

'Oh, no, she wasn't,' the more rational were saying by the 1960s. This was a wartime case – it had to be to do with espionage. Why else could the dead woman not be traced? Why did no dentist recognize her teeth? Why were there no labels in her clothes? Because she was German or Dutch and had been parachuted into the area by the Luftwaffe to carry out acts of sabotage or at least report back to Berlin on key military installations.

What happens when a journalist, one of those people paid to 'juice up' stories, has links with the shady world of espionage? He writes fiction, but I am not talking about Ian Fleming, involved in Naval Intelligence during the war, who went on to create the most famous fictional spy of them all, James Bond. I am talking about a friend of his, Donald McCormick, who wrote the first – and worst – book featuring Bella in 1968: *Murder By Witchcraft.*

The clue is in the title. McCormick muddies the waters by linking the Hagley Wood case with another murder in nearby Warwickshire four years later. There is no comparison at all between the two, but that did not deter McCormick, who was able to use his spurious espionage connections to invent pure fiction.

And the generation of writers that followed fell for it. The two unrelated cases are linked forever in the public mind and ever-more-lurid ideas emerged, with seances being held at Bella's possible murder site, novels being written, at least one opera, several folk songs. None of this gets us remotely near to who Bella really was or why she was murdered or who killed her.

In 2005, West Mercia police, as the Worcestershire constabulary now were, declared the case closed. By that time, 'all persons involved' (to use police jargon) were assumed to be dead and with the Freedom of Information Act hovering in the background, the *facts* of the case at last came to light. Speculation and nonsense could now cease and a solution could be found.

Yes and no. The Worcester Archive is chaotic. The inquest is not there; neither is the first part of the police investigation. There is a great deal of duplication which serves no current purpose and a number of articles – letters, reports and photographs – that have no clear relevance to the case. Either the police did not keep all the information and it never reached the files in the first place or it has been removed/lost/misplaced since.

More unforgivably, the remains themselves have vanished. The bones, the shoes, the clothing fragments, which today could provide so much valuable information, are nowhere to be found. They were in the safe keeping of the forensic unit of Birmingham University, but they are no longer there; neither is the information relating to the burial of the bones. Bella has disappeared for a second time. The first was after her murder some time in the summer or autumn of 1941; the second had probably already happened by 1978.

And into the mix of lost evidence, poor quality original photographs and fanciful storytelling, comes that melting pot of confusion, the Internet. What ought to be a storehouse of information, unparalleled in history, is a disastrous mess, where anybody can post any nonsense they like in pursuit of a pet theory. So you can listen to excerpts from Simon Holt's opera on Bella, but you cannot find out who she was. You cannot even find out very much about Professor James Webster, who carried out her post-mortem, even though he was a Home Office pathologist, one of the most distinguished men of his generation.

For too long, the story of Bella in the wych elm has been shrouded in mystery, made worse by anecdotes without sources, pamphlets written and published by well-meaning amateurs.

Have I, Hercule Poirot and Jane Marple-style, solved the case? And can we now, at last, put the shade of Bella to rest?

You'll have to decide that for yourself.

Chapter 1

The Wych Elm

I felt that I was in hell itself. All around me were great squat wych elm trees ... like round-bellied devils with beards and shaggy hair.

Was it such a night as this that death visited the woods, turning, for the first time in criminal history, a tree trunk into a coffin? What happened that night? Was the wood in fact the scene of ghoulish rites ... was the body brought ... from some other place of execution and carried through that very undergrowth now clinging and clawing at my ankles, to its secret resting place?

I stopped suddenly for the wood had become alive ... Red eyes pierced the darkness ... I could imagine her clearly there in the wood. Only one feature of her physical appearance seemed absent – her face. Instead ... I saw only a leering and enigmatic skull. It made me shudder as I thought of it.[1]

The myths kick in almost at once. Which of us has not stood in the dark tangle of a wood and heard the whispers in the trees, the sighing of the leaves? As though nature itself has recorded an unnatural horror and replays it over and over again in some ghastly time-loop. Such ideas raise the hairs on the back of the neck; they also sell newspapers. The words above were written for the Wolverhampton *Express and Star* by a journalist with the nom de plume Quaestor, which is at once enigmatic and false. The Latin words sounds as if the writer is a questioner, an avid seeker of the truth. In fact, a quaestor was a Roman tax official and in this context he was Wilfred Byford-Jones, a part-time columnist for the *Express and Star* in the early 1950s.

A wych elm is a standard English tree, the only variant native to the country. It can grow to a height of over 30 metres and has the Latin botanical name *Ulmus glabra*. Its bark is dark grey and its leaves irregular, broad and with a distinctive sudden point. Its flowers, a striking red-purple, appear before the leaves in early spring and grow in clusters. It is generally found in watery areas, mostly in the north and west of Britain.

And then, only a few lines into most websites on the tree, man's obsession with the supernatural begins:

Elm wood burns like churchyard mould
E'en the very flames are cold.[2]

The wych elm is a tree associated with melancholy and death, perhaps because its branches can drop suddenly, without warning. An old verse ran, 'Elm hateth man, and waiteth'. It was often used for coffins and in folklore was equated with prophetic dreams. Welsh longbowmen of the Middle Ages used elm for their weapons. The Old English wych (*wice*) has nothing to do with witch but means pliant or supple, referring to the springy qualities of the wood which made ideal bows. In the herbal medicine of the Medieval period, the outer bark of the wych elm was boiled down as an ointment for burns. The inner bark was ground into a compound for sore throats. In one or two modern accounts of what happened in the years before Byford-Jones walked there, the elm is confused with witch hazel, which is a different tree altogether; in fact, it is a shrub. Even botanical experts like Jacob Strutt confused the two as in his *Sylva Britannica* (British Woods) in 1822.

Websites will tell you that the wych elm is associated in Celtic mythology with burial mounds and the passage to the Underworld. In fact, this is just one of the legends that has grown up around the central figure in this book. As we shall see, the Celts worshipped the oak, the mistletoe, the ash, the yew and the hazel, not the elm.

The trees described above stood in the now re-landscaped grounds of Hagley Hall, Worcestershire. Today, it is difficult to find the heart of Hagley. True, we were looking for a particular spot in Hagley Wood, to the east of the village, but the reality is that the village is now strung out along the busy A456 stretching north-east towards Halesowen and the behemoth that is Birmingham. Everything in our time is geared to the car – the dual carriageways, roundabouts, traffic lights. The Hagley we wanted to find has all but disappeared in a mass of new building and housing estates. There was no sign of the school and the church, once at the centre of the community. Even the pub, the Lyttleton Arms, much altered and gentrified, stands oddly at a road junction beyond the village, like an afterthought because new road layouts have changed the lie of the land.

The story starts on Sunday, 18 April 1943, ironically on the day that the Russians announced that over 4,000 Polish soldiers found in a mass grave at Katyn were the victims of Nazi violence. They were not; the Russians themselves were responsible for the murders. None of what was happening in Eastern Europe had much effect on four boys wandering Hagley Wood that day. Some accounts today – the myths and mistakes continue – contend that there were only three of them, so for the record, they were Robert Farmer, Robert Hart, Fred Payne and Thomas Willetts. And they were not, as reconstructions claim, technically schoolboys. Two of them were fifteen and had left school the previous year, the school-leaving age at the time being fourteen. By April 1943 they were both at work, although what they did is not recorded.

Accounts differ, too, as to where the boys came from. They certainly did not live in the village of Hagley. Local historian Joyce Coley[3] has them coming from Lye, a village four miles away, with its curious placenames of Lye Waste and Careless Green. Lye's most famous son was the actor Cedric Hardwicke, but in 1943 he was on stage in New York, not coming back to Britain until the following year. According to Coley, Bob Hart lived in Pearson Street, Bob Farmer along Balds Lane and Fred Payne in Stocking Street. No address is given for Tommy Willets, the youngest lad. Other accounts have the boys hailing from Stourbridge on the edge of the Black Country with its distinctive dialect. The small town was famous for its glass-blowing industry, dominated by the Jeavons family, a parochial success story in the shadow of the Clent Hills and Kinver Edge. The boys had their dogs with them, lurchers called Trix, Jock and (unthinkable today) Nigger. If they came from Lye, they could have reached Hagley Wood in fifteen minutes or less than three-quarters of an hour with a casual stroll.

What were they doing in the Wood? Casual accounts call them poachers, but that is a twenty-first-century misreading of 1940s reality. One website today contends, ludicrously, that the lads were poaching to supplement their families' incomes at a time of extreme rationing. The boys were actually looking for birds' nests. It was spring, the egg-laying season and every red-blooded boy of that generation saw it as a mark of skill and courage to climb the tallest tree to reach the eggs. As a boy in the 1950s, I had a collection of twenty-five eggs, all lifted by me, 'blown' with the aid of a needle and kept carefully in cotton wool. We have only started to worry about such things recently.

In those more innocent days, the shock that Tommy Willets and the others had would stay with them for years; some said, all their lives. In the tangle of undergrowth stood one of those squat, round-bellied wych elms which 'Quaestor' described. Judging by its limited height and the 'shaggy' thicket of branches bristling out of its trunk, the tree was damaged and probably dying. The trunk had broken off at 3½ft from the ground. It also looked an ideal nesting site for birds – the lightly speckled blue of the thrush, the glossy white of the collared dove.

The photographs taken of this soon-to-be-notorious tree are themselves enigmatic. All versions that I have seen in newspaper accounts and subsequent books show another tree altogether. True to the sensationalism of bad provincial newspaper journalism of the time, Quaestor's caption in the *Express and Star* records 'The body was found in this repulsive tree, known as the wych elm, although its common name is witch hazel [*sic*] because hags of old days used hazel twigs for divining rods.' The reason for the wrong photograph is an innocent one. By the time the media cameramen reached it, the actual tree had been cut down by the police. It had been pollarded and dozens of branches radiated out from the decaying bole in the centre.

Most accounts today have Bob Farmer climbing the wych elm alone. In fact, according to the *Evening Dispatch* of 29 April 1943, the boy who made this climb was actually Bob Hart. In subsequent newspaper editions and magazine articles, both Bob Farmer and Tommy Willets are credited with the find, but the *Dispatch* was reporting from the coroner's court at the time and was covering a bizarre and important story that sold newspapers; surely it can be relied upon more heavily than subsequent re-imaginings. Hart had done this before, countless times. He forced his arm into the thicket of branches, peering down into the hollow bole below him. The hole was 2 feet wide at the top, tapering to 17 inches at the bottom. A skull stared back at him with sightless eyes. He poked it with a stick and it slipped to one side, severed by the years from its neck. Hart reached further and pulled it out, calling his mates to see what he had found. A fox, surely? A badger, perhaps? 'Come here. Have a look at this.'

They did and recoiled in horror as Hart brought the skull down to ground level. A clump of reddish hair still clung to the right temple. Some teeth were missing and the front two upper incisors overlapped. And, even allowing for the often-chaotic teaching in wartime Britain, there was no mistaking this find. The skull was human. Hart used some of the rotten clothing near the skull to push it back into the hollow tree with the aid of a stick. And the boys ran. To add to the ghoulishness of the scene, some later accounts have darkness descending on Hagley Wood at that moment. In fact, according to the boys' testimony to the coroner, it was midday. We reached Hagley Wood and the approximate site of the wych elm on April 21, seventy-nine years and three days after the boys were there. The trees were in full bud in the spring sunshine and the day was bright.

Bob Hart may have had more stomach than the others and he considered their predicament. They had discovered a body and the natural thing would be to tell the police. But they were in Hagley Wood and, technically, trespassing. Hagley Hall was – and still is – owned by the Lyttleton family, and the Palladian building which stood in the distance on that April Sunday had been built by the eccentric George, First Baron Lyttleton, who was Chancellor of the Exchequer in 1754. His great-grandson, also George, married Mary Glynne, whose sister Catherine married William Gladstone in a joint ceremony in 1839; the future prime minister was often a guest at the Hall. Typical of the general building style of the aristocracy in the Age of Reason, Hagley's grounds included a deer park, a castle folly, a temple of Theseus and a series of 'ancient' standing stones, all courtesy of the architect Sanderson Miller in the 1750s. The obelisk on top of Wychbury Hill, which he also built, still has echoes of the body in the wych elm to this day.

Today, Hagley Hall is a much-refurbished wedding venue and the old stable yard is home to a number of commercial enterprises. Its sumptuous interior reflects the glittering collection of paintings and porcelain, despite the fire that gutted the building in 1925, breaking the heart of the 9th baronet. The previous hall, which the Palladian mansion replaced in the 1750s, was no stranger to scandal and dark deeds. Two of the Gunpowder plotters who had tried to assassinate the parliament of James I in November 1605 had fled to the Hall for safety. They had been surrounded at Holbeck House but Robert Winter and Stephen Littleton had escaped and begged Stephen's brother Humphrey for help. He sheltered them but John Fynwood, the Lyttleton's cook, reported them and they were arrested in January 1606. Inevitably, both Halls, original and replacement, had a resident ghost!

On that April day, the Lyttletons still lived at the Hall, but there was a war on and much of the building, rather down at heel by now, had been commandeered by civil defence and served as function rooms for fundraisers for the war effort. Whether facing the officialdom of pompous men in khaki or a family that had owned the land since the days of John of Gaunt, Bob Hart knew that the deck was stacked against him. Stealing birds' eggs was not regarded as remotely criminal in the 1940s but trespassing was definitely illegal. He and his friends would say nothing.

There, if the boys' consciences had not got the better of them, the body in the wych elm might have stayed until it collapsed into dust. There would have been no mini-industry, no infuriating mysteries surrounding Hagley Wood. And this book would not exist. It would have been the perfect murder.

Chapter 2

There Was a War On

By the time the boys made their gruesome discovery, Britain had been fighting against Nazi Germany for three and a half years.

The unthinkable had begun in September 1939 when Adolf Hitler, the German chancellor, had refused to remove his troops from Poland despite an ultimatum from Neville Chamberlain, the British prime minister, and Britain consequently declared war on the Third Reich.

We have recently reassessed Chamberlain and Britain's preparedness for war. R.J. Mitchell had designed the iconic fighter plan, the Spitfire, before the war began and the country's industrial infrastructure and expertise meant that we were able to switch rapidly to war production, despite the grim years of austerity in the recession-hit 1930s. Even so, the 'people's war' was like no other in history. The reach of long-range bombers and Hitler's strategy combined to turn civilian Britain into the Home Front. Conventional warfare was being fought by armies, navies and air forces around the world, but death came to ordinary people from the skies. It was no longer a question, as it had been in the First World War, of women waving a tearful farewell to their menfolk as they marched away.

No one was ready for blitzkrieg, its speed and ruthlessness. Wars have always been bloody and have little to do with notions of chivalry and romance but from 1939 onwards, *everybody* knew that, not just the boys in khaki or blue. After Hitler's objective of invading Britain to consolidate his megalomanic aims had failed, he unleashed his Luftwaffe on the cities, pulverising London, Hull and Plymouth. A new word entered the language – to 'coventrate', meaning the flattening of a city as in Coventry, in November 1940. The once-magnificent Medieval cathedral was left a smouldering ruin.

And society had to adapt to a new way of life just to cope. The families of the Hagley boys learned, like thousands of others, that catastrophe and collapse were only a careless word away. Income tax rocketed to 7s 6d in the pound; the war cost Britain £2 million a day to fight, pocket-money by today's standards, but an unbelievable sum in the 1940s.

Propaganda became a way of life too. An army of 'little Hitlers' sprang up, wearing tin hats and carrying gas masks for a chemical attack that never happened. They had ARP (Air Raid Protection) painted on their helmets and shepherded terrified civilians to air-raid shelters in towns and cities. 'Put that light out!' they barked at careless people who had forgotten to close their curtains or lower their blinds. Posters appeared everywhere. The public were encouraged to turn their gardens into allotments and grow their own vegetables. They were urged to buy War Bonds and to donate their pots and pans to be recycled into tanks, battleships and aircraft.

'Careless talk costs lives', the huge posters reminded them. 'Keep it dark'. Walls, of course, had ears and everybody was expected to be 'Like Dad – Keep Mum'. Mum might well be driving an ambulance, working in munitions, typing the very propaganda which bombarded everybody. A few of them flew aircraft from factory to airfield. What they did *not* do was to train to fight, unlike their sisters in Communist Russia. Neither did they work in the concentration camps, like their Nazi counterparts. Most people expected things to return to normal after the war. It would be an Allied victory, of course, and it would herald in a brave new world. People had believed that in 1918 too – and the only meaningful result was the Second World War.

By the time the boys found the body in Hagley Wood, their families had become sickeningly used to privations. Butter and bacon were rationed from December 1939. The weekly allowance was four ounces of butter, twelve of sugar, four of bacon or ham. Meat was rationed from March 1940; tea, jam, cooking fat and cheese followed in July. Eggs? One a fortnight, unless you were 'lucky' enough to be in the RAF undertaking a raid over enemy territory; no flying, no egg.

The country became obsessed with food, or rather the lack of it. 'War and Peace' pudding from Canada was a Christmas treat throughout the 1940s. Carrot Croquette and carrot fudge were regular suggestions in newspaper recipes, even when newsprint was limited and newspapers shrank to a quarter of their peacetime length. 'All Clear' sandwiches and Woolton pies (named after the government minister responsible for food) were heavy on parsnips. Bread was not rationed; it had been the country's staple diet for centuries and folk memory was long. Ration bread and riots would ensue – law and order would collapse. Even so, the 'British loaf' was grey, coarse and unappetising.

Children like the Hagley boys got the best of a bad lot. They had daily milk and orange juice, even if the latter had nasty little circles of cod liver oil floating on the surface! The Spam and dried egg made available under America's lend-lease programme must have seemed heaven.

Clothes, too, were hit by wartime austerity. Out went the ridiculously wide 'Oxford bag' trousers of the 1930s. Turn-ups disappeared, as did pleats in skirts. Without lipstick, girls painted their lips with beetroot juice. Stockings became a thing of the past, because silk was needed for parachutes and barrage balloons. Girls coloured their legs with gravy browning and got a friend to draw a seam up the back with an eyebrow pencil.

There were queues everywhere. The word might have been French, but the idea suited the British mentality; most people were conformist and behaved themselves. The joke ran that a woman could not pass a line of people without joining the end of it. People queued for hours a day, to get what they could from harassed retailers with their coupons and to whisper furtively to them, 'AUC?' – Anything Under the Counter?

The wireless was indispensable. Long before the BBC became 'woke', it genuinely spoke for and to everybody, even if all the broadcasters were male and still wore dinner jackets for evening broadcasts. The nine o'clock news on the Home Service gave the 'truth' to an anxious nation, who learned little or nothing from the censored letters of their loved ones overseas. Even then, although no one outside the corridors of power knew it, morale was being strengthened by outright lies. On 10 May 1941, the worst blitz of the war – and almost the last – hit London with devastating effect. The prime minister, Winston Churchill, toured the appalling debris in Westminster the next day as the BBC calmly told their listeners that twenty-eight enemy aircraft had been shot down during the previous night's raid; in fact, the figure was seven.

The Hagley Wood boys were too old to get much out of *Children's Hour* on the radio, with the kindly voice of Derek McCullough – 'Uncle Mac' – speaking to the country's little ones; 'Hello, children, everywhere'. They probably enjoyed the antics of *ITMA* (It's That Man Again) by 1943, with its national catchphrases – 'Can I do you now, sir?' and 'I don't mind if I do.' This programme was so popular that people had said in 1940 that if Hitler had invaded between half past eight and nine o'clock, he'd meet no resistance at all. High-brow listeners could listen to the *Brains Trust* on a whole range of imponderables and the BBC's biggest property during the war years was the 'Forces Sweetheart', Vera Lynn.

Anybody with a gramophone could still just about afford to buy a thick plastic disc spinning at 78 revolutions per minute, playing the ridiculous *Yes, We Have No Bananas,* the melodic *A Nightingale Sang in Berkeley Square* or (as popular in Britain was it was in Nazi Germany) *Lili Marlene*.

Undoubtedly, the biggest form of escapism was the cinema. Twenty-five to thirty million tickets were sold each week across Britain. Clark Gable did not give a damn about Vivienne Leigh in *Gone With the Wind* and there were stiff upper lips everywhere in propaganda films like Noel Coward's *In Which We Serve.*

The call-up slashed workforces and emptied streets, the dreaded buff envelopes falling on doormats all over the country. Conscientious objectors, morally opposed to war, were denounced as traitors, as they had been in the First World War and foreigners, anyone with a German-sounding name, were routinely rounded up under Regulation 18B and sent to well-guarded camps up and down the land. Italian ice-cream parlours disappeared overnight.

'I cannot offer [women] a delightful life,' the Labour Minister Ernest Bevin said from Whitehall, 'I want them to come forward with the spirit that they are going to suffer some inconvenience, but with a determination to help us through.' Nursery and child-minding facilities were increased and improved, but families like the Farmers, Willets, Harts and Paynes had less than £5 a week to live on. An average man earned £3 0s 6d a week; his average wife only £1 18s.

There have been spurious comparisons recently in the age of lockdown and responses to COVID, invoking the spirit of the 1940s. The two are not really comparable, but in the sense that Boris Johnson's government has re-introduced measures not used since the war, some similarities spring to mind. One of these was war-weariness. It was well described by Molly Lefebure, personal secretary to Keith Simpson, Medico-Legal adviser to Surrey Constabulary. She was in her early twenties at the time:

> One would feel a bout coming on, endeavour to fight it off, fall victim to it, shiver and shake in its grasp, finally to emerge from it bored, depressed and listless. It was a real illness ... and as the war went on, almost everybody fell victim to it ... Some it made

drink a lot. Others took to bed – with others – a lot. Some became hilariously gay [in the original sense] brave and hearty. Others became sardonic and bored. Some seriously depressed ... A few took to prayer ...

Molly Lefebure's war was the same as everybody's, yet radically different. With her boss, the legendary 'CKS' tramping over moorlands and woods to inspect murder victims, she developed a stoicism and a steely nerve that would have been beyond many of her contemporaries. There was a dramatic increase in crimes of all types. In 1939, over 300,000 cases were reported. By the war's end, in 1945, it was 475,000. There was also a great deal of unreported crime, either through indifference or the authorities' need to keep morale high. Simpson himself summed up the reason for the increase:

> Emergency regulations, uniforms, drafting, service orders and a life of discipline cramp the freedom of many young men and during the long periods of wartime training and waiting not a few of them got bored – 'browned off' was the common term. Some missed their wives or girlfriends and got into trouble with local girls and camp followers ... urged on by long periods of sex starvation ... there was a steady flow of rapes (some with strangling and other violence), of assaults (some fatal), of abortions and infanticide ... all arising from the changes in life that were thrust by service conditions on ordinary people.

Arguably, life became cheap. As Graham Greene wrote in *The Ministry of Fear* (1942), 'Nobody troubled about single deaths ... in the middle of a daily massacre.' There were 135 murders in the first year of the war; 141 in the last. The bloodiest year was 1942 – 159 cases. While police forces were hopelessly stretched hunting spivs and black-market racketeers, whom most people regarded as necessary evils in a time of deprivation, killings piled up. Leading Aircraftsman Arthur Heys strangled WAAF Winnie Evans at a Suffolk aerodrome. Samuel Morgan killed 15-year-old Mary Hagan in a blockhouse in Liverpool. Harold Hill strangled and stabbed two little girls in a Buckinghamshire field, leaving his gas mask behind to ensure his capture and execution. Officer cadet Gordon Cummings mutilated and murdered four women in London; the press called him the Blackout Killer. It would not come out until after the war, but John Christie was already raping women and burying them in his garden at 10, Rillington Place.

And in Hagley, Worcestershire, somebody had stuffed a body into the hollow bole of an old wych elm.

Like hundreds of villages all over the country, Hagley had to adapt to the sudden, bizarre and sometimes terrifying changes that the war brought. There was nothing unique or outstanding about the place that would have attracted the interest of the Luftwaffe, but Birmingham, only thirteen miles away, was a different story. It was the largest city in the country after London, expanded in the early days of the Industrial Revolution due to its position at the centre of the 'silver cross' of canal networks that crossed the Midlands. Over 8,000 businesses operated in its teeming streets, representing more than 1,200 trades. Above all, the city was an arsenal, as it had been in the First World War, making tanks, Bailey bridges, aircraft and components, badges and buttons, shot and shells. The letters 'BSA' – Birmingham Small Arms – were a byword for weapon and vehicle production. Half the country's gold and silver goods were made there, along with cars, motorbikes, glassware and chemicals.

Under its innovative nineteenth-century mayor, Joseph Chamberlain – 'Radical Joe' – Corporation Street was laid out broad and straight, like Paris's Champs Elysées. The town hall was a massive monolith with its Greek columns, the municipal bank not much smaller. Queen Elizabeth hospital, opened in 1938, was a monument to the vast block-buildings of that decade, heralding the obsession with flat roofs that would become the norm of post-war development. Libraries, a university and technological colleges, museums and institutes made Britain's second city a centre of cultural excellence as well as serious money-making.

No wonder Herman Goering's bombers were interested. Air raids, which killed 2,227 people, destroyed the Victorian market hall, with both cathedrals (Anglican and Catholic) taking major hits along with the art gallery and university. The population of over a million got used to the wail of the sirens, the roar of aircraft and the thud of anti-aircraft guns aimed at the night sky. The fire service was so inept in handling the first raid that its chief resigned in embarrassment, but it soon improved. By comparison with other cities, however, Birmingham got off lightly.

And the city kept working. One small factory made all the carburettors for Spitfire and Hurricane fighters; its output doubled in a fortnight in the summer of 1940. The normal working day became eleven hours a day, seven days a week.

There was an influx of women from all over the country in 1941–44. A large group was trained in from Scotland under the care of a female guide, who was their warden and friend. Reception officers got them settled in homes and church halls, but some of them missed their native hills and went home. 'Short of a military escort,' whinged one reception officer, 'who can make a woman do what she doesn't want to?'

Unwanted pregnancies rocketed during the war and nowhere more so than in Birmingham. Between 1940 and 1945, children born to married women, with husbands in the armed forces, tripled.

And to cap it all, the food in wartime Birmingham was grim. One former hotel chef wrote that he 'despaired of Birmingham's taste in food. He had been all over the world and catering in Birmingham was the worst in the world ... the workers at the factory only wanted fish and chips, cream cakes, bread and butter and brown gravy over everything ... they would not eat salads, did not like savouries.' They did not, in short, 'understand food'.

In Hagley, they would have heard the sirens, seen the glow of fires. There was an Ack-Ack battery at nearby Field House, complete with searchlights and watchful troops. They probably shared the view of Birmingham's population about food. The vicar, throughout the war, was Robert Burns, MA. His letters to his parishioners have survived and they make interesting reading. We have no way of knowing whether the Hart, Farmer, Willets or Payne families attended church, but it is likely that they did, at least from time to time. Lord Cobham and the Lyttleton family from the Hall would certainly have been regulars at the church of St John the Baptist or St Kenelm's near the Wood's boundary. In January 1943, three months before the boys found the body, Burns was telling his parishioners, 'The spring is at hand, pull yourself together and ask God for renewed faith and courage to hold on until, in His good time, His enemies and ours are in the dust.' He mentioned the same 'war-weariness' that Molly Lefebure wrote about and warned his people against defeatism, which was, after all, a criminal offence under wartime regulations. His curate, Mr Philpott, had been called up to become a chaplain in the army and the male ranks of the choir were thinning too.

In the village itself, local women organized soldiers' comfort groups, knitting socks, vests and blankets for troops stationed who knew where. If meeting in each other's homes was not convenient, the school served as a useful meeting centre. The local scouts were urged to do their bit. Unbeknownst to anyone in Britain in 1943, Walter Schellenberg, Head of Amt IV of the SS's Secret Service, had drawn up a hit list of individuals most wanted by the Third Reich who would have been rounded up and shot had Hitler invaded in 1940. The 'Special Search List' (*Sonderfahndungsliste GB*), known as the Black Book also contained institutions and organizations believed to be anti-Reich in their attitudes. Among them were General Baden Powell's Boy Scout movement. They were probably equated in the Nazi mindset with the brainwashed *kinder* of the Hitler Youth movement, in which every German child over 10 was being indoctrinated in Nazi ideology. This was far from the case in Britain, but Scouts *did* help the government. In the First World War, they knocked on doors looking for enemy aliens – 'Do you have a German living here?' – and in the 1940s, they plane-spotted and reported incendiary bombs and suspicious circumstances. We do not know if any of the Hagley boys were Scouts, but the discovery of human remains was something they should certainly have reported if they were.

There was an ARP post set up in the Parish Room and the senior warden was H.W. Burns (relationship to the vicar unknown). No bombs fell on Hagley, but the nature of bombing in the Second World War was haphazard to say the least. Enemy aircraft routinely jettisoned bombs after raids to lighten their loads for their return flights and Luftwaffe pilots did not much care where they landed. In case of fires, stirrup pumps were much in demand in Hagley throughout the war.

Colonel the Viscount Cobham inspected the Halesowen Home Guard in December 1943 as he did often. Were the fathers or grandfathers of the Hagley Wood boys involved in this? We do not know. Food Production Clubs in Hagley and surrounding villages had sixty members and the school playing fields had been turned into vegetable-growing allotments by May 1942. Fundraising events were held regularly, as on Bank Holiday, 2 August 1943 – by which time the Americans had arrived and the music was by courtesy of the US Army Dance Band.

A number of Hagley's buildings had been taken over by the government. The Station Inn, the Hall itself, the school and Hall Barn, all these were ARP posts or First Aid centres and the population had suddenly increased – and decreased – because of circumstances. A Billeting Committee had been set up in November 1940 to consider who could take in evacuees from Birmingham and even London. Concerns were raised over parochial trivia like Identity Cards for new brides. The girls must not alter names on the cards themselves, but take them to the National Register Office, presumably in Birmingham. As for the neat little holders for the cards, they could be obtained from Miss Bradley of Pendower, in Hagley's Middlefield Lane at 6d each. And in case anyone should accuse Miss Bradley of war profiteering, all proceeds from the sales went to the Red Cross.

The huge influx of Birmingham children to Hagley in 1940–41 never quite materialized. The expectation at the start of the war was that casualties would run into the thousands daily and vast numbers of cardboard coffins were mass-produced in readiness. When Birmingham mothers discovered that the village of Hagley had no air-raid shelters but only domestic cellars, they promptly marched their children back to the city, to take their chances in the streets they knew so well.

Even so, there was something risky about outlying villages like Hagley. Various modern accounts talk of people driving out from Birmingham to escape the bombing and sheltering in the woods nearby. This *may* have happened but today we have a distorted view of the impact of motor transport. Few people had cars in the 1940s and travel was restricted by limits on petrol allowance (a fall from 823,000 tons in 1940 to 301,000 three years later) and by the need to dim headlights at night. At the start of the war, there were over 2 million cars on the road; by 1942 only 718,000. That said, there were a number of strangers in the village, billeted on a long-suffering local population and, by comparison with the pre-war situation, the place must have seemed impossibly busy.

Then, on Monday, 19 April 1943, a knot of trench-coated and uniformed policemen came to Hagley, almost certainly in a black Railton car, looking for a particular wych elm.

Chapter 3

The Thin Blue Line

Tommy Willetts had 'cracked'. Bothered as he was by the sight of the skull in the wych elm, he was probably equally bothered by the knowledge that he and his mates had been trespassing. For the last four years of their lives, the country they knew had been regimented, bullied and watched like nothing else in its history. Men in uniforms were everywhere, tape stuck across windows to minimize bomb damage. Everybody carried a cardboard box containing a gas mask. Every adult (and two of the boys *were* adults now) had to carry identity cards and other papers and they had to produce them at the drop of a government regulation from the Ministry of Information. The underlying tensions, habits and life patterns of a largely rural village were swept aside in all this. And Tommy Willetts told his mum what they had found. She told his dad and Mr Willetts contacted the police.

Careless modern accounts claim that he rang the police, but this was unlikely; most people in the 1940s did not possess a phone. And anyway, Mr Willetts knew the local station sergeant, Charles Lambourn, well; in the way that village communities hung together in what now seems a distant age. Lambourn was probably Willetts' age, 47, and he had enlisted in the Worcestershire Constabulary in 1919, the year in which the first ever police strike had taken place in the Met – an incident that many people believed meant that the country was going to the dogs.

In February 1942, the prime minister, Winston Churchill, had delivered one of his many morale-boosting broadcasts to the nation, singling out the police in particular for their heroic efforts. They 'have been in it everywhere all the time. And as a working woman wrote to me … "What gentlemen they are".'[1]

To honest citizens like the Willetts, the police were the avuncular 'bobbies' of Lawson Wood's contemporary cartoons, wide-girthed, seemingly middle-aged and kindly. The pre-war generation remembered the 'White Horse' Wembley in 1923 when PC George Scorey, riding a grey, had prevented catastrophe by gently steering the crowds off the pitch. They knew that coppers cuffed kids around the ear for 'scrumping' apples and knew that they were perhaps none too bright, but they were a symbol of safety and solidarity at a time when both of those commodities were singularly lacking.

The 183 police forces up and down the country were stretched to breaking point, but this was their finest hour. The relationship between law enforcers and the public was brilliantly summed up by a cardboard sign slung outside a bombed London police station that read 'Be Good; we're still open'. It was a largely male institution; in 1939 there were only 282 women police officers; at first carrying out clerical duties and making the tea, they soon joined their male colleagues in the front line. The outbreak of war meant that chief constables of counties like Worcestershire lost the semi-autonomy they had enjoyed previously; now, it was all run by the Home Office. There were 60,000 officers in 1939, 9,000 of them army reservists or liable for call-up if under twenty-five. A Reserve was added and a Special Constabulary to offset those who had volunteered or been drafted into the armed forces.

The Police and Firemen (War Service) Act of 1939 made it impossible for officers to retire unless on medical grounds, which explains why all the named policemen in the Hagley Wood case were in their late forties or early fifties. By 1941, police numbers had soared to 92,000, an unprecedented high.

Men like Charles Henry Lambourn had to be of British birth and descent, over 20 on enlistment, but under twenty-seven. They had to be at least 5ft 9in in their bare feet, be able to read and show reasonable proficiency in dictation and simple arithmetic. They all had to undergo medicals, the police doctor checking for hernias, flat feet, poor eyesight and deafness. They had to sign a form, solemnly swearing 'that I will, to the best of my power, cause the peace to be kept ... [and to] discharge all the duties thereof faithfully according to the law'. Each constable carried in his pocket a copy of *Police Laws* (1939) written by Cecil Moriarty, Chief Constable of Brighton and he was expected to know it off by heart. 'Offences against the person', which effectively was what Sergeant Lambourn would be facing in Hagley Wood, included assault, murder, rape, abduction, prostitution and indecency. There was a separate section for offences against children. Some of this was obsolete, based on Victorian legislation (for example, employment of child chimney sweeps) which is a reminder that the Second World War, like any other moment frozen in time, is a strange mix of the present and the past.

The war put a huge additional strain on the officers of police stations like Lye. Coppers had to know the law concerning the carrying of a camera (in case it was being used for sabotage or espionage purposes). They had to be as familiar as ARP wardens with blackout regulations. They had to be up to speed on legislation pertaining to Aliens and Regulation 18B which, as we shall see, effectively rules out one suspect in the Hagley Wood case.

By now, it was Monday, 19 April and Lambourn and Willetts took Bob Hart to show them what they had found among the bluebells. In the dark bole of the wych elm, perhaps 3½ feet from the ground, they could see a skull and a bone, as well as material and what looked like a shoe. This was clearly a crime scene and Lambourn needed a higher authority. He contacted Sergeant Richard Skerratt, his old oppo from Clent police station, and he arrived with Constable Arthur John Pound, known as Jack. Because of the vagaries of online research, we know more about this man than any other policeman on the case. He was born in Abberley, Worcestershire in January 1895 and was recorded as a labourer in the census of 1911. He joined the Worcester force in 1920 by which time he had married. At the outbreak of war, he is listed at the police station in Bromsgrove Road, Hagley, but because of his age and his times, had seen more of life than many of his younger colleagues. In November 1914 he had rushed to the colours, along with thousands of the naïve generation who had been told that war was a great adventure. He enlisted in the Royal Garrison Artillery at Gosport, Hampshire, so we have physical details that are missing from the others. At the age of 19 he was 5ft 10in tall with a 35in chest. He served throughout the war as a Bombardier and was one of those unsung heroes who did his bit for king and country twice – first in the army, then in the police.

A photograph of Sergeant Skerratt has survived from his time as a constable. He is wearing the 'bobby' helmet designed in the nineteenth century in an attempt at self-defence and is wearing his double-breasted greatcoat, complete with whistle and chain. As a sergeant, his uniform would have been identical except for the three chevrons on his sleeve. He and the others knew very well that nothing could be touched in the Wood until the detectives were called – and that meant guarding the potential crime scene.

We are all familiar today, thanks to endless television crime series, with the blue and white tape (yellow in America) fluttering across leafy glades, usually in crime-ridden Midsomer! There was no tape in 1943 and scene of crime officers today would be horrified at the amateur handling of such places eighty years ago. Skerratt, Lambourn and Pound trampled all over potentially crucial evidence in their size elevens, as (with probably smaller feet!) did Willetts and Bob Hart. The CID in Worcester could arrive in under an hour, but there would have to be a pathologist on this one and Professor James Webster could not get there until the next day.

It is now, with the body in the wych elm untouched by anybody except Bob Hart, that discrepancies creep in. While they waited for someone to stand guard overnight, Skerratt and Lambourn took careful measurements of the tree. One account has that guard being Lieutenant Colonel Wilfred Byford-Jones, who would morph into Quaestor as a jobbing journalist after the war. As a Home Guard officer, this was the sort of work he might be called upon to undertake, but his exalted rank makes this unlikely. If he was as genuinely rattled by night-time in Hagley Wood as he later claimed in the *Express and Star* (see Chapter 1) he made an unlikely volunteer. Joyce Coley, writing on the case in 2007, claims that the real guard was Eric Douglas-Osborne, a Special Constable waiting for his call-up papers from the RAF, someone who will feature later in this book.

It was not until Tuesday, 20 April that the black Railton – or more probably Railtons, complete with hearse – drove off the Bromsgrove Road along the narrow Hagley Wood Lane that runs along the edge of the wood. Today there is a gate into the wood about 200 yards from the main road which is locked and blocked by a 'keep out' sign. There is a broken wire fence around the wood itself and it can be entered easily at any point north of the gate. Contrary to Quaestor's hysterical journalese, Hagley Wood is a peaceful place, the elms severely thinned by comparison with 1943, and carpeted with bluebells. The Lane itself, twisting up to a car park on the Clent Hills, is clearly a rat-run for locals today, judging by the volume of traffic using it. In 1943, it would have been very quiet, although there are a number of sightings of cars parked along it in the 1940–43 period.

A body in a hollow tree must have sounded bizarre to Worcester CID. It remains the only such example of corpse disposal in British criminal history. And if we have a mental picture of the 'boys in blue' in the 1940s, our image of the detectives is equally strong. Unlike today's largely anonymous police forces, who usually trot out chief constables or PR specialists used to dealing with the media, the plainclothesmen of wartime were often legendary. Inevitably, much of this focused on the Metropolitan police and especially Scotland Yard, the 'most public institution in the world' but there was a tradition at the time that 'the Yard' was called in to provincial murder cases because of its expertise and experience. For reasons which are unclear, that did not happen in Hagley Wood. And I believe that this led to someone literally getting away with murder.

Typical of the 'type' was Chief Constable Edmund Greeno – 'the guv'nor' to hundreds of subordinates and criminals alike. When the pathologist Keith Simpson's secretary, Molly Lefebure, met him in the spring of 1942, she wrote:

> More than anything he resembled a huge, steel-plated battle-cruiser, with his jaw thrust forward like a prow. He spoke little, noticed everything and was tough, not in the Hollywood style, but genuinely, naturally, quietly, appallingly so ... The grim light of battle glimmered in his eyes and he started asking me questions in a rather rasping voice that sent shivers down my spine. He was on the warpath and I thought, 'God help the poor fool he's after.'[2]

Greeno's experience as a Londoner with the Met would have been different from that of the detectives from Worcester, but there would have been similarities. Greeno would not have passed selection today – he had a gambling problem and his betting on the horses doubled his detective's salary of £2,000 a year. When he joined the Flying Squad, known as the Sweeney or the Heavy Mob, he spent most of his time chasing armed robbers and cracking the heads of the London racecourse gangs, spearheaded by Darby Sabini, the 'godfather' of his day. He was rarely involved in vice although he did close down a high-class brothel in Dover Street. Inside the elegant premises, he found 'whips and racks and spiked girdles and the biggest bed in the world, currently occupied by the Misses Mary, June, Betty and Helen' as well as 'a glistening six-foot Negress in thigh boots and nothing else'. In fact, only the raiding police were fully clothed and in court later, one of the accused who had written 'incredibly filthy letters' to the black girl, objected to being referred to by the police as 'this man' whereas, in fact, he was a solicitor!

During the war, Greeno caught twelve high-profile murderers, by no means all in London. Eleven-year-old Sheila Wilson was sexually assaulted and strangled in Lewisham, Kent. Mark Turner was an 81-year-old who had mistakenly befriended a deserter from the Canadian army who killed him in Halifax, Yorkshire. Fourteen-year-old Daphne Bacon had her skull shattered in a Suffolk cornfield.

But if Greeno was a celebrity in the press of the time, he was not alone. George Hatherill had been everywhere and done everything during his stint with the Belgian police in Brussels and Antwerp. He spoke several languages and was one of the 'big five', the Yard's leading men, by 1943. He had attended the 1936 Olympic Games as a guest of Heinrich Himmler, the Third Reich's top policeman and brought down one of the cleverest conmen of the war in the unlikely shape of Harry Clapham, the vicar of St Thomas's, Lambeth. The dodgy divine was sending out nearly a million begging letters a year and had no less than ninety-one different bank accounts.

Like the men working out of Worcester, Robert Higgins had a provincial background. He came from Oakham in Rutland, the country's smallest and best-behaved county. Scraping into the Met in terms of height and weight, he was an inspector for the Flying Squad in C Division by 1941, based in the Tottenham Court Road, centre of 'van-dragging' (theft from unattended vehicles). 'Though death and horror were often all around, society had to be maintained and murderers and felons were still pursued relentlessly.'[3]

John du Rose – known as 'Four Day Johnnie' for his speed of catching crooks – joined the Met in May 1931, walking his beat in Mayfair and Soho – places crawling with prostitutes, high-class shoplifters, pickpockets and conmen. The section house he shared as a young copper was harsh. He had a bed and a locker and a long walk to the toilet. The water was invariably cold and the washbasin was a lead trough. His take-home pay before the war was £3 a week, but this was cut to £2 'in the interests of national economy'; these were, after all, the years of the Slump. His day was fourteen hours long with half an hour for lunch. 'New kinds of villains were bred during the war,' he remembered in his autobiography. 'Looting after air raids became prevalent and the old standards of honesty began to slip. We moved into the era of the spiv and the smart alec, the get-rich-quick types.'[4] What struck du Rose, as it would policemen on the Hagley Wood case, was how secretive whole communities could be, even when faced with a common enemy. Covent Garden was a ghetto of silence.

Reginald Spooner was physically the opposite of Bob Higgins. At 6ft 5in tall, he dwarfed virtually everybody he met, far too conspicuous for the undercover work he was sometimes called on to do. Colleague Iain Anderson had no idea how he did it. 'When he went into the office [for undercover selection] he seemed about 3 inches shorter than normal; he was wearing wide trousers [Oxford bags] and he somehow bent his knees without showing it and hunched his shoulders.'[5] Just before the war, he worked in the Soho-centred 'dirty book trade' which would become the Yard Vice Squad years later. A workaholic, as most of these detectives were, he rarely saw his family and in 1940 was central to the West London Aliens Tribunal, sorting out the complex stories of foreigners in the capital who might *just* be enemy agents. When France fell in May, he was seconded to Wormwood Scrubs to work with MI5 in B57, an anti-espionage and anti-sabotage unit. At the end of the war, he wrote, 'I haven't seen my wife in daylight since 1939.'

Against men like these, the detectives who gathered at Hagley Wood that Tuesday in April 1943 are mere shadows. That is not at all to denigrate them. They were simply modest men who got on with their jobs and did not write autobiographies. In fact, despite the existence of dozens of these, the attitude of the Home Office and the police generally was that officers should not write up their cases for public consumption and certainly should not brag about their clear-up rate. This is partly why Scotland Yard's famous Black Museum (actually called the Police Museum) is not open to the public.

Divisional Detective Inspector Jack Henry can have won few plaudits when he published his autobiography in 1945. 'The small and petty crimes could be left safely in the hands of the [locals]. Scotland Yard undertook the detection and apprehension of the more skilful type of crook and scientific thug.'[6]

How skilful and how scientific the crook and thug who stuffed someone into a hollow tree in Hagley Wood was remained to be seen, and the men to oversee it were Detective Superintendent Sidney William Inight, 47, and his leg man, the one whose signature appears more times than anybody else's in the police files of the CID, Detective Inspector Thomas Nock Williams. Inight had joined the Worcester force in 1919, Williams nine years later. Together, they stood with the constables under the opening buds in Hagley Wood on that spring day. No doubt they wore long trench coats and trilby hats, the unofficial uniform of a plainclothesman. Perhaps at least one of them had the ubiquitous pipe.

But it was the man with them who commanded everybody's attention, a thick-set, avuncular-looking man with receding hair who would now direct proceedings and kickstart the Hagley Wood case. He was Professor James Matthewson Webster, the Home Office Pathologist and he had some questions to ask of the bones in the tree.

Chapter 4

Old Bones

He was the greatest detective of us all; the man who solved more cases than anyone the Yard has ever produced ... His word was accepted by judges and juries throughout the country, more often than not without question.[1]

Superintendent Robert Higgins' view of Bernard Spilsbury is a perfect encapsulation of the adulation that attached to this man – and, by inference, his lesser-known colleagues – in the first half of the twentieth century. Despite the international obsession with crime scenes and laboratory work – think 'CSI' and add any placename you like – the *real* pathologists of today are shadowy, behind-the-scenes people. When the body was found in the wych elm, they, like senior detectives, were household names. Ironically, as technology and science has improved, the less we trust pathologists' research. A number of high-profile cases, from the 'babes in the wood' murders of Nicola Fellows and Karen Hadaway in 1986 to the disappearance of Maddie McCann in Portugal in 2003, have collapsed or stalled because of the inconclusiveness of forensic evidence.

Not so in the days of Spilsbury. He made his name in the solution of the Crippen case in 1910, which led to Dr H.H. Crippen being hanged for the murder of his wife. The case was a sensation, involving Scotland Yard, the first use of radio communication to apprehend the fugitive Crippen, and the stoic certainties of Spilsbury in the witness box at the Old Bailey. In fact, at least one modern crime writer has expressed serious doubts about the Crippen case, believing that Mrs Crippen's body in the basement of 63, Hilldrop Crescent, was actually that of a man.

By the 1940s, Spilsbury was not a well man. He had a stroke in May 1940, collapsing over a mortuary table, but continued to work his ludicrously long hours anyway. The Met's traffic cops routinely ignored his parking tickets and his driving of his Armstrong Siddeley the wrong way down one-way streets. He was impossibly arrogant and treated the new generation of pathologists with contempt. 'I find it difficult,' he told Keith Simpson, 'to separate fact and opinion in your report [into the Harold Loughans' murder of Rose Robinson in November 1944]. No, don't bother me now. I'm involved.'

'I was dismissed,' Simpson wrote later. 'The "headmaster" had finished with me.'[2]

Spilsbury never got round to writing his definitive opus on forensic medicine, committing suicide in his laboratory after the war ended. Simpson, by contrast, wrote five books and in that he was shadowed by his indefatigable secretary, Molly Lefebure. He also wrote novels under the pseudonym Guy Bailey. Guy's was his teaching hospital and the Old Bailey was the scene of many of his spectacular court appearances.

Simpson's colleagues Francis Camps and Donald Teare were just as well known. Camps worked in Chelmsford and Teare at St George's Hospital, London. The police called them 'the three musketeers' and *their* hero was not Spilsbury but Sydney Smith, head of Forensic Medicine at Edinburgh University.

One of the most bizarre aspects in researching this book has been the dearth of material on Professor James Webster who carried out the forensics on the body in the wych elm. Unlike Simpson and Camps, who wrote on their famous cases, Webster seems to have written nothing. He covered several high-profile murder cases in the 1940s and 1950s and had some stern criticisms to make over the running of various hospitals in the Midlands. Other than that, we are forced back to the brief entry in *Who Was Who 1971–80*.

He was born in 1898, making him of the same generation as Simpson and Co. and of most of the policemen in the Hagley Wood case. He was educated at St Andrew's University, one of Scotland's oldest and most prestigious colleges, with their scarlet gowns and the tradition there of awarding all their alumni Arts degrees, even if they read Sciences. In 1926, by which time Spilsbury was *the* doyen of pathologists, Webster was awarded his FRCS and in 1943, obtained his MD from Birmingham University. That was the year in which he became head of the West Midland Forensic Science laboratory a behalf of the Home Office. The Hagley Wood case would have been one of the first he handled in that capacity.

At Hagley Wood, on 20 April 1943, the first job was to take photographs. Today, this would be done by a scene of crime forensic photographer, but in the absence of anyone like that, Webster took the photos himself. Either the day was cloudy and the wood dark, or photography began late in the day, because neither the photograph of the tree nor the bones are very clear.

From the very first, irregularities have occurred, not with the pathologist's work but with subsequent newspaper articles and books that have consistently used the wrong photograph. Because of what happened later, the actual tree was not available for later photographs and the one shown, usually with the label 'body found here' is another tree. It is the first of many errors that have become associated with Hagley Wood and accepted as fact by almost everybody.

Webster climbed up to point his camera into the tree's hollow bole. We have no idea what type of camera he used. He was not a young man by this stage in his career and, from his own photograph, looks quite portly. Whether he needed help from the policemen present is not recorded, but if he did not, it is evident how easily a younger, fitter man could lift the body into its hole in the first place. Webster's second photograph shows the discoloured skull lying in the debris of the rotting tree. This is not of course how it was when the body was placed there, but the result of a rattled Bob Hart pushing it back in with a stick. In the third picture, the skull has been moved so that we are looking at the top of the cranium. Sections of vertebrae and cloth material are clearly visible, including the stripes of a 'top' and the paler colour of a skirt. The toe of the right shoe is obvious too, minus laces.

The pathologist clearly could not reach all this easily or he wanted a clearer view so he ordered the tree to be cut away. The police had anticipated this and Constable Pound, with a labouring background, had brought his axe. The infamous wych elm was chopped and hacked, all the material extracted and taken away for forensic examination. It was probably now that the skull was photographed. If there was any hope of identifying the victim, this was the best bet.

In 2017, this photograph and all the others taken of the bones, was submitted to Professor Caroline Wilkinson, Director of the School of Art and Design at Liverpool John Moores University. The professor is an expert in craniofacial identification who became famous in 2013 for her work on the 'king under the car park', Richard III's remains in Leicester. In that case, although she tried not to be swayed by existing portraits of the king, she did have a basic pattern known to everyone. The body in the tree had no pictorial back-up and Professor Wilkinson was working in the dark. Her problem was that the bones have now vanished, so the literal hard evidence has gone. The photographs, in black and white, were taken under a leafy canopy as night was falling and the quality is poor.

To a layman like me, the most obvious physical appearance focuses on the teeth. Webster reported that the left lateral incisor was missing as was the second right molar. The incisor was found in a subsequent search and when placed in position clearly presents a 'snaggle-toothed' appearance. These front teeth would have protruded slightly in life. Clinging to the left temple was a tangle of hair, reddish in colour as a result of the chemicals in the tree itself. For many years, as the tombs of the Egyptian pharaohs were opened and their mummies unwrapped, it was assumed that many of them, too, were auburn. Again, it was the oxidation in their tombs that caused this. Both Professor Webster and Professor Wilkinson, nearly eighty years later, came to the conclusion that the hair was actually light brown, often referred to as 'mousey' by the police at the time.

Oddly, Webster focused at first not on the teeth of the upper jaw, but on the lower ones, which, he said, exhibited irregularities. This is not apparent either in the *in situ* photograph or later ones taken in the laboratory. Interestingly, Professor Wilkinson made no such comment on these teeth in 2017. One tooth was missing from the lower jaw; this had been extracted 'long before death'.[3]

When the skeleton was cleaned and laid out in the laboratory at Webster's West Midlands Forensic unit in Birmingham University, another photograph was taken. Perhaps because we are now used to Richard III's scoliosis (spinal curvature) I was drawn to a similar curve in the case of the body in the tree. In fact, since neither of the professors comment on this it must simply be the way the vertebrae have been placed on the table that creates this effect. The hand bones are missing, as are the feet, although a number of small bones placed between the lower legs are clearly carpals and metacarpals. The left tibia is absent.

What did the jumble of old bones, cleaned and reassembled, tell a man of Webster's experience? His report, typewritten at the science laboratory in Newton Street tells us that he got to Hagley Wood at 6.30 p.m. and found a human tibia (shin bone) 12 yards from the wych elm. Two days later, the police handed him a left pelvic bone, a right femur and a right fibula. It is not clear exactly where these were found, but presumably in the bole of the tree itself. Although the skeleton was now mostly complete, one patella, one tibia and some of the small bones of the hand and feet were missing, as was part of the hyoid bone in the throat.

The skull, Webster was sure, was that of a female. He notes the missing teeth in the upper jaw. These had dropped out post-mortem and had not been knocked out in a struggle. There was slight evidence of pyorrhoea (gum disease) but the teeth were clean. There were no marks of injury to the skull so the blunt force trauma often associated with violent death could be ruled out. The blood traces inside the skull were badly decomposed and it could not be ascertained whether this was ante- or post-mortem. The clear suture lines meant that the deceased was not middle-aged, probably being between 25 and 40 years old. The teeth, however, gave no clear indication of age at all. In the case of the lower jaw, Webster seems to have gone overboard. The first right molar had been extracted before death (the socket had fully healed) but the incisors overlapped slightly. This would have produced a 'noticeable irregularity' which is commented on in later reports, notably the notorious 'police reconstruction' which I will examine later.

Then, Webster stuck his neck out and, I believe, got it wrong. Tightly pressed over the lower jaw in the mouth cavity was 'part of the khaki or mustard coloured dress the deceased was wearing at the time of death'.[4] In fact, this is not a dress at all, but a skirt. 'So far as this [material] thrust over the teeth margin and so fairly adherent to the teeth was this part of the apparel that I do not consider it likely – I cannot say impossible – that this came into the mouth accidentally after death. It appears much more probable that this had been forced into the mouth prior to death, and if so, this would have been capable of causing death from asphyxia.' I do not know if Webster was aware that Bob Hart had shoved the material there himself before returning the skull to the bole of the wych elm. He admitted as much to the press years later.

The clavicles and scapulae were all present and irrelevant in terms of identification or cause of death. Webster found part of the hyoid bone, believing the rest of it to have been taken away by the 'ravages of animals'. Because there was no ossification between hyoid and cornu, the deceased was under forty. Arm bones were not worthy of comment and Webster took the measurements. 'The curvatures of the spine are normal' and there would have been no abnormality in the woman's posture.

It was the pelvis above all that made this body out to be female. The uniting of the epiphyses proved that she was over 22, but there were no distinguishing features. The leg bones were normal and the left tibia, found separately from the body, had been partly chewed away by animals.

The foot bones, likewise, showed no malformations, such as bunions and this was borne out by an examination of the shoes.

Webster's conclusions established that the body in the wych elm was female, aged between 22 and 40. He plumped for 35 'plus or minus a few years'. It was the dead woman's height that should have made identification easier than things turned out. Webster used Karl Pearson's formula, a standard calculation based on the length of leg bones in particular and posited 60 inches. In fact, in a subsequent report, the pathologist reduced this to between 4ft 9in and 4ft 10in tall. If Webster was right about age, she would have been born in 1908 and, depending on her social class and environment, would have been subject to all kinds of dietary deprivations. Even so, 5ft was short for a woman in the 1940s and she should have been more noticeable for that.

Webster then posed the time-honoured question – accident, suicide or murder as the cause of death. First, nothing in the skeleton or clothing gave a hint on this, but it was the position of the body as found that was the real clue. Nobody, not even a boy climbing a tree looking for birds' eggs, falls into a hollow trunk not to be found except by chance. And are we seriously supposed to believe that a woman in her thirties would be doing that? Accident was ruled out. The same arguments stand for suicide. The woman may have killed herself 'when the balance of her mind was disturbed' but would she have climbed inside a tree to do it or to create her own natural elm coffin? It defied belief, especially as such a little woman would have serious difficulty climbing in the first place.

Murder, however, was distinctly unlikely. The woman would have been pushed in feet first. Although Webster does not say so (this was the job of the police) it would have taken a strong man or perhaps two to get that done.

Webster then made what I believe was a mistake. He wrote that the body could only have been placed in the tree before rigor mortis had set in or after it had passed; and he opted for the former. Rigor mortis (literally the stiffening of death) is notoriously difficult to measure, because it depends on a number of variables such as external temperature, position of the body and even cause of death itself. Webster could not say with certainty whether the dead woman had been killed near the tree or elsewhere, because without flesh on the bones, the lividity of the body which might have offered clues was entirely missing. In normal conditions, the fingers, toes and facial muscles begin to stiffen within one to four hours; the limbs in four to six hours. After twelve hours, the body is rigid and it would have been impossible to shove it into the bole of the wych elm. After approximately another twelve hours, rigor mortis relaxes in the opposite way from which it developed. Webster's supposition is that the woman was murdered and deposited within perhaps two to three hours after death. This is possible, but the implication is that the killer knew of the existence of the tree and took his victim there deliberately. This supposition was music to the ears of those who, as we shall see, came to the belief that this murder was linked to witchcraft and the supernatural.

It is, of course, equally possible (and here I believe Webster opted wrongly) that the woman was murdered and left perhaps overnight. The killer realized that the spot was very near to Hagley Wood Lane – the body would be found, sooner rather than later, and there was a need to hide it. When he got there, animals had already been at work. They had chewed the left leg below the knee, taken away the right hand entirely. He looked around in panic and noticed the rotten wych elm with its handy hollow. It was not perfect, but it would have to do and it was better than leaving a murdered woman lying in the open. And, had it not been for four lads birds-nesting, it might have been the perfect hiding place for ever.

Webster's argument for pre-rigor stashing is based on the fact that putrefaction would have set in almost at once after death 'and it is extremely unlikely that the murderer would have kept the body until it had got into this condition'. Clearly, Professor Webster lived too early to witness the grisly examples of Jeffrey Dahmer and Ted Bundy who kept corpses close to them for days or weeks and had sex with them.

The time of death was contentious and it opened a can of worms for which the police at the time were not ready and which has led virtually all the writers on the case in the wrong direction. Because of the condition of the bones and the fact that the wych elm had sprouted through the clothes, Webster estimated that the murder had happened between two years and eighteen months previously. This meant that the woman was murdered in the summer or autumn of 1941 and, although the war was well and truly underway by then, it was at a very different phase which might have a bearing on the killing itself.

Webster, factoring in the clothes found in the wych elm, gave a 'likely' description of the deceased.

> A woman aged between 25 and 40 years, most probably around 35 years of age, 5ft in height, with light ('mousey') brown hair;

no undue prominence of the teeth but noticeable irregularity of the front teeth in the lower jaw; clad in a dark blue and light khaki or mustard coloured [this last added to the type in handwriting] striped woollen cardigan with cloth-covered buttons and a belt of a slightly brighter shade of blue than the blue stripes in the cardigan itself, a light khaki or mustard coloured woollen cloth skirt with a side [left] fastener, a peach-coloured taffeta rayon underskirt, navy blue interlock cotton knickers, corsets and black crepe-soled shoes. The above person has been missing for at least 18 months. She was wearing a rolled gold enamelled ring.

In a second report, dated the same day as the above, Webster went into more detail on the clothes. There were portions of five garments apart from the shoes, all seriously decomposed. The knickers were interlock cotton, 'a cheap type'. The drawing made of them (not attached to this report) shows a voluminous 'bloomer' style which presumably was common in the 1940s. The slip was of silk taffeta material, used to line coats. It was a common material used to make slips by women at home; that is, it was not of a professional manufacture. Webster could find no trace of shoulder straps and believed it was rather long for someone 5 feet tall. The colour may once have been pink, but was more likely peach. Parts of a corset were present, little more than tufts of material still clinging to metal stays and suspenders. It was similar to the wrap-around pattern of the 1940s, sold for between 8 and 10 shillings.

In wartime, clothing was a problem. Material itself was, as we have seen, reduced in quantity, but prices had rocketed. Fourteen guinea (£14 14s) coats and skirts cost £42 by 1943; a guinea handbag was £6. A nightdress that cost £1 5s before the war was now £12. Handmade garments for the wealthy were subject to long delays because the seamstresses themselves had been called up in the war effort. All clothing was bought using coupons. In November 1943, an overcoat required eighteen points, a woollen dress eleven and even a pair of knickers was two. The dead woman's clothes bore all the hallmarks of 'make do and mend', one of the many mantras of the war, but the odd thing was that they had no labels at all, a fact which gave the espionage-obsessed observers of the Hagley Wood murder all the ammunition they needed.

The skirt was of good quality wool of 'pale khaki, perhaps with a tinge of beige'. The female units of the army wore such skirts, whereas most

Land Girls wore breeches instead, often corduroy. The belt buckle, which might have given a clue, was mentioned, but clearly yielded no useful information. There were no sleeves with the cardigan, which was unusual and Webster merely comments that such garments usually had sleeves. The two crayon-coloured versions of this cardigan in the police files are not only very different from each other, they both have sleeves, which runs counter to Webster's observation. There is nothing in the files to say when the drawings were made or by whom. There was no sign of stockings, but in wartime that was hardly to be wondered at. The clothes were generally poor and the dead woman was dressed for outdoors, given the time of year presumed to be summer or early autumn. Oddly, Webster makes no mention of a brassiere. No respectable woman would be seen without one in the 1940s.

The dead woman's hair was present in large quantities, not merely the portion attached to the right temple. There was no sign of permanent waving and the hair had not been dyed or bleached. Webster found some hairs 7 inches long but this was not consistent and he could only conclude the hair to be of average length. The presence of a corset implied that the body was not that of a young girl.

All this was digested into a police report which covered national criminal events. Under Worcestershire, the headline reads 'Body Found'. The age of the dead woman is listed as 'Age 1903 to 1918, most probably 1908' and the damning mistake by Webster already perpetuated 'no undue prominence of the teeth but noticeable irregularity of the front teeth in the lower jaw'. The ring is described in more detail – a 'faceted wedding ring, 2mm wide "Rolled gold" stamped inside, when new would have cost about 2s 6d; this type of ring came into fashion about 10 years ago and the cheap model on the market about 5 years ago.'[5]

Bizarrely, the article claims that the Hagley area was 'visited nightly by a large number of people from Birmingham, West Bromwich and Smethwick about 18 months to 2 years ago during the enemy raids on those districts'. The area is 'also much frequented by pleasure seekers and courting couples'.

Fast forward to 2017 and there was little that Professor Caroline Wilkinson could add to Webster's forensics. Her brief, of course, was very different from that of 1943. She had to reconstitute a living face from a *photograph* of a skull and we can have nothing but admiration for her efforts. Her conclusions were that the dead woman was of broad Caucasian origins with some Middle Eastern or Indian characteristics. Professor Wilkinson makes the obvious point that Webster did not. 'The upper incisors were prominent, with some overlapping of the central incisors producing an overjet over the lower teeth and mild prognathism (forward protruding oral cavity).'[6] The nasal bones suggested a short nose, deviated slightly to the right.

Using Photoshop's mask, wrap, liquify and resize tools, Wilkinson could make an intelligent guess at the dead woman's eyes, ears, hair and skin tone but on her own admission, this is an approximation only. 'It must be noted that this facial reconstruction is NOT an accurate portrait of the face of the person, but rather a representation of the face based on the available skull images.'

What is it that stands out about a person? Their hair, their eyes, their teeth when they smile; in other words, the very things that craniofacial reconstruction cannot pin down. Fascinating though the science (and art) is, we are no nearer to knowing who was dumped into a wych elm in Hagley Wood.

Chapter 5

The Victim From Another World

On Wednesday, 7 October 1942, the Marines were patrolling the sand dunes on Hankley Common near the village of Thursley in Surrey. The soft ground had been churned up by tanks manoeuvring in the area and in one of the twisting ruts, POX 100381 William Moore saw a human hand protruding from the mud. The thumb and two fingers had been gnawed away, probably by rats. There was a foot visible too. Moore reported his grisly find to Sergeant Jack Withington who in turn relayed the message to Lieutenant Norman McLeod. He called the police.

The Surrey Constabulary were as stretched as any other police force during the war, but a body was a body and action had to be taken. Sergeant Benjamin Ballard from Milford police station arrived at the scene with Constable A.W. Bundy, Thursley's beat bobby.

As in Hagley Wood six months later, by nightfall on that Wednesday, a cluster of policemen were standing under the evergreens on the slope of Hankley Common. It was a measure of how seriously everybody regarded the finding of a body that the chief constable of the county, Major Nicholson, was there, along with two superintendents, Richard Webb and Thomas Roberts, together with a police photographer. Eric Gardner, consulting pathologist at Weybridge Hospital was in the company of a man we have met already – Keith Simpson, lecturer in forensic medicine at Guy's Hospital, London – and his long-suffering secretary, Molly Lefebure.

'The stench of putrefaction was strong,' Simpson reminisced in his *Forty Years of Murder*. 'The air was buzzing with flies and the remains of the body were crawling with maggots.'[1]

Molly Lefebure stood loyally by CKS, making notes, collecting specimens of beetles, maggots, earth and heather and sealing them in buff envelopes. Everybody else moved away from the smell.

The body was that of a woman. She was wearing a shabby green and white summer frock with a lace collar. There was a piece of knotted rope around her waist serving as a belt. Under the frock were wide-legged French knickers, a slip, a vest and a bra. Her ankle socks still clung to her feet but her shoes had gone. Simpson estimated that her skull had been shattered by a heavy, blunt object, perhaps a wooden stake. Gardner estimated that the woman had been buried five or six weeks earlier, so that she had probably been murdered in late August or early September of that year. She was taken to Guy's, with the permission of the local coroner Dr Wills Taylor, and 'by tea-time, thousands [of maggots] were struggling for life in a carbolic bath in [the] Hospital mortuary'.

Having examined the body more carefully in laboratory conditions, Simpson moved the probable murder date to the middle of September. The thirty-eight pieces of the skull were painstakingly reassembled by him and Gardner and what was left at the back was a gaping hole, 5¼ by 1¼ inches. The single blow would have caused immediate loss of consciousness and death minutes later, from shock and brain damage. There was also a series of peculiarly shaped stabs to the forehead and the front teeth were missing. Simpson estimated that the victim had been attacked by her assailant from the front, using some sort of knife and had then been finished off with the heavy object from behind. Her teeth would probably have been knocked out because she was already on the ground, face-down, when the fatal blow had been struck.

X-rays of the victim's bones and teeth, as well as the measurements of the pelvis, told Simpson that the dead woman was between 19 and 20 years old. She was 5ft 4in tall and slim. Her hair, what little of it was left, was a mousy brown. Significantly, it was her missing front teeth that gave the most important clue. Their position in the skull clearly told Simpson that they protruded slightly, rather like the woman in Hagley Wood.

The most common assumption in the finding of a female murder victim is that the killing was sex-related. Yet the girl's underwear was intact and there was no sign of assault. Neither was there in the Hagley Wood case.

What clinched the identity of the girl on Hankley Common was her clothes, the green and white frock. The sharp-eyed Superintendent Webb remembered seeing a frock like that – and recently. He checked his diary. He had been at the station on 23 July when a constable brought in a girl wearing that very dress. She was 19 and had brown hair and protruding teeth. She was one of those girls who became increasingly common during the war, a runaway. Her name was Joan Pearl Wolfe.

In the days that followed the finding of the body, sixty coppers in uniform trudged through Houndown Wood and on to Hankley Common, elbow to elbow, turning over the leafmould with sticks. On 12 October, they found a tooth, a piece of skull and a tuft of hair. And two shoes, about ninety paces apart. Later that day, more was found, corroborative evidence for Webb's memory. There was a canvas bag containing a rosary, a bar of soap and a water bottle. Three days later, the most vital evidence of all, an identity card and National Health Insurance card with the name Joan Pearl Wolfe. Ironically, only in wartime would those things exist; nobody in peacetime Britain routinely carried identity information, least of all 19-year-old girls. Six days later, Constable Joseph Armstrong of Surrey police found the murder weapon, a broken branch of a silver birch tree measuring 38½in long. Joan's hair still clung to the peeling bark.

The police were even able to find two places where Joan had spent her last days. On high ground in Thursley village was an old cricket pavilion, beaten by the wind and rain. Inside was a pair of stockings, an elastic garter and a knitting instruction booklet. And on one of the wooden planks of the pavilion's walls, a child-like drawing under a smiling sun and the words 'Our little grey home in the west'. It was a schoolgirl's dream, of sharing for ever with her lover; with the man who had killed her.

The identification of a victim is a *huge* step forward in a murder case. It creates a set of parameters within which the police can work. Relatives, friends and colleagues can be located and interviewed. Murder by a random stranger is far rarer than most people think, so the chances are that, during those interviews, the police will happen across the killer they are looking for.

Eight years before the body was found in Hagley Wood, a dismembered body was found in a shallow river near Moffat on the Carlisle to Edinburgh road in Scotland. It was 29 September 1935 and over the next few days, no less than seventy body parts were found scattered in the area, as well as clothing and newspaper pages. Tasked with identifying the remains, Professor John Glaister of the forensic medicine department at Glasgow University and Professor James Brash of Edinburgh University's anatomy department, set to work to produce a milestone success in forensic science.

The remains were of two bodies, both female, and all parts had been found except a right foot. Teeth had been deliberately extracted and hands had been mutilated to disguise fingerprints. The eyes and lips had gone too. Both women were short, one 4ft 10in to 4ft 11in, making her the same height as the Hagley Wood victim. The younger was between 18 and 25 at the time of death and the older, 35 to 55. This woman was taller, perhaps 5ft 6in. Time of death was ascertained as just after the middle of September, because some of the remains, badly decomposed because of the effects of immersion in water, were wrapped in a copy of the *Sunday Graphic* dated 15 September. This and the clothing led the police to Dr Buck Ruxton, a Parsee general practitioner. There was no sign of Mrs Ruxton or the housemaid, 20-year-old Mary Rogerson, but there was nothing concrete to say that either woman had died in Ruxton's house.

Brash had a theory. He got a photograph of Isabella Ruxton and photographed the second skull from the same angle. Superimposition showed a near-perfect match and when he made models of the victim's feet from a gelatin-glycerin mixture, they fitted the dead woman's shoes. Ruxton was found guilty of both murders and hanged on 12 May 1936. The case even led to a spoof version of a popular love song of the time:

> Red stains on the carpet,
> Red stains on the knife.
> Oh, Dr Buck Ruxton,
> You murdered your wife.
> The housemaid, she saw you,
> You thought she would tell.
> Oh, Dr Buck Ruxton,
> You killed her as well.

What had the police to go on in the case of the Hagley Wood victim? The problem with wartime, unlike the peacetime Ruxton case, was the presence of many servicemen, not just from the British army, navy and air force but the Canadians, the Americans (from 1943 onwards), not to mention Poles, Free French and any number of hangers-on from the eight foreign governments that were now operating out of Britain. Men in uniform, without wishing to sound *too* sexist, have always attracted some women, especially young ones and naïve idealists like Joan Wolfe. Conversely, prejudice against soldiers is centuries old. They were 'brutal and licentious' even when they were defending the Empire or, as was the case in the Second World War, largely civilians in uniform. 'Going with a soldier' was regarded with horror by stately matriarchs and vicars all over the country and the fact that so many did posed nightmarish problems for the authorities trying to keep such girls safe. They often came before harassed police desk sergeants and irascible magistrates, causing nuisances in pubs and cafes and hanging around army camps and railway stations. They might pay a fine or spend a day or two in a cell or at a hostel, but all too often they were gone and the cycle of 'little girl lost' would start all over again.

Professor Webster had concluded that the woman in the wych elm had died, in all probability, in the summer or autumn of 1941, so the police search had to extend backwards by between eighteen months and two years. The bodies of Joan Wolfe, Isabella Ruxton and Mary Rogerson were found much more quickly than that, so the trail was far less cold.

What exactly was the situation in the autumn of 1941 and where could the search begin? In June of that year, there were 2½ million men in the army – 'brown jobs' as they were known – with 395,000 in the navy and 662,000 in the RAF. The 'Brylcreem boys' who flew aircraft were the most popular, with a flair and glamour of their own. Hitler's invasion of Russia, in Operation Barbarossa, took some of the heat out of air raids on Britain and a kind of lull became the norm. By contrast, there was even more pressure on the Home Front to work harder to produce more materiel to aid Stalin's war effort, now that Russia was an ally. Pearl Harbor had not yet happened and Churchill and others could get no more out of Franklin Delano Roosevelt than he was already supplying under the lend-lease programme.

Unbeknownst to anyone in Britain, except a few in the Whitehall corridors of power, all Jews in occupied territories were now forced to wear yellow armbands stamped with the star of David. Experiments were being carried out using a gas called Zyklon B in the camp at Auschwitz in Poland. The German war machine swept east, taking Crimea and Ukraine before concentrating on Moscow itself. The RAF's bomber command was hitting Kiel's shipyards and the industrial centres of Hamburg and Emsden, but the cost, in planes and men, was high. And the Allies got a bloody nose in August 1941 when the 'reconnaissance in force' raid on Dieppe went badly wrong. There were 4,384 casualties out of 6,086. It was a valuable lesson of how *not* to invade Europe.

The police may well have made a sketch based on the body in Hagley Wood and that had to be seen in the context of what was happening in the area all those months earlier, which was difficult. When I consulted the police files on the Hagley Wood murder in the Worcester Archive (which did not become available until 2005) there was *no sign* of this sketch. The first time I came across one was in Donald McCormick's *Murder By Witchcraft* and, as we shall see, that work is riddled with so many errors and assumptions that it is almost a crime in itself. The sketch, which *may* have been produced by the Worcestershire CID appeared in newspapers in the year that McCormick went into print. It is notoriously unhelpful. The face is of course left deliberately vague because nobody before Caroline Wilkinson's work in 2017 had any real idea about the features. The hair, however, is appalling. It is dark (the only versions of the sketch I have seen are in black and white) and medium length but the style does not belong to the 1940s or 1930s and gives a totally wrong slant in terms of identification. A label reads 'Noticeable irregularity front teeth, lower jaw', proliferating Webster's mistake, and the drawing in any case does not show it. The cardigan, which Webster says was sleeveless, has three-quarter sleeves and there is clearly the collar of a blouse beneath it where no blouse was found. The woman has a classic 'hour-glass' figure which we cannot determine from a skeleton. The skirt, with its distinctive seams, has none in the sketch and the peach-coloured taffeta underskirt is visible beneath it, even though Webster specifically stated that the skirt seemed rather long for someone who was 5ft tall. Unforgivably, the black crepe-soled shoes are now labelled blue. Is that because some typist was careless with a comma? Should Webster's note have read 'black crepe-soled shoes' or 'black, crepe-soled shoes'? There is a difference. The belt has a square buckle, although Webster does not specify its shape at all.

The inquest was held at Stourbridge on 28 April, but no details of it have survived in the Worcestershire records. Webster would certainly have been called to give his professional opinion and what he said can be gathered from the minutes of a police conference at Birmingham on 3 May. Along with the pathologist were superintendents J.J. Hollyhead from Worcester and F. Richardson from Birmingham. DI Williams was there too. Webster concurred that the inquest verdict – 'murder against some person or persons unknown' – was correct, but everyone knew that such a verdict was a holding exercise only, designed to kickstart a police investigation that was obviously already underway. Because at that stage there was no suspect with a defence team, the proceedings reflected the prosecution angle only – that a crime had been committed – so coroner's courts in those days were often called police courts.

Webster believed that the choice of the wych elm indicated a previous knowledge of the area. It was the only effective hiding place in the wood.

By the time of this conference, the pathologist had had the skull X-rayed and had come to the conclusion that the dead woman's wisdom teeth had not erupted and probably would not even had she lived into old age. He also modified his observation on pyorrhoea, believing now that it was slight and might have caused bad breath or a dirty appearance of the teeth. Since dental hygiene was low on everybody's list in wartime, this was not particularly helpful. Webster now acknowledged (at last!) that her top teeth protruded. She had never had ear or sinus trouble.

He then ventured out of his comfort zone. For reasons of televisual convenience (not to mention the cost of employing another actor) virtually *all* the forensic work in the early *Midsomer Murders* series was carried out by one man, Dr George Bullard but in reality this has never been the case and a whole team of forensic experts are required to assist. A pathologist's job is to investigate human remains only, not to speculate on lifestyle, but I suppose the police of 1943 were keen to pick up any small crumbs if they led to identification. Based on her clothing, the Hagley Wood victim was 'neither in the "higher flight" nor was she a ragamuffin'.[2] She was, perhaps, 'rather neglectful as to her appearance and habits'. One of her teeth was infected, which would have caused pain and 'given her a nasty taste in the mouth'.

There was nothing in the skeleton to suggest hard manual work with no suggestion of 'excessive' muscular development, but she had had at least one child. Webster had been hesitant about this at the inquest (why is not clear) but he was sure now. In terms of the time of death, he retained the timescale but now veered nearer to eighteen months ago, which fixed the murder in late summer/early autumn 1941. It was ironic that there was no actual cause of death, but nothing in the remains (apart from the cloth stuffed into the mouth cavity by Bob Hart) gave any indication of that.

According to Donald McCormick, writing in 1968, Worcestershire CID mocked up a dummy based on Webster's forensics. A wig and correctly coloured cardigan, skirt and rayon underclothing were placed on a mannequin. Again, there is no mention of this in the police files. The cardigan was, in fact, striped dark blue and mustard colour, which the sketch does not mention and the skirt was also (contrary to the black and white sketch) mustard coloured or khaki. The whole construction was expertly done, bearing in mind how little Webster had to deal with, but it produced very few results. Had the skirt been khaki originally, it might have pointed to one of the female auxiliary units, the Women's

Land Army or Women's Voluntary Service. Land Army girls – there were hundreds of those sent all over the country to keep the nation's food supply going – traditionally wore corduroy jodhpurs rather than skirts because the work was hard and messy. There were 43,000 girls in the auxiliary outfits, a third of them (the Auxiliary Territorial Services) with the army, who of course wore khaki.

Just as rape could be ruled out in the case of Joan Wolfe, so could it with the woman in the wych elm. Her knickers were still there – blue – as were her corsets, which tended to suggest a conventional dresser more likely to be mid-thirties than younger.

There is no suggestion that the Worcester constabulary did not pull out all the stops to identify the woman. Unfortunately, there are serious gaps in the records deposited in the Worcestershire Archive when the case was closed in 2005. We have to take the word of later writers, some of them not very reliable, concerning the direction of the police investigation. There is nothing about routine visits to clothiers, haberdashers or shops of any kind in the record, but at the 3 May conference in Birmingham, Professor Webster praised the work of Special Constable Goldfar who had clearly been carrying out enquiries. At that conference, the pathologist produced a number of items including the peach-coloured slip, which he believed was home made from a coat lining. Had the dead woman not tucked this up, it would have appeared below her skirt; her corset probably prevented this. DI Williams, veering in what I believe was the wrong direction, thought that this was in keeping with a woman flinging on clothes over a nightdress in a hurry to escape an air-raid.

Three days after the Birmingham conference, Superintendent Inight was writing to chief constables across the country asking for help with 'case 17' (Hagley Wood). He described the shoes found near the wych elm as 'of a blue semi-chrome Gibson shape, having three rows of pin punchings [eye-holes] on the uppers, with crepe soles and heels. The size was 5½ and stamped with the Maker's No. D.956 on the inside of each shoe upper.'

These shoes, looking so hopeful in terms of identification, fill the newspapers and anecdotal memories for years and are good examples of the nonsense engendered by unsolved murders. The police themselves were tireless in their search for these shoes, even though it could not be said with certainty that they actually belonged to the dead woman.

Two days after Professor Webster's report, DI Williams was keeping his boss, Sidney Inight, abreast of events on the shoes. He had been to Bacup,

Lancashire, to meet the chief constable, R.W. Priest, who had arranged that the managing director of a shoe company, Maden and Ireland, should be present. They assured Williams that the shoes in question had been made in the Rossendale Valley, but not by them. The tell-tale number D 956 was theirs, but it pointed to distribution by W.R. Wilford Ltd of Leicester, wholesale dealers. From the shoes themselves, it looked to these experts as if the shoes had had at least six months of hard wear.

One typed report without date or signature but probably written by Williams, talks of a visit to Mrs Anne Boles of King Street, Wednesbury, a shoe-shop manageress. She remembered that in 1940 when crepe-soled shoes first appeared on the market, the 'ice' colour was very popular, the blue less so. From information now missing from the police files, a Mr Allen provided these shoes in the area, but he obtained them from a variety of makers across the Midlands. Williams and Detective Constable Sutherland traced Leonard Pass of Elwell Street, Wednesbury, who repaired shoes for Allen and Co, specifically for poorer clients who could not afford new shoes or expensive repairs. Pass's records were excellent, going back five years and among the thousands of invoices were four pairs of the blue Gibson pattern, but none of these was size 5½. Pass knew his customers and was able to assure the officers that they were all still alive at the time of asking. The superintendents of Wednesbury and Bilston were alerted to the shoe problem, especially in relation to missing persons on their respective patches.

On 1 May, just before the Birmingham conference, DI Williams was hunting shoes in the Leicester area. Messrs Wilfords of Charles Street did indeed produce Gibson footwear with stamps 956, 955 and 957 but none of them had the prefix D and none of the soles was blue. With DI Haywood of Leicester CID, Williams traipsed around shoe shops all afternoon. At one point, the police thought they had hit paydirt. The director of Bray Ltd told them that the photograph the police showed him was very similar to those his company made, down to the identifying numbers inside. A tour of the workshop revealed that Brays had made these shoes – D596, blue semi-chrome with three rows of pin-punching on quarter and vamp. The pair was made on a 97 last with leather through crepe sole, Fair-stitched fore-part and crepe heel. The first of these was made in April 1940, Brays were the only company to sell them and the first order was placed in June 1940. This was a remarkable piece of good police work, but it did not end there. Allen's company in Bilston had sold only six pairs of these shoes in size 5½. There were other firms too, scattered all over the country: Lills of Coventry Road, Birmingham; Ambrose Wilson of London; Darnell and Sons of Shoreditch. Some of these were mail-order, but all kept records and the police were in the process of following this up. Gibson shoes cost 13/11d in 1940 and stood out as perhaps the only expensive item in the dead woman's possession.

Tracing the manufacturers and sellers of the shoes was important, but the next step – who bought them – was the vital one and it was never solved. Because of this, in the years ahead, all sorts of enquiries were relaunched to pin down the Gibsons' owner. A number of writers on the case claim, dubiously, that 6,000 such shoes were traced and only six pairs could not be accounted for, sold for cash in a Dudley market. One version has the shoes made by Silesburys of Northampton, although that company appears nowhere in the police files. That same source has a woman swapping her Gibsons at the door with a lady who seemed down on her luck and exchanging them for a cup and saucer. No date, no time, no place – just an anecdote of someone who longs to be involved in something exciting and gruesome.

Then there is the story, covered more fully in Chapter 11, about an impoverished singer who performed at various pubs in the Midlands in the 1940s. A landlady felt sorry for her and said "'Go into the kitchen and put your feet up on the fender ...' Feeling very sorry for her [the landlady] gave her a pair of crepe-soled shoes which she was not very fond of.'[3] This story, complete with dialogue, came from a Brierley Hill resident in his eighties who was reminiscing about humdrum events over sixty-five years earlier.

And the old man remembered something else. He joined the RAF towards the end of 1941 but he was back on leave three years later, when there seems to have been a burst of new activity on the Hagley Wood case. His sister had bought a copy of the national newspaper the *Daily Sketch* and saw an article by Professor Webster relating to the case and the shoes. The airman and his sister were convinced they were the shoes their mother had given the singer. They contacted the police and the paper, but heard no more. That was because their mother's shoes were two-tone brown and cream, not the dark blue of Hagley Wood.

In August 1978, the *Black Country Bugle* carried an article about a Mr Cogzell (no Christian name supplied), a shoemaker who believed he had some answers. Cogzell had seen a television programme which Joyce

Coley says was made featuring Professor Webster. The pathologist died in 1973 but had retired by 1955, so this was a *very* early example of this sort of 'crime watch' programme, in which Webster showed the shoes to his television audience (watching of course on small, grainy screens in black and white, 405 lines). As a shoemaker, Cogzell was fascinated and thought he recognized the distinctive stitching. He was adamant that the shoes he was shown by Dr R.T. Davies of Birmingham University's Medical School and purporting to come from the wych elm were not those he had seen on television. The colour was right, as was the dilapidation, but a particular cut on one of the uppers, which had been stressed on the programme, was not there.

The *Bugle* was able at least to clear up the fact that the television programme had been aired in 1969 or 1970 and both the BBC and ITV were trying to trace it. Cogzell's story was that, nursing his sick wife, he forgot about the programme until the *Bugle*'s article on the case in June 1978 had jogged his memory. He had lived in Lye for years near a cobbler and knew that the girls who worked in a local sheet metal works wore shoes that were damaged by sharp metal. The cobbler repaired them using a particularly distinctive type of stitch and Cogzell believed he could recognize it if he had access to the original shoes.

The wedding ring yielded nothing at all. An expensive piece of jewellery might have led to identification – jewellers keep careful records of such things – and Birmingham of course was linked with the gold and silver trade. But this was cheap rolled gold, worth about half a crown, the sort of 'cover-all' that many young women used to con nosy hotel and guest-house proprietors that they were married to the man they had come in with. It was not far above a plain old curtain ring, except that photographs show that it had designs all the way around it.

Inight and Williams probably put most faith in the peculiar teeth. Dentists keep careful records, like jewellers, and not only did the dead woman have overlapping incisors, she had also had a tooth removed within a year before she died, from the right side of her lower jaw. The problem was that many dentists, like doctors, had been called up for military service and we have no way of knowing how accurate record keeping was, given that manpower shortage. Then, there was the problem of amateurs, people who took out teeth with no anaesthetic and only a rudimentary idea of what they were doing. Like back-street abortionists, they kept no records at all.

What is astonishing is that, apart from requests in police newspaper reports, there is *nothing* on dentists in the Worcestershire Archive. Since it is likely that these would have been in a file unique to that source, an equal likelihood is that this has become separated over the years and subsequently lost. But the reality in 1943 was that, yet again, nothing was forthcoming.

The assumed scene of the crime was slightly more forthcoming, though. While the Surrey force had been able to construct a reasonably accurate thumbnail sketch of Joan Wolfe, only two items, other than scattered bones, were found in Hagley Wood. One was a green glass bottle which probably had no links to the case. It is described nowhere and such bottles, usually with ribbed exteriors, often carried poison. Even in the 1940s, it was possible to buy various dangerous chemicals over the counter in pharmacies. Professor Webster could not find a definitive cause of death, but poison would leave no trace on bones or the limited scraps of clothing found. The problem with any crime scene is that it can be littered before and after the event by just about anybody. According to contemporary reports, Hagley Wood was used widely by courting couples, 'pleasure seekers' and evacuees from bombing; the bottle could have been anybody's.

Altogether more fascinating is the identity card. We know that Mrs Bradley of Hagley made covers for cards like this and it had to be carried at all times to be shown to officials in a country paranoid about a fifth column operating in darkness. This particular one had a woman's name on it and an address. The police made enquiries.

Actually, they did not. Donald McCormick wrote the first book on the Hagley Wood murder in 1968. *Murder by Witchcraft* linked Hagley Wood with the killing of labourer Charles Walton in Meon Hill in 1945, a fatal misconception that has dogged both unsolved murders ever since. According to McCormick, whose fabrications are analysed in Chapter 14, the owner of the card lived at 'an address in the Midlands'[4] and voluntarily gave her name. When the police called on her and asked to see her card, she could not find it. She admitted the card was hers, but she had no idea how it had ended up in Hagley Wood, a place she had never been to in her life. At this point, according to McCormick and others who have followed him, the police seem to have shrugged and wandered away.

This defies belief. Not having an identity card was a criminal offence. Being unable to explain how it got to a place where a murder had happened was, to say the least, suspicious. And, surprise, surprise, there is no mention of this incident in the Worcester Archive.

What there *is*, however, – and this, I believe, is where McCormick's vague nonsense came from – is the finding of a lady's handbag in 1944. It was 17 November and Special Constable R. Sheppard of Hagley was in the wood investigating shooting rights when he found the bag 'some distance below' the wych elm. The bag measured 9½ inches wide by 6½ and the moss covering on one side indicated that it had been there for some time. So much for the thorough search of the ground in April 1943, although conceivably the bag may not have been there that long. A letter T had been carved into the bark of a silver birch nearby.

Clent police had a record that a handbag had been reported stolen on 16 December from a car parked in Hagley Wood Lane. The woman who reported it was Dr Dorothy Edith Markham of 25, Elgin Rd, Alexandra Park, London N22. Police enquiries revealed that the doctor now lived in Compton Court, Compton Road, Wolverhampton. The bag itself was empty but Dr Markham had said that it had contained about fifteen shillings in cash, a fountain pen and a driving licence. To be fair to McCormick, he had no access to police files when he wrote his book because Hagley Wood was still an open case, so the driving licence morphed into the much more likely identity card.

Constable Jack Pound was sent to interview Dr Markham on 22 November and she identified the bag as hers. Pound was satisfied that the bag had no links with the body in the wych elm but leaving it at that seems just as irresponsible as McCormick's version in which the police make enquiries of an anonymous woman in a Midlands town (Markham in Wolverhampton) and accept that being without an identity card for months was not unusual and no cause for concern. Few people had driving licences in the 1940s and motorists were not obliged to carry them. Even allowing for the fact that Dr Markham was working in the area in 1939, what was her (vacated) car doing in Hagley Wood Lane? It was December, hardly a time for a nature ramble. The fact is that Jack Pound may have been too easily fobbed off by a professional woman who was unlikely to have been intimidated by the sudden arrival of a policeman. Whatever the links between the doctor and the wood, the actual driving licence was never seen again.

In *Murder By Witchcraft*, Donald McCormick refers to a man who saw an article on the Hagley Wood case in the papers. Typical of McCormick's style, we have no name, no date, not even the newspaper in question. He was, McCormick says, and everyone else has followed him, an executive of an industrial company who was living in lodgings on Hagley Common in the summer of 1941. He was walking to his digs, perhaps on 16 July and heard a woman's screams coming from the wood. Minutes later, he met a teacher walking in the opposite direction and he had heard the same thing. The pair decided to call the police and a sergeant came to investigate. The three found nothing. Was a dead woman already lying, contorted in the confined space of the bole, inside one of the many wych elms they trudged past?

Knowing what we do about McCormick's habit of running with all the rumours and half-baked truths, this story requires investigation. There is *no* report of the incident in the police files, no screams in the woods, no keenly searching sergeant. What time of day was this? If the executive was returning home, it was presumably after the day's work, so early evening. The teacher would have finished his day too, by then, the school term still in operation on 16 July. To call the police, they would either have gone to whichever of their homes was nearest or to find a call box. Buttons had to be pressed and '999' had to be dialled. The operator's voice would have clicked in – 'which service do you require?' – and wires would be pulled to make the police connection. The days are long in July so it would be entirely feasible for a search to be conducted that evening. But if the screams were the last sounds made by the woman in the wych elm, her murderer would still be at large in the wood. Did he stuff the body in the tree and make a run for it while the walkers were finding their red-painted telephone kiosk? Possible, but unlikely.

It is possible that the teacher and the executive are figments of McCormick's imagination or a misreading of a newspaper article. We shall come across two teachers in the Hagley Wood Archive later, but there is no one who fits the pattern of the executive.

In the end, like so much else in the Hagley Wood murder, it was all smoke and mirrors. Asked for his comments late in 1943, Superintendent Sidney Inight admitted they had no real clue as to the identity of the dead woman. She might as well, as someone in the original investigation put it, have come 'from another world'.

Chapter 6

The Writing on the Wall

Sixty-three years before the Hagley Wood murder, a series of killings took place in London's East End which have assumed iconic status. Seven women[1] all of them prostitutes, were attacked and mutilated in the adjacent parishes of Whitechapel and Spitalfields by a blitz-style killer who, thanks to over-the-top journalese, came to be known as Jack the Ripper.

On the night of 31 September, the killer struck twice. His first victim was Elizabeth Stride, known as Long Liz, whose body was found by a passing carter in Dutfield's Yard off Berner Street. It is likely that the arrival of Louis Diemschutz, with his pony and trap, interrupted the killer who hid until the coast was clear, then moved west, probably out of his comfort zone. This brought him out of the jurisdiction of the Metropolitan police and into that of the City force.

In Mitre Square, the Whitechapel murderer came across Catherine Eddowes, whose particular patch that was, and he killed her. This time, there would be no interruptions and despite the frequency of police patrols in the area, 'Jack' cut the woman's throat, slashed her cheeks, earlobes and eyelids, ripped open her abdomen and removed a kidney and ovaries. Where he went then must be conjecture, but a piece of evidence came to light which has an indirect link with the Hagley Wood killing.

Constable 254A Alfred Long of the Met was patrolling his usual beat along Goulston Street, to the east of Mitre Square, and he noticed a scribbled sentence, written in chalk, on the black brick facia of Numbers 108–19 Wentworth Model Dwellings, a tenement block typical of dozens all over the East End. Lying in the basin of a stand pipe below it was a piece of bloody cloth which had been ripped from an apron. Subsequent research proved that the cloth – and the blood – came from Catherine Eddowes. In all probability, the murderer had a considerable amount of blood on his hands and had taken the cloth away to wipe them. Heading to what was almost certainly his home in Whitechapel, he chanced upon the stand pipe and washed his hands more thoroughly.

Had he also written the chalk message of the wall nearby? Unfortunately, detectives who arrived to view the scene did not record accurately what the words said; neither, although the technology was available, were they photographed. According to the official police line, backed by the Home Office, the words read 'The Juwes are the men That Will not be Blamed for nothing.' The misspelling of 'Jews' was noted but changed at least three times by the time of the coroner's inquest. Fearing that this overt anti-Semitism would inflame the non-Jewish population of the area (where over 90 per cent were Jewish) the Commissioner of the Met, the clueless Charles Warren, ordered the words erased.

As with the writing that appeared in the Hagley Wood case, the Goulston Street Graffito opened a can of worms and has itself reached iconic status in the febrile world of Ripperology. A number of detectives at the time did not believe that the words had any connection with the Whitechapel killings, and this, of course, is the problem with all sorts of evidence at crime scenes. To take another example from the Ripper case, a leather apron was found near the body of another victim, Annie Chapman, in a yard behind No 29 Hanbury Street, Whitechapel. This 'evidence' was leaked to the press who brazenly asserted that the apron belonged to the killer. Accordingly, a local named John Pizer, who not only, as a shoemaker, owned such a garment but actually had the nickname 'Leather Apron', was attacked by a mob and had to be rescued by the police. It was later discovered that the apron belonged to one of the seventeen occupants of No 29 who had washed it and left it out overnight to dry.

I have not been able to pinpoint the first appearance of the Hagley Wood graffito but it was certainly there by Christmas 1943 when the message was reported on an external wall of Upper Dean Street, Birmingham. It was written in block capitals in chalk, each letter approximately the height of a brick. It read 'Who put Bella down the Wych elm – Hagley Wood'. There was no question mark, implying perhaps that the author was not much of a writer, but 'wych' was spelled correctly, as it usually was in later editions of the question. One, slightly nearer to Hagley – Old Hill, Birmingham – read 'Who put Luebella down the Wych Elm?' and was followed by 'Hagley Wood Bella'. The most common form of the dozens that appeared in the weeks and months that followed read 'Who put Bella in the Wych Elm?'

The first reference (of many) in the police files is dated 28 March 1944, eleven months after the body was found and nearly three years after she died. Detective Constable Frank Kedward wrote to Superintendent Hollyhead at Stourbridge to tell him that Wilfred Lawson White, a 40-year-old fruiterer of Beale Street in the town had seen some wall writing that morning on his way to work at Smithfield Fruit Market in Birmingham. The inscription was on the wall of Messrs Francis Nicholls Ltd, but the confusion over the address – 'either Pershore Street or Dean Street, Birmingham' – is a cause of confusion itself. The words were identical to those found in the same area since the previous December – 'Who put Bella in the Wych Elm Hagley Wood'.

Both DI Williams at Worcester and Birmingham City Police were informed. Worryingly, Williams's version of the same incident on the same day reads differently – 'Who put Bella in the Wytch Elm tree at Hagley Wood?' The devil, as is the case with all murder enquiries, was in the detail. And the detail was careless and confused. Detective Inspector Dillon of the Birmingham force was to look into the matter.

Three days later, DI Williams was in Upper Dean Street, Birmingham with the local officers Chief Inspector Davis and DS Renshaw. The writing was on the wall of empty premises next to those of Messrs Williamsons. The manager was helpful, as were the Boffeys, father and son, who worked as warehousemen on the premises. Raymond Boffey, the son, had his attention drawn to the writing by a lad named George Bond (both boys were in their teens). Boffey had written 'No parking here' nearby, obviously tired of the world and his wife blocking the Williamsons' yard. Boffey denied writing anything else, but admitted he had read about the Hagley Wood murder recently in an old newspaper. Under pressure from the police, the 16-year-old cracked and admitted his writing the 'Bella' message. He subsequently withdrew this statement, so Williams got him to write it down. This proved to be a disaster. 'He is absolutely,' the inspector wrote in his report, 'an illiterate youth, having only reached the third standard at school.' Boffey's scribble is still attached (one of four made) and only in one was the spelling correct, simply because Williams had told him how to spell the words!

Enquiries in the area drew a blank. No one in the markets and coffee houses knew anyone called Bella. The next day, Williams had a phone call from Sergeant Renshaw; another message had appeared, on the wall of Messrs Whites near the Williamson buildings. This time it just read 'Hagley Wood Bella' and must have been written late on 29 March or early on the 30th. So, back Williams went on the next day, a Thursday.

The enquiries at Whites' included interviews with lorry drivers who came from all over the Midlands, as far away as Shrewsbury in the west. Out of this came a possible suspect, for the writing if not the murder itself. On Saturday, 25 March, a man had called at the offices of the *Birmingham Gazette* and asked to see the file on Hagley Wood. He was between 30 and 40 years old, wearing work clothes and an overcoat, had dark hair and was 5ft 10in tall. He spent half an hour perusing the cuttings, and Frederick Anderson, the desk reporter, asked if he could help. He told him that he had been passing Hagley Wood at about the time of the murder and felt that 'something terrible was going to happen'. He had been talking this over with workmates and wanted to check on the dead woman's wedding ring. Anderson was naturally suspicious and asked to see the man's identity card. The name was John Jones, of Reservoir Road, Selly Oak but Anderson had not written down the National Registration Number nor the actual address.

Williams took Anderson to Reservoir Road but he could not identify 'Mr Jones' at all. There were two hundred houses along the road but the local fire-guard officer was very helpful and whittled down the likely address to 264 or 266. No one was in at either house, so Williams called it a day; by now it was 8.30 p.m. and getting dark. In wartime, of course, with a blackout in force, that meant very dark indeed.

When Williams reached the station, he got a phone call about yet another outbreak of graffiti, this time in Old Hill, Staffordshire, with the phrase 'Who put Luebeller in the Wych Elm'.

The next morning saw him with Detective Constables Kedward and Venables looking at the writing on the wall of an old cottage on the Old Hill to Halesowen road. Williams believed the handwriting to be identical to the others he had seen. He contacted an old teacher friend of his, John Cox, head of Old Hill School and asked his professional opinion. Contrary to the report that Williams had only received the day before, Cox told him that the graffito had been there since before the previous Christmas. Still following his hunch about Jones of Reservoir Road, Williams conferred with Inspector Bache of Halesowen in respect of a firm, Gaskell and Chambers, who had recently moved premises from

Dalesend to Hayseed, only a quarter of a mile from the Old Hill writing. Williams was sending telegrams in all directions, keeping everybody in the loop, including the journalist Anderson, in case the elusive Mr Jones should call back. He suggested keeping watch on various premises in the area for a possible return of the graffiti writer.

Two days later, on what was, ironically, April Fools' Day, Sergeant Renshaw was letting Williams know that he had taken photographs of the Upper Dean Street writing and had taken scrapings of the chalk itself, trying to pinpoint the origin of the material.

The previous day, teacher John Cox of Haden Hill, Old Hill, made an official statement to Detective Archie Venables. His involvement went way back, in fact to the previous summer (1943) which, if correct, makes it the closest graffito we have relating to the finding of the body. At the time, Cox did not equate it with Hagley Wood. But he was not the only eyewitness to this. Venables also interviewed James William Rowley, a laboratory assistant aged 18, of High Haden Road, Old Hill. Rowley was walking to work on 30 March 1944 carrying a copy of the early edition of the *Birmingham Gazette* and had just read of similar writings. There it was on a cottage wall – 'Who put Luebeller in the Wych Elm'. Venables' search of the Burgess List, a sort of street directory, revealed no one called Bella, Luebeller, Christabella or any other likely variant. Enquiries at the Food and Registration office also drew a blank.

Venables added in this report that he had heard of a conversation in the Star pub in Halesowen on that day, in which one of the men concerned said that he knew who the murderer was. Inspector Bache, whose manor this was, was dealing with it. We have already noted the paranoia of wartime Britain and 'guilty' conversations of any sort were taken very seriously by the authorities. As a footnote, are Messrs Rowley and Cox the *actual* origin of McCormick's duo who reported the screams in Hagley Wood? Cox was a teacher and even though Rowley, as a laboratory technician, hardly equates with a company executive, it is easy to see how one member of an establishment could be confused with another. They *had* both gone to the police with information linked with Hagley Wood, although not as directly as McCormick would have us believe.

On 12 April, another graffito was reported and this one had a cynical, if sinister, twist. At some time after 10 a.m., the following words appeared on a wall at Mucklow Hill, Halesowen. It was, as usual, in white chalk and read 'Who put Bella in the wytch elm, Hagley Wood. Jack the Ripper. Jack the Ripper. Anna Bella. Died in Hagley Wood?'

Bearing in mind the Goulston Street Graffito (see p49) and its red-herring goose-chase by the police in 1888, this one underlines the point of the Bella writings; virtually all of it was a joke. Jack the Ripper was – and remains – the best-known unknown murderer in the world; and Bella's killer was unknown too. Two things, however, emerge from the Halesowen daub of 12 April 1944 – the second name Anna (later to have sinister echoes) and the valid, unanswerable question, did Bella actually die in Hagley Wood? Detective Constable John Lee was to follow this one up.

He reported that the lettering was very roughly done about 5ft 6in from the ground. It had appeared soon after a group of lads from local factories had been seen loitering in the area (as they did routinely during their lunch break) and one of them was likely to have been responsible. DI Williams had seen this message too, on his way to a detectives' conference in Birmingham with Sergeant Skerratt from Clent. In his opinion, the writing style was nothing like the others he had seen.

There seems to be a lull in the graffiti outbreak because the next police reference is dated 1 August. Williams reported that the writing had been photographed on a wall in Wolverhampton and read 'Hagley Wood – Luebella – her address was opposite the Rose and Crown, Hasbury'. Hasbury is a village on the road to Halesowen, about four miles from Hagley. Inspector Bache told Williams that a similar message had appeared on a gate opposite the Shelton Inn, Belle Vale, Halesowen and that DC Lee had seen it. Was this, at last, a breakthrough?

PC231 Albert Pitcher, on Bache's instructions, visited Hasbury the next day. On a bridge wall near the gate was the incomprehensible 'I use to Hagley Wood' but the next part of the sentence was more interesting. 'Lubella was no pross[titute]'.

The ever-diligent Constable Pitcher visited all the houses opposite the Rose and Crown and dutifully recorded details of all the residents (although the report is somewhat garbled). He had gone back six years. The Willetts family (four adults and one child and no known relation to Tommy who had helped find Bella's body) had lived at Number 390 for forty years. Ernest and his wife had one child; Walter and his wife had no children. Harry Moore had lived four doors away for thirty years, along with his wife and four daughters. Mrs Withers lived at 396 with her small child; her husband Colin was serving with the armed forces and the family had lived there for five years. Hilda Argent's husband had been killed by enemy action in 1941; she lived with her child at 398. At 400 lived Alfred Hardwick, his wife and three children. Next door was Albert Allsopp, his wife Annie and daughter who had lived there for thirty-five years. Their son, Samuel, was a leading Aircraftsman based in Suffolk. At 406 lived Arthur James, his wife, daughter and son-in-law. They had been there for twelve years. Number 408 was the home of the widow Mabel Basterfield and her son. John Laight, his wife and three small children lived at 410, except that the husband was somewhere with the armed forces. None of them knew anyone called Lubella.

The only Bella that Pitcher came across was a woman – Bella James – who occasionally visited the Allsopps who were distant relatives of hers but they had heard nothing of her for over four years and she was aged between 60 and 70. Subsequent enquiries found her alive and well in Kidderminster.

On the same day that Pitcher was knocking on doors in Hasbury, 24-year-old chemist Stanley Ray, employed at Mander Bros by the Ministry of Supply made a statement to DC L. White to the effect that he had seen another Rose and Crown graffito the previous day in Sun Passage, under an archway belonging to the railway. Chief Inspector Penderel visited the site with the words in white chalk and believed that they had been recently done. Penderel made sure that DI Williams was kept in the loop but by now everybody involved in the case must have been heartily tired of pranksters' work appearing all over the place. The Wolverhampton *Express and Star* reported the latest outbreak on 7 August – 'it can only be supposed that these chalkings are yet another hoax.'

Williams' visit to Halesowen, however, elicited some potentially useful information. Opposite the Rose and Crown were the premises of J.T. Willetts (Pitcher had talked to the family at 390). This was a timber yard and Mr Willetts senior knew Hagley Wood well. He told Williams that either the wych elm was a piece of luck for the murderer or that the tree was known to him in advance. Willetts believed 'that the woman was taken to the Wood and that some person attempted to have intercourse with her against her will and that her death occurred as the result of some violence being used'. He was convinced that Bella was not local. Williams knew the Willetts family and knew he could trust their knowledge. Against that, however, was Professor Webster's assertion that the presence of the woman's undamaged knickers precluded rape or any attempt; Willetts obviously did not know that.

In his report, Williams had been talking things over with Inspector Bache and they agreed that using local papers, especially the *Express and Star* with its big circulation, would be a good vehicle to prompt the public and elicit any information. Most CID units did this by the 1940s, but some were reluctant to give too much away as it brought out the prurient and frankly deranged – as would be the case with Bella.

One of these was the mysterious Mr Jones who had called at the *Birmingham Gazette*'s offices in search of the paper's Hagley Wood murder file. He had been traced back in April 1944 and Williams had interviewed him. He was 'a peculiar youth, over 6ft, protruding ears and teeth and looked abnormal'. John Jones lived at 106, Reservoir Road, Erdington, a suburb of Birmingham and worked as an electrician in the BSA works in Small Heath. Somewhat bizarrely, bearing in mind Williams' opinion of him, he was attached to the Intelligence Section, 26th Battalion, C Company, Birmingham Home Guard. As to his sense that 'something was going to happen' near Hagley Wood Lane, Williams concluded that he had 'either been reading too many detective novels' or had read a journal called *Armchair Scientist* and saw himself as an amateur psychologist/sleuth. Jones had rung Digbeth police station over twenty times offering his advice and assistance. Williams got Jones to write out the Hagley Wood message found in Upper Dean Street (the first one that appeared) and believed he was responsible; Professor Webster disagreed although he was not an acknowledged graphologist. Attached to the police file on Jones is an extract from *Armchair Science*, August 1939 which attempts to identify murderers from their glandular peculiarities. When a certain type of man turns to crime, reads the section annotated in pencil by Jones:

> ... his will be the 'perfect crime' of fiction, carefully planned and carried out without a hitch. He'll rob, but only for six-figure sums, and when he kills, you'll find that love or its step-sister [hate?] was the motivating impulse ... And if the police don't catch him in the act, they're hardly likely to catch him in the next six months. But when they do and if they're glandularly minded, they'll put him in a cell with a ream of paper and a dozen pencils. Then he'll give himself away. Oh, no, he won't confess. He never confesses. But he can't resist the urge to write.

It is difficult to say who was more 'peculiar'; John Jones or the author of *Armchair Science*!

Again and again, we come back to that first wall writing in Upper Dean Street. Later ones were almost certainly the work of hoaxers – and if the purpose was to distract the police and lead them in the wrong direction, it worked – but why Upper Dean Street? And was that first one actually written by someone who genuinely knew something? The street was a short one, just over 300 yards long, in the heart of the city centre, near the Rag Market and the Bull Ring. Tat of all kinds was sold in the area, as it had been for centuries and the Bull Ring itself rang to the shouts of costers and the rumble of their carts in the 1940s. There was a synagogue there and among its once more opulent Georgian homes, a pub called the Coach and Horses. The police determined that the chalk used for the graffiti was the bog-standard type, universally used in schools on blackboards and in pubs to mark up darts' scores. What could be easier than for someone to sneak a piece into his pocket after a pint and use it to pose the question on nearby brickwork after closing time?

At the heart of the graffiti was the name itself. Later assertions (see Chapter 14) were that the name was associated with witchcraft, but this is an almost nonsensical generalization. It means 'beautiful' (as in 'belle of the ball') but this is a much later interpretation. '*Belli*' is the plural of *bellum*, a war. A Bellatrix was a female warrior (largely, in Roman times, a literary convention). All of it came from Bellona, a war goddess. So, there was something appropriate about Bella's body being found during the biggest war in history. The 'beautiful' meaning comes from *belle*, meaning well or nicely and is a far more Italian convention.

As an English name in the 1930s and 1940s, it was unusual, a derivation of Elizabeth, alongside Eliza, Isobel, Lubella and the commonest version, Betty. Today, Bella is rated sixty-second among popular girls' names; in 1940, it is not even in the first hundred. Was the scrawled name on that wall in Upper Dean Street a generic one, almost like the Australian 'sheila' which fitted any female? Or did the writer know exactly who had been hidden in Hagley Wood and was that actually her name? If the writer of the original graffito knew Bella and was concerned that she had not, by Christmas 1943, got justice, why did he not contact the police with what he knew? Or was it just a matter of taunting the authorities, who had so far failed to catch anybody? In the case of the Whitechapel murders, the police and the press received upwards of 220 letters and postcards, most of them chiding the Metropolitan and City forces for their incompetence. What we do *not* have, unlike the Ripper killings, is anyone coming forward to admit responsibility. Often, the higher the profile of a murder and the more coverage it gets in the press, the more the pressure is on some people – usually men – to confess. In the case of Peter Sutcliffe, the Yorkshire Ripper who battered women to death in Leeds in the 1980s, the most blatant – and damaging – of these was the spurious confession on tape from 'Wearside Jack', whose identity would only be discovered years later and who had nothing to do with the Leeds murders at all. As far as we are aware, no one came forward to say '*I* put Bella in the wych elm' and the police were no further forward.

But in October 1944 came an unusual twist. At Halloween, a letter was sent to the chief constable at Newton Street, Birmingham:

Sir,
Just a line you are letting me Be at ease I mean about who put Bella Down the Wych Elm in Hagley Wood, you know the writing on the wall in Smithfield St. some months Back that was me Mr Wood. Well here is your chance to meet me in Market St of[f] Collshill St tomorrow Nov 1 at 5.30 and you shall hear the truth all for Now.
Yours truly
Mr Wood

Needless to say, the police followed this up and needless to say, no one turned up at the rendezvous. Neither could anyone called Wood be located in the area. Wood was the 'Wearside Jack' of his day, an oddball who probably took delight in taunting the police.

The war undoubtedly added to the complexities of the case. While it is true that no one could wander the countryside as freely as they had before 3 September 1939 and everybody and his wife was on the lookout for fifth columnists and suspicious activity, police forces were stretched and records were not kept. There was, for instance, no national census for 1941 because so many people were serving overseas in the armed forces and administrative units were needed elsewhere. Likewise, in Birmingham, there were no updated electoral rolls between 1940 and 1944. And the shady characters of the underworld had a knack of staying firmly under the radar, even given that it was Britain that invented it!

Grim as it was, the Second World War was a golden opportunity for some people. Professional criminals saw the openings at once. They became Black Marketeers, thieves and pilferers, getting around the restrictions of rationing. The unscrupulous factory worker could sneak out of his workplace with metal goods, fabric, machine parts under his coat. The dodgy stevedore could 'mislay' whole crates of imports. And there were 'larks' everywhere. The bomb lark saw people still living in untouched houses claiming compensation for bomb damage that had not happened. The billeting lark witnessed landlords and landladies claiming expenses for troops in their homes who had long moved on. After any air raid, the rate of looting was horrendous. Who knew how many peopled trudged past the Coach and Horses in Upper Dean Street, casually reading the chalked question that somebody had posed, with a few jars of jam in their pockets or a fur coat rolled up in an otherwise empty pram? The penalty for looting was fourteen years at His Majesty's Pleasure, but it was a risk worth taking because the police could not be everywhere.

Women like Bella – the name stuck; the media and the police widely used it – were particularly at risk. A London magistrate warned about air-raid shelters. 'The things that are going on now in those public shelters are very dreadful. For a young girl to go into a … shelter … without her father and her mother is simply asking for trouble.' Because of the war, there was, at any given time, a sizeable number of missing persons. Some had been blown to pieces in the Blitz and their bodies never found. Others, down on their luck and deprived of the financial support of husbands and fathers, wandered the cities and the peripheries of army camps. The arrival of the Americans, with their gum, their nylons, candy, smart uniforms and, above all, their money, made this worse.

Let us look at the women we know were victims of murder in the same period. We have already met Joan Wolfe, whose body was found in Houndown Wood, Hankley Common in October 1942. She was the product of what today we would call a broken home, her mother Edith marrying three times. The man assumed to be Joan's father suffered from what at the time was called sleeping sickness. He gassed himself while Joan was still at school. Edith's letters to her daughter constantly carped about the girl's behaviour – she stayed out late with older men and, at 16, began to 'go with soldiers'. She was already engaged but broke off her relationship and went first to Aldershot, the 'home' of the British army, then to London to work, for a month only, in an aircraft factory. Edith was appalled, believed that her daughter had venereal disease and was probably a nymphomaniac. When she became involved with a number of Canadian soldiers, including August Sangret, who eventually killed her, she lived rough, in 'wigwams' in the woods, and was infested with lice. She only owned one set of clothes, the ones she was wearing when she died. She spoke French, wore a crucifix and did not, in her own words, understand men.

When Superintendent Fred Cherill, the fingerprint expert at Scotland Yard, first saw Nita Ward, she was 'lying across a bed ... with not even a sheet as covering ... She was a ghastly sight. She had been the victim of a sadistic attack of the most horrible and revolting nature.' She had been strangled and her killer had mutilated her with a tin-opener and a piece of broken mirror. Her real name was Evelyn Oatley, aged thirty-six. She had been an actress and a Windmill girl, performing nightly in the famous theatre that refused to close even at the height of the Blitz and she had left her husband. Lack of cash drove her to prostitution. There were 143 brothels operating in London in 1942 before the Met closed some of them down. Many more were in business two years later and the majority of their customers were Americans who were being ripped off by their outrageous charges. The 'Hyde Park Rangers' and 'Piccadilly Commandoes' as they were called, flashed torches at would-be clients in blacked-out alleyways. Some of them serviced fifteen men a night and the money was good. The fact that Evelyn had a flat in Wardour Street, London, on the edge of Soho, implied that she was a cut above the usual street girl.

Margaret Lowe was 43, 'a handsome and finely built woman' according to Cherril and everybody knew her as Pearl. She was widowed and had once kept a boarding house in Southend. Her body was found in her flat in Crosfield Street off Tottenham Court Road. She was working as a prostitute and there was a darned silk stocking tied tightly round her neck. Her naked body was hideously mutilated.

Doris Jouannet was the wife of a French hotel manager. Her husband had taken British citizenship in the 1930s and the couple lived in Sussex Gardens, already known for its availability of cheap rooms, often by the hour. Henri Jouannet had an alibi for the time of his wife's death and had no idea that she was 'on the game'. She had been strangled with a scarf and ripped open like the others. Her killer had nearly sliced off one of her nipples with a razor blade.

The three women above were all victims of the man dubbed the 'Blackout Killer' by the press – Aircraftsman Gordon Cummings. He was an extraordinarily inept murderer, leaving fingerprints, items of uniform and a gas mask behind at scenes of crime. Two failed attacks on women sealed his fate and he was hanged by Albert Pierrepoint at Wandsworth on 25 June 1942.

It is true that Cummins' first victim was the respectable Evelyn Hamilton, a 42-year-old pharmacist who was about to move back home to the north, where it was safer than much-bombed London. She had £80 on her when she met Cummins in an air-raid shelter (despite the caveats of the magistrate quoted above) and he strangled her, ramming her silk scarf into her mouth to stop her screams. But it is also true that the maniac's other victims were all 'good time girls', as the Americans called them, as were the lucky pair who got away from him. The risks that these women took were huge.

'Nita', 'Pearl' and 'Mrs M' and 'Mrs H' (Greta Haywood and Mrs Mulcahy, also known as Kathleen King) were aliases used by women who offered their bodies to men for money. Was that also true of Bella?

Chapter 7

All the Bellas in the World

Every commentator of the Hagley Wood murder has followed Donald McCormick's lead that the police tried to trace the 2,000 women missing in Britain between 1941 and 1943. This was within, according to McCormick, a radius of 1,000 miles from Hagley, which would have taken the enquiries well into occupied Europe – to be precise, halfway across Poland and the whole of France – which was, of course, a no-go area for any police force in wartime. Even if McCormick meant 1,000 square miles, it is still too vast an area for overstretched forces. That said, it is clear from the Worcester Archive that cooperation between constabularies was good and other forces would help if they could.

And because it was wartime, there were two conflicting elements operating, which actually made it quite difficult for a woman to 'disappear'. One was the camaraderie, itself a product of fear, which made people group together and look out for each other. The other is the paranoia we have already noted, a natural extension of many people enjoying nothing better than to snoop – and to report certain activities to the authorities. In the recent COVID experience, equated, as we have seen, with the Second World War, it has been everybody's delight to report on 'Partygate' and 'Beergate', catching the great and good of government out breaking their own rules.

We can see this happening in the case of Joan Wolfe that we have discussed already, a case which, unlike Bella, had a successful outcome. When Joan first ran away from home, her mother, Edith Watts, contacted the police who traced her to the army camps at Aldershot. The army brought her back. When she ran again, this time to London, Mrs Watts managed to trace her via a series of landladies. Admittedly, Joan kept up an intermittent contact with her mother through letters – as of course Bella might have done with somebody. When the runaway got to Godalming in Surrey, near to a Canadian army camp, she stayed with Kate Hayter, an old lady in nearby Thursley who looked out for her. A patrolling policeman saw her with a soldier in a Godalming park and he moved them on. Constable Timothy Halloran of the Surrey police took the pair to the station on another occasion. He quizzed her as a vulnerable person under the Children and Young Persons Act. Halloran was able to trace Joan's mother in Tunbridge Wells but the girl did not want to know and the constable had no choice but to let the pair go (she was nineteen). She was ill two days later and booked herself in to the emergency ward of Warren Road Hospital, Guildford, where the staff looked after her. She had ignored Halloran's advice to find quarters with the Church Army in the town.

Once out of hospital, Joan lived with her lover August Sangret in a wigwam the Meti soldier had made for her in Houndown Woods. Various guards at Witley Camp moved them on because soldiers were forbidden to 'set up house' with civilians. The police took Joan into custody and returned her to hospital in something akin to desperation. They could not hold her at a police station as she had committed no crime. Days later, she was living (on and off with Sangret who slipped out of his barracks) at a cricket pavilion in Thursley; the ARP warden, William Featherby, saw them there and kicked them out. Two children had seen them looking for digs in the village. True, the involvement of a number of people, including the police, failed to keep Joan Wolfe alive, but her lifestyle, in the weeks before her death in September 1942, was documented and known. Surely, a similar pattern could be found for Bella in the wych elm?

The obvious difference was that the Hagley Wood victim had no identity, but the name Bella caught the imagination of police and public alike. If that actually *was* her name, tracing her could not be that difficult; and three Bellas came to light.

The first was Bella Tonks. When the Hagley Wood investigation was closed in 2005, West Mercia police (as the Worcestershire force was now called) produced a detailed report (see Chapter 16). It reads 'Bella Tonks was raised as a possibility following a media circulation' and it says a great deal about how determined – or desperate – the police of 1943 were that the 2005 report says, 'The name "Bella" was seemingly derived from the chalk writings on the walls throughout the West Midlands conurbation and as such the link to the enquiry was questionable.' It was as though the Met in 1888 were looking for a man called J.T. Ripper! Bella Tonks was found, living under her maiden name (not given in 2005) in Heath Hayes, a village near Cannock nearly twenty miles away from Hagley. There are no further details, but presumably some long-suffering plod had to go door to door in the same way that Constable Pitcher had in Hasbury.

The Worcester Archive says that this Bella was a teacher at Clent School, very close to Hagley and that she was in her mid-fifties in 1943, which would make her too old for the woman in the wych elm. She was described as plump, with gold-brown hair and 'a good set of even teeth'. She was 5ft 4in tall. On all counts, Bella Tonks could not be the woman in the tree. She was 'very fond of the company of men', however, and that probably rang alarm bells for investigating officers. She was believed to be living in Wednesbury, near Heath Hayes and was married with four children. This was on 4 April 1944 and she was found, very much alive, soon afterwards.

Bella Luer was an altogether better bet, if only because several of the chalk writings had the name Lubella attached. According to the 2005 closure report, she moved from London, almost certainly to escape the Blitz, to work in a factory in the Birmingham area, which has an air of frying pans and fires about it! There is a letter in the Archive from Alfred Richardson of Stamford Hill, N16, to the effect that Bella Luer was a neighbour of his. She had planned to get married but had subsequently disappeared. She lived in lodgings with Mrs Dora Harris, a 50-year-old housekeeper who received a Christmas card from Bella in 1942. This effectively ruled her out as the Hagley Wood victim, who, at 24 was *just* under Professor Webster's estimation of age. She was also, however, 5ft 4–5in tall with a 'good set of teeth, her own, not false' and was a Jewess. Since the last line in the report of May 1944 reads 'She lives at 10 Railway Cottages, Goring-on-Sea' we must assume that she was still alive and that the police had drawn a blank again.

What about Bella Beech? Like Luer, she had left London when the Luftwaffe targeted her stomping ground in West Ealing. The police could find no one named Beech in the Birmingham areas where the first graffiti had been found, but James Beech, a railway porter, lived in Stourbridge. He was Bella's twin brother and *had* lived for a while at Upper Dean Street. Someone else who lived nearby was Harry Trueman, who had fallen out with his wife and lived with another woman, who may have been Bella. The Worcestershire Archive is infuriatingly vague about him, probably because in May 1944, Isobel Eleanor Beech was found alive and well, working as a nurse in a hospital in Muswell Hill, London. The process of elimination of these women was all very laudatory – and probably necessary – but it cost the overstretched constabulary a vast amount of time and resources.

Nor could the police afford to concentrate *just* on missing Bellas. Other reports of missing persons came their way constantly in the turmoil of the war years and all of them had to be checked. In *The People's War* (2000), Angus Calder estimates that there were about 60 million changes of address between 1939 and 1945 at a time when the population was only 38 million. Much of this was evidenced by the two Bellas cited above – a drift from London, but it also worked from east to west. The industrial North East, East Anglia and Kent were considered the areas most likely to be overrun by an invasion – Devon and Cornwall seemed a paradise by comparison, but of course, work was limited there. London had only 67 per cent of its population by the summer of 1943, although the industrial Midlands increased, adding to the workload of the Worcestershire constabulary. Overcrowding became a real issue and small towns like Stourbridge, even villages like Hagley, became overwhelmed. The Mass Observation unit reported that sleepy hamlets up and down the country looked like London railway stations with an 'atmosphere of irritable bustle, impersonal pushing and hurrying'. The newcomers extended queues outside fish and chip shops; they filled up cinemas. Host towns and villages had to take essential war workers and evacuees who had been bombed out, but they did not have to like it. And in 1941–43, nobody could have foretold how much worse it would be when the Americans arrived!

Into the muddle of the Bella investigation stepped another time waster. He was Private Heywood, Christian name not recorded, of the 2nd Battalion, Oxford and Bucks Light Infantry based in Nottingham. In the Worcester Archive is a letter from the Reverend A.G. Harper who was the regiment's padre and who was making enquiries on Heywood's behalf. In fact, he need not have bothered because Heywood had already contacted the police using his own name and then a second time with an alias as though to shine a spotlight on the woman he was looking for. Harper's letter describes Heywood's missing girlfriend as being 23 but looks 18, about 5ft 2in tall with blue eyes, very long and very black hair, very white pearly teeth, none missing. She was a fruit and hop picker, last heard of at Illey Farm, Illey, Worcestershire (two miles from Hagley). The kindly padre was just doing his bit for one of his men, but one glance at the missing woman's description, her black hair, her pearly teeth, should have had Inspector Bache throwing the letter in the bin. Instead, the police wasted their efforts following this up. The padre had been right – the girl was 'of the "gypsy" class'. Her name was Mary Lee (a very common Romany surname) and by the time the police found her in Stow-on-the-Wold, she was living under an assumed name – Mary Wenham – and had moved on from Light Infantryman Heywood at least three times! The feeling was that Heywood knew all about this, had no concerns that Mary may be Bella and was just trying to get back with her again.

'Sheila' was another missing person the police were looking for and her existence came to light under rather unusual circumstances. Vivienne Cross, also known as Biddy Williams, shopped Kenneth Patten, also known as Pat Graham, over the disappearance of a Land Army girl in the summer of 1942. Again, the date should have ruled this enquiry out, but again, no stone could be left unturned. The population migration was a perfect opportunity for people to assume aliases, although the paperwork they carried, especially identity cards, was a problem for them. That said, most people who have aliases have a shady take on life and some of them have criminal records. That was certainly true of Kenneth Patten who was at the time residing at His Majesty's Pleasure in Wandsworth Prison in London. He and the Land Girl 'Sheila' had been working on the Hagley estate where he used to walk Vivienne Cross's dog. He also helped himself to somebody else's overcoat which is why he was in Wandsworth. When police interviewed him, they found that he had no clear recollection of Hagley Wood, had been working on T.F. Parsons' dairy farm in the area for three weeks that summer and had no idea who 'Sheila' was or where she had gone. Despite being a teller of tall stories, including one in which his racing-driver fiancée had been killed in a crash, leaving him heartbroken, Patten had no case to answer and the matter was dropped.

Dinah Curley was someone else with an alias and there are a number of references to her in the police files. She fills available space too in the closure file of 2005 even though the conclusion there is that it is likely that Dinah Curley, also known as O'Grady, probably never existed. PC71 Thomas Kelly of the Stockport County Borough police in Manchester was following up a missing person's report on Dinah Curley. Mrs Mary Lavin of Stanley Street, Manchester had reported Dinah missing after an air raid. The horrific damage done by the Luftwaffe in Manchester, as elsewhere, meant that bodies were not always found or identifiable and distressed relatives and/or friends often went to their local police station in the hope of finding someone. One bizarre case happened in London in

July 1942 when a woman's body was found in a bombed Baptist church in Vauxhall Road. She was Rachel Dobkin, identified by superb forensic work on the part of the pathologist Keith Simpson. But she was not a Blitz victim – her body had been placed there by her fire-watcher husband Harry and he duly hanged for her murder.

Constable Kelly found Mrs Lavin at 40, Laurence Street, Stockport, only to discover that she had never heard of Dinah Curley and had never lived in Manchester. In May 1941, when Dinah was reported missing, Mary Lavin had been living at the same address where Constable Kelly now sat, no doubt having a cup of tea. She was single then, Mary Dowling, and all her family lived in Ireland. The most peculiar thing about all this was that whoever had lodged the missing person's report had Mary's identity card details, with the registration number LCIL.9/1; she showed it to Constable Kelly. The bobby's enquiries of in-laws elicited the same response; no one knew Dinah Curley.

There is considerable confusion in the 2005 closure file over this one and nothing in the original archive to clarify it. Mary's husband, Jack Lavin, seems to have been a dodgy character who at some point in 1942 was working as a contract labourer in St David's, West Wales. Mary Lavin had moved in with a family called Lynch in Robert Street, Manchester in that year and when the Lynches moved to Haverfordwest, Mary went too to join Jack. The police were able to trace Mary's movements until 30 March 1943 when she moved to Ripon, Yorkshire. By that time, the Lynches had gone to Kettering, Northamptonshire. Jack Lavin was wanted for non-payment of fines in Northamptonshire (what these were is not recorded). The identity card number is proof that Mary Lavin *did* in fact report Dinah Curley missing and the police were remiss in not pressuring her on this point. Perhaps the Lavins had some idea of cashing in on the disappearance of a non-existent friend in some hopelessly confused extension of the 'bomb lark', whereby people claimed compensation from the government for damage to property which had never happened.

Bella Lawley was also known as Kendrick and Shamwell, living in Trafalgar Road, Moseley, Birmingham. She may or may not have been engaged in prostitution in Ladywood and Bristol Road, but her sending a Christmas card to a friend in December 1942 implied that she was very much alive. The sending of the Christmas card has echoes of Bella Luer. Was this simply another alias of the same woman or a misremembering of her surname? The police files make no comment. We can assume the same for the other twenty missing persons in the police file were found alive and well too, representing, presumably, only a fraction of McCormick's alleged 2,000. Their last known addresses are the length and breadth of the country and if they were all as dodgy as Mary Lavin and Bella Luer, the police had their work cut out. What happened to Elsie Robinson, Mary Claypole, Gwen Parish, Miss P.D. Montgomery, Helen Ormsby and so many more from the police missing persons list? We will probably never know; their names light up briefly in the course of somebody else's murder enquiry.

But what we can be sure of is that none of them was Bella, or whatever the *real* name of the woman in the wych elm at Hagley Wood.

Chapter 8

Bloody Foreigners

There is a concept in the long history of murder that the killer is never a local, never 'one of us'. How often will journalists quote a neighbour where a body has been discovered as saying 'This sort of thing doesn't happen around here'? But, of course, it does, as the events make transparently clear. Not in my back yard, not in my street, not in my stretch of woodland – this remains the position generally taken. The extension of that argument is that the killer cannot be a local either – it must have been a stranger.

The stranger-killer is extremely rare, yet the idea is everybody's bogeyman. Generations of us have been so indoctrinated by television, slasher movies and home invasions, that we all have a morbid fear of the wandering lunatic intent on random slaughter. In recent years, this has been, sadly, reinforced by the perception of the danger posed by the mentally ill being badly diagnosed and released from institutions and by the rise of militant Islam, where any atrocity is accepted by some as being the will of Allah.

Nowhere is this fear of the stranger-killer more noticeable than in the Whitechapel murders of 1888. Since the area had a 95 per cent Jewish population and since most of them, from pogrom-plagued Russia and Poland, had only recently arrived, it was assumed by many that a Jew must be responsible. This was not helped by the fact that Israel Lipski, who murdered Miriam Angel in Batty Street, Whitechapel in June 1887 was one such recent arrival. He was hanged at Newgate just two months later. The surname 'Lipski' became a cry of contempt by anti-Semites for years afterwards. Modern studies of serial killers suggest strongly that they choose their victims from their own social class and race. There *are* exceptions, but the norm holds good in 95 per cent of cases. None of Jack the Ripper's victims was Jewish, but the finding of the infamous leather apron near the body of Annie Chapman led to John Pizer being attacked by the mob. He not only wore such an apron, as we have seen, but his behaviour was odd and he was Jewish.

But fear of the stranger-killer was not confined to hatred of the Jews. Into the frame as a possible Jack suspect steps Dr William Holt, a junior surgeon at St George's Hospital. On 11 November 1888 he approached a woman named Humphreys, who may or may not have been a prostitute. She screamed and reported that a white-eyed man with a black face had accosted her. Holt was eventually traced. He was a well-meaning (and harmless) do-gooder who prowled the area trying to do what the police, apparently, could not – catch the Whitechapel murderer. Holt was actually wearing glasses – hence the 'white' eyes – and he was not in black face; the rest was in Mrs Humphreys' fevered imagination.

It would be nice to think that prejudice of this sort – and the total misunderstanding of a killer's behaviour – would have changed for the better by the 1940s, but, if anything, it was worse. One of the casual observations in the Worcester police archives is that a witness had a 'Dago' name. At heart, it was institutional racism, but it was regarded as a factual statement by a society that had never heard of 'woke' and had other things to worry about rather than political correctness. Setting aside outright foreign invasions – by Celts, Romans, Saxons, Vikings and Normans – over a 4,000-year period, migration to Britain was a constant and although racial trouble broke out sporadically, most outsiders were welcomed, even if they tended to cluster together, forming ghettoes. This was particularly true of the Irish, who drifted to England's major cities in the 1840s as a result of the failure of the potato crop at home. The Jews likewise settled in London's East End, in effect driving the Irish out.

There is little doubt that the First World War was something of a turning point. Such was the anti-German feeling in Britain that German shops were attacked and proprietors beaten up. In October 1914, a mob of nearly 5,000 burnt down a German shop in Deptford High Street and the army had to be called in to restore order. Around the country, fifty golf clubs closed their doors to Germans and Austrians. Many hotels sacked their Teutonic staff. It did not help that the propaganda of the Great War created the myth of the German ogre, a savage monster like an enraged King Kong, complete with pickelhaube helmet and bloody fangs. There were stories of the Kaiser's troops crucifying Allied soldiers, even though they were just as Christian as their opponents; indeed, one of their battle cries was '*Gott mitt uns*' (God is with us).

This attitude never went away. In a country like Britain, internationally known for its generosity and sense of fair play, there were always those who not only flew the flag but detested foreigners. The comic duo Flanders and Swann, from a later generation, sang 'The English, the English, the English are best; I wouldn't give tuppence for all of the rest.' Even used ironically, these lyrics are unthinkable today, but in the 1950s everyone roared with laughter and nobody thought it was remotely distasteful.

When it came to particulars, foreigners were naturally suspected to be guilty of *anything*. Murder, claimed xenophobes, was not the British way, ignoring the bloody history of centuries. Recent articles on the Hagley Wood murder, mostly online, have pointed the finger at many people's bêtes noires: the Americans. Before Pearl Harbor, when the Japanese bombed the American naval base in Hawaii without the civilized courtesy of a declaration of war first, the government of Franklin D. Roosevelt provided cash and materiel under the lend-lease programme while Winston Churchill continually urged the president to join the war on the Allied side.

The alliance with the United States was part of an ongoing love-hate relationship. Traditionally, the GIs who came first as a trickle, then as a torrent, were 'overpaid, oversexed and over here'. The satirical magazine *Punch* summed up the situation perfectly in 1942:

Dear old England's not the same.
The dread invasion, well, it came.
But no, it's not the beastly Hun,
The god-damn Yankee army's come.

Britain was the same size, geographically, as Minnesota; Texas, three times as big. The guidebook given to the GIs spelt out the differences for a people who were, for all their advanced technology, surprisingly insular and isolationist. 'The British,' they were told, 'are tough, strong people and good allies. Don't be misled by the ... tendency to be soft-spoken and polite ... The English language didn't spread across oceans and over the mountains and jungles and swamps of the world because these men were panty-waists.'

In June 1942, there were fewer than 60,000 American troops in the country; by the build-up to D-Day, 6 June 1944, there were 1,526,965. More than 1,100 cities, towns and villages were home to these 'invaders', occupying country houses, schools, aircraft hangars, Nissen and Quonset huts and bell tents. The Americans were better dressed, better equipped, better paid. In 1942, a British Tommy earned 14 shillings a week; his GI oppo got the equivalent of £3 8s 9d. This bred resentment, especially when it came to local girls. They were easily lured by handsome young men in chocolate-coloured tunics, speaking the same kind of language they heard every week at the 'pictures'.

In terms of law and order, Parliament passed the United States of America (Visiting Forces) Act in 1942, which laid down that Americans be tried by their own military courts, not the British legal system. The Military Police, known as 'snowdrops' because of their white helmets, patrolled areas where their servicemen hung out and were considered over-zealous in their use of their night sticks. American servicemen found guilty of rape and murder were hanged at Shepton Mallet prison, either by Master-Sergeant John C. Woods of the US Army or Albert Pierrepoint, the British executioner.

In July 1943, four months after 'Bella' was found in Hagley Wood, GI John Waters shot his girlfriend, Doris Staples, who worked in a draper's shop in Henley-on-Thames. He then turned the gun on himself. Astonishingly, his head wound was not fatal. He faced trial, was found guilty and sentenced to death. Even more astonishingly, the townspeople of Henley organized a petition begging for mercy, understanding perhaps the enormous pressures on men thousands of miles from home.

The racial tensions of the American forces sometimes spilt over into British life. In Birmingham, so close to Hagley Wood, white soldiers kicked their coloured comrades off the 'sidewalk', calling them 'black trash'. A soldier of the 11th Armored Division told his dance partner, a girl from Chippenham, 'Ma'am, we shoot niggers where I come from.' But black soldiers were more courteous and polite when dealing with British girls. One young lady wrote, 'I don't mind the Yanks, but I can't say I care much for the white chaps they've brought with them.'

Three men were hanged for rape during the war and they were all Americans. Privates Elijah Brimson and Willie Small attacked 16-year-old Dorothy Holmes in March 1944 after a dance at Bishop's Cleeve, Gloucestershire. Thomas Madison 'got fresh with' Beatrice Reynolds at Gunnislake in Cornwall but she remembered his face too well and reported him. 'The only thing that was cheap in Britain,' disgruntled Americans joked, 'were the women.'

But all this faded into the background in contrast with the thrill-killers Jones and Hulten. In his *Decline of the English Murder*, George Orwell wrote that this pair 'committed their murder to the tune of V-1 and were convicted to the tune of V-2'. The terrifying pilotless rockets known as 'doodlebugs' were whining overhead, but a different danger lurked on the ground. Both killers used aliases. Private Karl Hulten was from Sweden, taken to America by his parents as a toddler. Cruising the bars of London, he called himself 2nd Lieutenant Ricky Allen of the 501st Airborne and most of the Britons he met, unfamiliar with American rank badges, went along with that. His partner in crime was Elizabeth Baker, from Neath, North Wales, although she styled herself as an exotic dancer called Georgina Grayson and had briefly been married to Lance Bombardier Stanley Jones. A rape victim at 13 who had 'done time' at an approved school, she was perfect for the *folie à deux* which happened on 7 October 1943. They robbed and killed a taxi-driver, George Heath, whose cleft chin led to the press name for this callous killing – 'the Cleft Chin Murder'. He bled to death from the single shot in the back from Hulten's gun.

Uniquely in wartime, the Hulten case came under the British courts rather than that of the American military. A presidential election while the case was pending led to the government waiving its jurisdiction. Both were found guilty of murder, which under British law they were. Graffiti appeared, even in Betty Jones's hometown, with figures hanging from gallows. In the event, 18-year-old Jones was given life imprisonment after the intervention of the Home Secretary, Herbert Morrison. Hulten, at 22, was hanged by Albert Pierrepoint at Pentonville on 8 March 1945. Men like Hulten gave Americans a bad name. A deserter from the army (he had been AWOL for six weeks before Heath's murder) he claimed to have run with the Mob in Chicago, which would have been familiar to his new girlfriend and others through the Cagney/Raft/Robinson movies of the 1930s and 1940s.

So, who was the GI who killed Bella? Nobody, because there were no American troops in Britain at the time. Professor Webster was only able to pinpoint the woman's death at some time in the summer or autumn of 1941, but the attack on Pearl Harbor did not take place until 7 December of that year, 'a day,' broadcast Franklin Roosevelt, 'that will live in infamy.' Tradition has it that the first GI to set foot on British soil was Private

First Class Milburn H. Henke of the 34th Infantry. Ironically, his father was a naturalized German. In fact, there were already 500 men of his Division's advance guard in Belfast before the photographers and media arrived. The possible link between Bella and an anonymous American are born, like much else on the Internet about this case, out of ignorance, but they may originate in another case that came under the watchful eye of Professor James Webster. There are superficial similarities between the cases. On 26 October 1944, while police enquiries were still ongoing into Hagley Wood, 33-year-old nurse Florence Porter went out with an American called Hal. They were seen drinking and laughing in the George Hotel, Lickey End, Worcestershire, and later walking towards the woman's home. Screams were heard at 10.30 p.m. but it was a wild, wet night and nobody investigated. Florence's body was found by two schoolboys the next morning. Her clothing was disturbed, but she had not been assaulted. Webster, working in his laboratory at the old workhouse on the Birmingham Road determined that the cause of death was seven stab wounds from a slim-bladed knife.

Descriptions of Hal – a 1st or 2nd lieutenant in full uniform – were circulated in local US camps and identity parades held. The American army used metal detectors and drained a pond nearby in search of the murder weapon. Nothing – apart from Florence's handbag – was found.

Police had two suspects in mind, but both, according to an enquiry in 2006, had cast-iron alibis. If that consisted of the word of fellow soldiers, I am afraid I do not believe it. There are many instances in other cases of soldiers literally closing ranks to protect their own. Hal had got away with it and the Americans had failed in what was a basic test of alliance.

If not the Americans, who? Britain had a love-hate relationship with its armed forces as well as with its former colonies. Soldiers were notoriously 'brutal and licentious' even when so many of them were conscripts and so, really, civilians in uniform. There was an RAF base at Hartlebury, less than eight miles from Hagley. The crimes of RAF serviceman Gordon Cummins had shocked the nation the previous year and, nonsense though it was, some people believed there was no smoke without fire; *all* men in uniform could behave that way, their minds hardened by war and the cheapness of human life.

Hartlebury was hardly a conventional RAF station. There was no airstrip and no planes, at least not complete ones. Unit 25 was what today would be called a logistics hub. It was part of Maintenance Command, responsible for supplying all air force equipment except guns. Propellors, Rolls Royce Merlin engines and much else rolled off its conveyor belts. In 1941, Hartlebury had a workforce of 1,230. Most of the men were over fifty and there were 300 women. When Jack Lazenby DFC got there, prior to a posting to a fighting unit, he was astonished to find a football match in progress, between two female teams; such things just did not happen in wartime England!

Having said there were no Americans in the forces in 1941, there were two civilians, known as Elmer and Alabamee, stationed at Hartlebury. The whole atmosphere was very civilian. The camp guards were Air Ministry wardens, mostly ex-servicemen armed with revolvers and they did not patrol at night. The team reported to a civilian in a bowler hat for their pay and discipline was extremely relaxed. The dance hall called the Glyderome in nearby Kidderminster was popular, as of course were pubs and cinemas. Could one of the Unit 25 team have met 'Bella' in the town, taken her to Hagley Wood and killed her? Of course, but the fact that nothing about the woman in the wych elm gave any hint of a local identity ruled this out as a likelihood.

Billeting was another wartime convention and meant that, at any given time, there were strangers in the area whose behaviour and motivation were unknown. Some of this was military. Half a mile from Hagley Wood was the village of Pedmore, already absorbed into the outskirts of Stourbridge. Eleven of its residents were killed in various actions during the war, including Lance Corporal Alfred Sangwin in North Africa. He died of wounds days after Bella's body was found. The largest bell in Pedmore's St Peter's church is inscribed 'I to Church the living call and to the grave do summon all.' The Welch Regiment was billeted here but information on the unit is difficult to come by.

In preparation for what might turn to war, a government committee reported on billeting in 1938. It stressed that there had to be priorities involved and it perhaps had an over-pessimistic attitude to the threat of civilian bombing. Even at its height, in cities like London, Plymouth and Hull, the Blitz did not drive everybody out. Even the children, evacuated at first, often drifted back, 'townies' feeling hopelessly lonely and adrift in the countryside. Evacuation areas were those most likely to feel the need for billeting. Reception areas were those that took refugees in; and neutral areas neither sent nor took evacuees.

Inevitably, most accounts of the time refer to evacuated children, their little worlds turned upside down by being thrust into a strange environment they did not know and could not understand. In some cases, mothers came with them, but neither a woman nor a child was likely to have killed Bella. There is no direct information for the Hagley area in the context of billeted adults whose homes had been destroyed, but, given that the Blitz proper did not start until September 1940 and was petering out by the early summer of 1941, numbers cannot have been that high. Author Paul Newman in *Under the Shadow of Meon Hill* points out the locals' fear of foreigners – Jews, Slovacs and Poles – but in reality there were probably few, if any, of these outside Birmingham.

Most Poles did not accept the offered British naturalization, longing instead to go home once the Germans had been removed. Most of them lived in camps, without barbed wire or gun-emplacements of course, and were infamous for scrounging in their neighbourhoods, especially firewood. Over a short period, they moved to hostels and disappeared into civilian life, setting up delicatessens, cafes and clubs that we still see in all major cities and larger towns today. They even had a Polish university in Earl's Court and twenty-one schools for their children. There were Polish comedians and nearly 200 Polish pubs. Inevitably, some locals took exception. An alleged 56 per cent of the nation wanted them to go home, but the point was that the Poles were very like the British – white, Christian and rabidly anti-German. To those who complained about Polish demands, the magazine *Truth* had an answer:

A little sensitive? Are we surprised?
Four times partitioned, murdered, robbed, despised …
No man has taken Oxford from us, yet;
No man says 'Give us Scotland, and forget.'
But if he did, I fancy we should strike
The same proud poses that you so dislike.

The Czechs were regarded in much the same way, although there were fewer of them than Poles, but the Jews might be regarded as a special case. When Oswald Mosely's Fascists had marched through Cable Street in London's East End, intent on giving local Jews a hiding, large numbers of gentile East Enders backed the Jews against the blackshirts. But it was not always like that. Such was the intensity – and longstanding – of anti-Semitism that some people could fully accept that Bella was killed by a Jew, just as their grandfathers had believed that a Jew was Jack the Ripper. Between 1933 and 1939, 60,000 Jews came to Britain, all of them on the run from the Nazis. Three future prime ministers – Harold Wilson, James Callaghan and Margaret Thatcher – all put up refugees in their homes. Among the Jews were intellectuals whose names appeared in Walter Schellenberg's 'Black Book'. 'Thank you, Hitler,' said the Minister of Pensions, 'for sending us men like these.'

The arrival of Poles and Czechs in Britain as a result of Hitler's invasion of both countries added to the numbers of foreigners who could potentially cause trouble. Two spectacular examples were Henryk Malinowski and Marion Grundkowski of the Free Polish Army. Deserters, they got involved in London's racketeering and were hanged in 1946 for the shooting of rival Reuben Martirosoff ('Russian Robert') in Notting Hill. Technically, the war in Europe was over by then (November 1945) but the Poles had not gone home, potentially to face the music over desertion, but shared a flat in Ilford, Essex. The pair were easily caught for the murder and proceeded to blame each other. Under the law of joint culpability, whoever had actually pulled the trigger was irrelevant – both men had to hang. This kind of killing was, of course, very different from the murder of Bella, but we shall have cause to return to London's underworld later in this book.

Any of the strangers passing through the Hagley area in the summer and autumn of 1941 could have been Bella's killer, but there is no hard evidence against anyone. One group, however, stood out; they were the Children of the Moon.

Chapter 9

The Children of the Moon

The Reverend Burns' churchwarden, A.H. Hodgetts, took the stranger-killer theme in a specific direction. With the police drawing blanks in all directions and the graffiti on local walls increasing, fireside and barside detectives all over the area were free to speculate. Hodgetts spoke to the local press in the early 1950s when the case was already cold and the war over – 'I think [Bella] was a gypsy and that she was tried and condemned by her tribe of Romanies.' His photograph appeared in the Wolverhampton *Express and Star* putting the finishing touches to a grave plot in Hagley churchyard, as though his theory was laying Bella's murder to rest. And in one sense, I believe it was.

Just as the Jews became scapegoats for the atrocities in Whitechapel in 1888 – and were blamed for both world wars and much else by certain elements of an unhinged Gentile society – so the gypsies were everybody's bugbear in the 1940s. Sensibilities have changed. Today, they are the travelling people, or travellers; Roma whose status has been elevated. In Britain, as elsewhere, they are regarded as a minority with the same raft of human rights as anybody else. But it was not always like that …

In August 1621, the playwright Ben Jonson presented his *Masque of the Gypsies Metamorphosed* to James I as summer entertainment for the court. 'Gaze upon them,' the narrator says, 'as on the offspring of Ptolemy, begotten upon several Cleopatras in their several countries.' Jonson had no first-hand knowledge of these travellers, who had begun to drift into western Europe, probably from India, in the fifteenth century, but he bought in to the commonly held belief that they were originally Egyptian, hence 'gypsies' and that they possessed extraordinary skills in magic not understood by most people. Those not involved in producing spectacle for the king had a more disparaging view of them – 'wretched, wandering wily vagabonds'. They seemed to be everywhere in late Elizabethan England, their faces painted red and yellow, their bodies, horses and carts dangling with ribbons and bells. The magic angle was one that they themselves promoted because it gave them an edge in their rare dealings with locals. A man would think twice before upsetting them in case they put the evil eye or some sort of spell on him.

From the eleventh century onwards, we have occasional reports of gypsies all over Europe, renowned as ventriloquists and fortune-tellers. The high spot of Medieval life was the local fair that might last for days; the gypsies would have been at all of them. It is likely that whole tribes were driven west by the conquests of Timur-e-Leng (Tamburlaine) in the fourteenth century and their sudden presence in the west was not appreciated. In Paris in 1427 they were refused entry to the city. Individuals were rounded up and gaoled at La Chapelle. They were *cajoux*, undesirables.

By Henry VIII's reign they had reached England and Scotland, where they were known as Saracens, western Christendom's enemies for centuries. A law of 1530 spelt out the problem that had not, even by the 1940s, completely gone away:

> For as much afore this time diverse and many outlandish people calling themselves Egyptians, using no craft nor fact of merchandise, have come into this realm and gone from shire to shire ... in great company and used great subtle and crafty [illegal] means to deceive the people ... and have committed many and heinous felonies and robberies to the great hurt of decent people ...

Those already in England were given sixteen days to leave. The fact that this did not happen tells us a great deal about the more liberal and humane attitudes of the public in comparison with government and church. Even when the gypsies tried to leave, however, port authorities at Boston, London, Hull and Newcastle were hostile to them and would not provide ships. Anyone sheltering a gypsy was liable to be fined £40 (over £25,000 today) after another parliamentary act in 1554. Any gypsy who was caught was to be summarily executed – no trial, no defence.

Yet, the 'children of the moon', as they were called, survived. They were reported in large numbers at the Devil's Arse in Derbyshire and on the open fields at Blackheath in south London. The nomadic lifestyle appealed to locals stuck in a drab existence of monotony and some joined the travelling bands. Several people called themselves Egyptians but were actually just vagabonds. Elizabeth's government, with no effective police force or even a standing army, feared the mob – 'the many-headed monster' – and the children of the moon were just the tip of the iceberg.

The dialect of the gypsies was a conglomeration of the various languages of Europe and, rather like the street-talk of underground groups in cities the world over, it acquired a status of its own, increasing the 'them and us' attitudes of the travellers and sedentary people. In the first book written about the gypsies, in 1547, Andrew Boorde wrote 'they be light-fingered and use picking [pockets], they have little manner and evil lodging and yet they be pleasant dancers.' There have been suggestions that the origins of the folk cult of Morris dancing (from Moorish, the gypsies in Spain) lies with the 'Egyptians'.

Sixteenth- and seventeenth-century gypsies were linked inextricably with something that was to surface again in the case of Bella, an involvement with witchcraft and the black arts. Thomas Harman wrote of their 'deep dissembling and long hiding and covering their deep deceitful practices ...' When Thomas Dekker wrote *Lanthorn and Candlelight* in 1608, he included the odd observation that gypsy women wore 'rags and patched filthy mantles uppermost' but that their undergarments 'are handsome and in fashion'.

It was the sheer numbers that alarmed the Elizabethan and Jacobean authorities. Groups of thirty to forty were common, but some were over a hundred strong and must have caused alarm in the small villages and even towns they passed through. Dekker accused the gypsies of bloodthirstiness – 'nothing can satisfy them but the very heartblood of those they kill'. He was actually talking about the slaughter of animals, not people. They carried long-bladed knives called skenes (as in the Scottish *sgian dubh*) but every man in Elizabethan England carried a knife and we cannot read anything sinister into this. Naturally, according to Dekker, the barns where gypsies slept 'are beds of incest, whoredom and adulteries and of all other black and deadly-damned impieties'. Traditionally, in the travelling communities marriage was not for life – couples divorced by shaking hands over the carcass of a slaughtered animal and went their separate ways.

In the eighteenth-century Age of Enlightenment, the gypsies were analysed for the first time as anything other than as a dangerous and unwelcome nuisance. Jacob Bryant decided in 1785 that they originated from India, but most of them could be found in the Balkans, especially Romania. George Borrow romanticized their existence in his two novels

Lavengro (1851) and *The Romany Rye* (1857) and produced an English-Romany dictionary, *Romano Lavo-Lil*, in 1874. A lover of the open air, which he called 'the wind on the heath', he was a friend of prize-fighters and dodgy horse-dealers and was largely shunned by the literati as a result.

Borrow was criticized by the next generation of Gypsylorists who doubted his veracity and found him altogether too quaint and 'twee'. As the nineteenth century wore on, more people came to regard gypsies as a vanishing breed, rather as white Americans saw the plains tribes they were rounding up on to reservations at the time. Ironically, Borrow's romanticized view of Romany led to gypsy concerts, fancy dress and parties becoming the thing to do with the 'in' crowd. At one concert in 1850, even before Borrow went into print, while the song *We Gypsies Have a Life of Ease* was receiving a rapturous reception in a Birmingham music hall, only a few miles away, genuine gypsies were being turfed out of their encampment – yet again.

Despite the work of the Gypsylorists, most people's awareness of gypsies in the later Victorian period was newspaper accounts of trouble. Even as late as the twentieth century, it was a commonly held belief that while all gypsies were thieves, they especially stole children. They did not eat them (that custom was reserved, according to the Nazis, for the Jews) but converted them to their own way of life as a race apart. The abduction of children had its origins in the nursery, a bogeyman to frighten children into obedience or (however unlikely!) sleep – 'Go to sleep, or the diddikois will get you.' Technically, a didikoi (spellings vary) is only part gypsy. Social groupings among the tribes are complicated, with pure-blooded, half-breed, poshrats and didikois. The bogeyman gypsy was a frequent theme in literature and even carried on into the films of the silent era. It is highly likely that churchwarden Hodgetts of Hagley saw at least one of these as a child and believed it implicitly. *Stolen by Gypsies* gripped audiences in Birmingham in 1905, as did *Kidnapped for Revenge* eight years later. As the philologist Heinrich Grellman had written as early as 1783, why would gypsies steal children? They 'have enough brats of their own'.

By the early twentieth century, gypsies were considered a race, sharing a common culture, manners and customs. The gypsy language, usually today called Roma, was derived from Sanskrit, an Indian language. Other travellers joined the bands, especially the Irish, whose only real link with genuine gypsies was an instinctive distrust of authority and a love of horses.

Actual crime statistics in the nineteenth and twentieth centuries tell a distinctive story. In a four-year period, out of 1,682 prosecutions, 216 were for theft, burglary and receiving stolen goods; 349 concerned obscenity and drunkenness; and 76 involved cruelty to women, children and horses. Only eighteen were linked with murder and (since it was still a capital offence) suicide.

The 'gutter-scum Gypsies', the 'off-scourings of the lowest form of society', as George Smith described them in the 1880s, were genuinely guilty of a whole variety of crimes in the late nineteenth and first half of the twentieth century, but none of them included murder and none carried more severe punishment that a fine or one year's imprisonment. Drunkenness was common, as was neglect of children, and fighting (which *could* lead to death) relatively frequent. The point is that exactly the same pattern of misdemeanours was the norm for many elements of the working class. The grinding poverty of Victorian England, the relentless rhythm of the machines, forced men and women to drink as an escape from the downward spiral of life. It was only centuries-old racism and fear of the different that made men like churchwarden Hodgetts point a finger at the gypsies.

There had been an upsurge of foreigners drifting to Britain in the years before the First World War and they were not welcomed by British gypsies, despite claiming to be of the same ethnic heritage. Polish gypsies were reported near Birmingham in 1904, and when the Surrey police tried to break up a camp of Serbians near Esher, the travellers unleashed their six dancing bears on them and His Majesty's Constabulary beat a hasty retreat!

The law crowded in against the gypsies, whether home-grown or newly arrived. America, supposedly welcoming everyone's 'huddled masses' refused to take them, embarking as it was on a new isolationism, so that many emigrant-wannabes had to stay in Britain. The Law of Property Act 1925 made it an offence to 'drive any carriage, wagon, cart or truck or to set up camp and light a fire' in certain areas, thereby severely curtailing the gypsies' freedom of movement.

They had their defenders, especially in the race-goers who liked a gypsy presence at Epsom or Goodwood. Four years after the above-named Act was passed, Oliver Locker-Lampson defended them in court and won the undying gratitude of all travellers. Locker-Lampson may have been an eccentric – he led a motorized cavalcade against the Bolsheviks in the

Russian civil war – but he represented a new and more humane stance in the case of gypsies. The partial removal of the vagrancy law in 1935 helped their cause too and explains why there was a gypsy encampment near Hagley at all.

The biggest gypsy camp nearby was Black Patch. Officially, travellers' links with the area, in Halesowen, Birmingham, came to an end in 1907 after the landowners evicted them and turned the area into a respectable park. Esau Smith had been elected king of the gypsies there in 1901 and his widow Henty took over the mantle as queen. The royal caravan was burned down in the ongoing trouble over the eviction and Henty put a curse on anyone who built on Black Patch. There was an ongoing dispute, however, and gypsies kept returning to the area for years afterwards, certainly during the inter-war period.

One of the most common charges against gypsies concerned poaching; we can imagine that the gypsies parked near Hagley in 1941 had little compunction about setting the odd trap in Lord Cobham's woods. Driving without a licence (although the vast majority still drove the traditional horse-drawn vardo wagon), lighting fires too close to a road and hawking without a licence were all fairly commonplace.

There are a number of references to gypsies in the police files. Mary Lee, a possible Bella who was drifting from man to man and pursued by the lovesick Light Infantryman Heywood was probably of Romany stock, Lee being perhaps the most common of all travellers' surnames. Another potential Bella was Ann Forrest. She lived with her husband (unnamed) in West Hagley in July 1941 and both of them worked at Spout Farm in the area. The pair were known to have frequent, violent rows; a neighbour, Mrs Lewis, heard screams and once saw 'the female' (presumably Ann) with bleeding neck wounds. Part of the problem was that residents who did not actually employ gypsies regarded them as a race apart, describing them almost as animals in a zoo, with terms like 'the female', 'the male' and 'the young'. It transpired, however, that Ann Forrest was 5ft 7in tall with 'a nice set of even teeth' and she was found alive in April 1944.

As late as 1949, memories of travellers in the Hagley area were still coming to light. John Swindon, a library caretaker of Church Road, Smethwick, had seen a soldier and a 'plain woman' (probably a euphemism for gypsy) get off a bus and go into Hagley Wood on 16 June 1942. William Sherwood, of Hancox Street, Worley, told the police in September 1949 that he had seen gypsies fighting in a field called the

Nimmings next to Hagley Wood. Whatever information he had led to DI Williams, DI Mobbs, Superintendent Inight and the local bobbies Skerratt and Pound visiting the wood with him on 2 October.

Jack Pound himself had visited the Nimmings in December 1942 (before Bella's body was found) and talked to a family called 'Smith'. The fact that the police reports have the words in speech marks indicates that they did not believe it for a moment! There was one horse-drawn wagon and two canvas tents. Three men there were employed cutting sugar beet for Felix Tate of Holliers Farm nearby. The woman with them was in her fifties.

The Smiths must have been making a nuisance of themselves elsewhere because Constable Benbow of Severn Stoke, between Pershore and Malvern, was also nosing around them. He saw no children and no signs of bad behaviour. Arkus and Wisdom Smith were polite to him, as were the women Ellen Smith, Ivy Butler and another called Davies. Benbow's report has one cryptic, unexplained (and, today, unacceptable!) line on somebody else in their company – Bill Fletcher, 'a Dago, who was one of the suspects in the case'. As there is no list of suspects as such in the Worcester Archive, and no other mention of Fletcher, it is difficult to know what this is all about.

The Smiths had left litter in the area, having thrown rubbish into Hagley Wood itself and they were possibly the same family who had been seen by other eyewitnesses. Flora Reece of Pen Orchard Farm, Clent, remembered them at the Nimmings. There were two women, one tall and thin, about 40, and the other in her twenties, with blonde hair and a fresh complexion. John Palmer, licensee of the George Inn, Halesowen, who might be expected to pick up more gossip than most people, remembered 'there was some talk afterwards that the gypsy woman had been found and she had gone away to have a baby'. Was this a garbled misremembering of a newspaper cutting to the effect that Bella had once given birth? Mrs Sarah Porter, of Hayley Green, Halesowen, told police that gypsies had bought from her shop soon before the body was found. The women she saw wore shawls and one of them had a ration book in the name of Davis.

Despite the perceived prejudice of locals, the gypsies are a scrupulously clean people. A plate from which a dog has eaten will never be used again by humans. Such an item is *mochadi*, defiled. A similar ritual is involved in childbirth and female underclothes, but these vary slightly from one group of families to another. One custom that survived the centuries and was probably still in use in Hagley in 1941 was the burning of a caravan belonging to a deceased gypsy. The fear of ghosts, which is a widespread human condition, is particularly strong among the travelling people. Among their traditions is the wearing of holed pebbles, called adderstones, to protect against the Devil. Meeting a donkey or a woman with a squint on the road presaged death, while the moon, frogs, falling stars and white horses all prefigure health and happiness.

The problem with the case of Bella is that it is full of anecdotes which cannot now accurately be evaluated. We have already come across, courtesy of Donald McCormick in 1968, the anonymous teacher and company executive who heard screams in Hagley Wood in July 1941. But there are others. Paul Newman cites a story told to him by David Taylor, 'the local parasearcher [paranormal researcher]' who was approached by an old lady in the Hagley area who remembered, as a young girl, travelling to work by bus in the 1940s. As she passed Hagley Wood, she saw a 'gypsy' girl covered in blood being chased by a 'man with a stick or club' but she decided to say nothing 'because it was the war'! This story is so vague as to be useless. Who was this old lady? How old was she at the time? Where was she going and what time of day was this? Above all, what was the date? There is nothing in Professor Webster's post-mortem to suggest bone damage or any trauma caused by a heavy object. Look again at the damage done to Joan Wolfe's skull by August Sangret's silver birch branch. It caused a hole nearly 5 inches long and 1½ inches wide.

In the war itself, little is heard on the national stage of the gypsies. Some, especially those who had intermarried with *gorgjos* (non-gypsies) served in both world wars. Along with everybody else in 1939, gypsy men were liable to be conscripted. Some fled to Ireland to escape this; others reported to barracks as ordered. As to clothing, the colourful ribbons, jewellery and blackened faces belonged to the sixteenth and seventeenth centuries. Descriptions of gypsies and photographs in the twentieth century show no distinction between them and ordinary working-class locals. Some of them, at least, became sedentary, returning to the road from time to time as their fancy dictated.

One of the traditional beliefs, possibly still current in the twentieth century, was that gypsies killed farm animals and claimed their bodies later from their owners. To ensure that the cause of death of a sheep, for instance, looked natural, they would suffocate the animal by forcing wool down its throat. This has echoes in Professor Webster's assertion that

Bella was asphyxiated in a similar way, although we have already discussed the problems with that thesis.

Reports from the nineteenth century have gypsies making cheap jewellery and passing it off as genuine gold. They hammered coins and pewter and made wedding rings out of them which they then sold to a gullible public. Was this the origin of Bella's wedding ring, worth half a crown? Hardly, because it was stamped 'rolled gold' on the inside.

The case of the woman in the wych elm seemed destined to be shrouded in legend and rumour. All that is missing are the facts! Churchwarden Hodgetts blamed the gypsies through ignorance and deep-rooted racism. He believed the gypsies to have their own legal code and that Bella had somehow transgressed against her people. Even in paperwork-obsessed 1940s Britain, it was possible for a traveller to slip through the cracks and disappear. And in one respect only, he may just have been right.

Chapter 10

Anna and the Flying Dutchman

By 1953, Wilfred Byford-Jones had hung up his Home Guard uniform and had become 'Quaestor', writing occasional articles for the Wolverhampton *Express and Star*, adding titbits of second-rate journalese to inject a spookiness into a story that had none in its original form. If anyone is responsible for beginning the nonsense that has been written on the Hagley Wood murder, it is Byford-Jones.

In November a letter arrived on Quaestor's desk:

> Finish your articles re the wych elm by all means. They are interesting to your readers, but you will never solve the mystery. The one person who could give this answer is now beyond the jurisdiction of earthly courts. The affair is closed and involves no witches, black magic or moon night rites.

As we shall see in a later chapter, 1953 saw the first suggestion of a supernatural solution to Bella's murder, hence the comments above.

> Much as I hate having to use a nom-de-plume [the writer called herself Anna] I think you would appreciate it if you knew me. The only clues I can give you are that the person responsible for the crime died insane in 1942 and the victim was Dutch and arrived illegally in England about 1941. I have no wish to recall any more.

Intrigued, and obviously scenting a bigger scoop, Byford-Jones contacted the police. Tom Williams was by now a superintendent and doubtless had moved on to other problems but, like Quaestor, he could not leave this one alone. Donald McCormick, without access to police files, adds to the frisson of mystery. Anna was traced but would only talk to the police 'at a place far out into the country outside Wolverhampton in a waiting room which could be viewed from outside without risk of detection and

Above left: The wych elm in Hagley wood where Bella's body was found. Most accounts of the murder show the wrong tree.

Above right: The site of the wych elm today. The tree itself was destroyed in removing the skeleton in 1943. This image was taken seventy-nine years to the day from the day the body was found – note the buds and growing foliage, giving the lie to the writers who speak of gloom and death!

Right: The Nimmings, a field next to Hagley Wood where gypsies often camped during the 1940s.

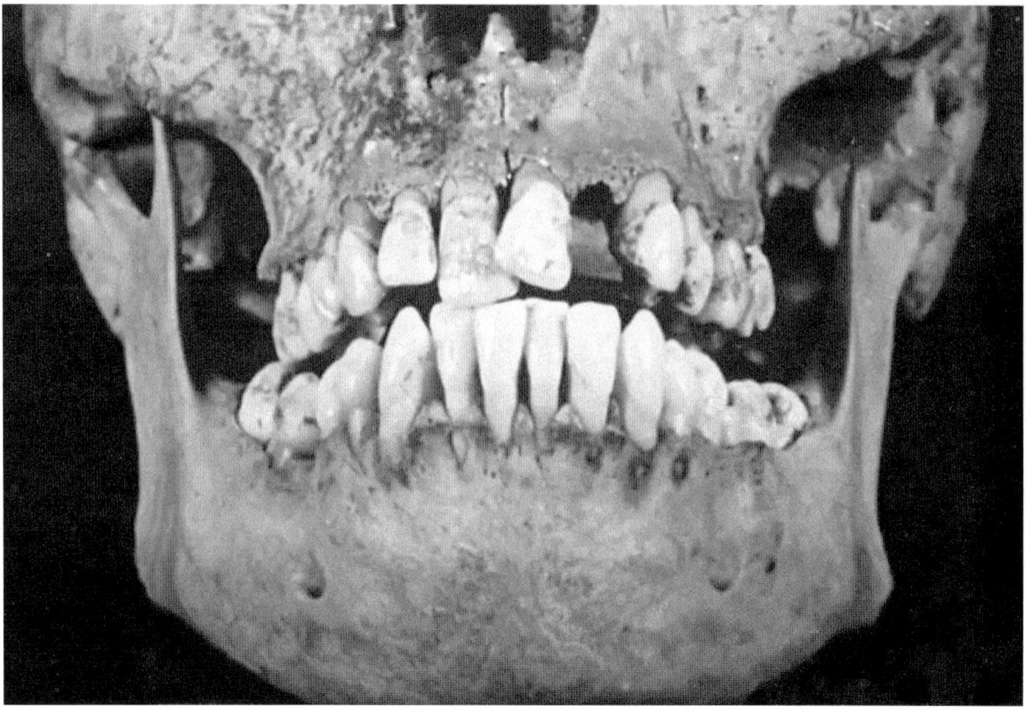

Bella's skull with the missing front tooth replaced. Confusingly, the pathologist, James Webster, talks about overlapping *bottom* teeth, whereas the abnormality clearly lies in the upper jaw.

Bella's skull photographed in situ in Hagley Wood. Note the hair still clinging to the bone.

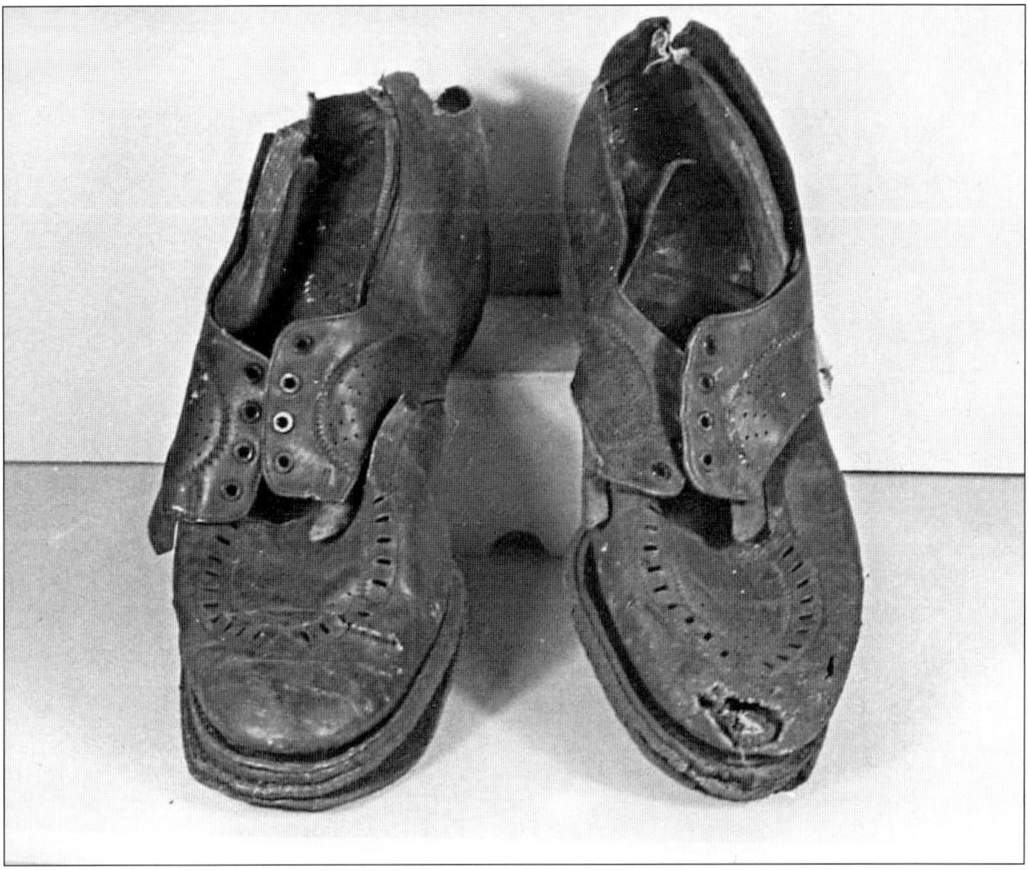

Above: Bella's shoes were more expensive than the rest of her clothing. For years, police and journalists followed stories of these shoes, to no effect.

Right: A sample of knitting in the style of Bella's jumper. Donald McCormick suggests that the stripes are vertical, but that would take twice as much wool, unlikely within wartime conditions. This sample was created for this book to prove the point.

Left: Bella as she may have looked at the time of her death. According to Professor Webster, her cardigan had no sleeves and her skirt was too big for her. The hair is always a guess, but in this drawing, the artist has taken into account her uneven teeth.

Below: Bella's cheap 'wedding ring', redrafted from an unclear photograph in the police gazette, April 1943. Such rings cost half a crown.

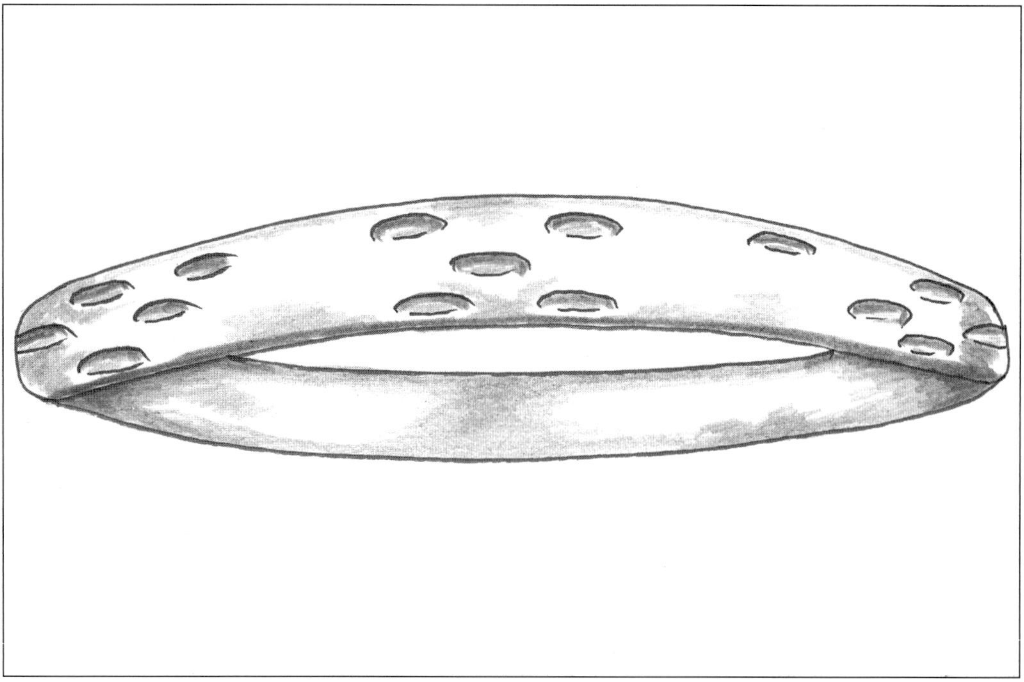

> PUT
> WHO ↑ BELLA DOWN THE
> WTFE WYCH ELM AT
> HAGLEY

Above: One of the many examples of wall writing relating to Bella's death. This one was written on paper by a possible suspect under direction from DI Williams. The suspect could not spell various words.

Right: The 'McCormick Mannequin'. In 1968 Donald McCormick claimed that this was from a police sketch of the 1940s. The hairstyle and clothing are wrong for that decade and have added to confusion ever since.

Above left: Professor James Webster of the Midland Forensic Crime Lab attached to Birmingham University. One of the foremost pathologists of his day, he was considerably more modest than the rest of them.

Above right: We do not know how Dr Margaret Murray was dragged into a possible witchcraft angle regarding Bella's death. She was an academic with a background in Egyptology and anthropology and gave various interviews to local and national newspapers. Several of them misquoted her, as, I suspect, did Donald McCormick.

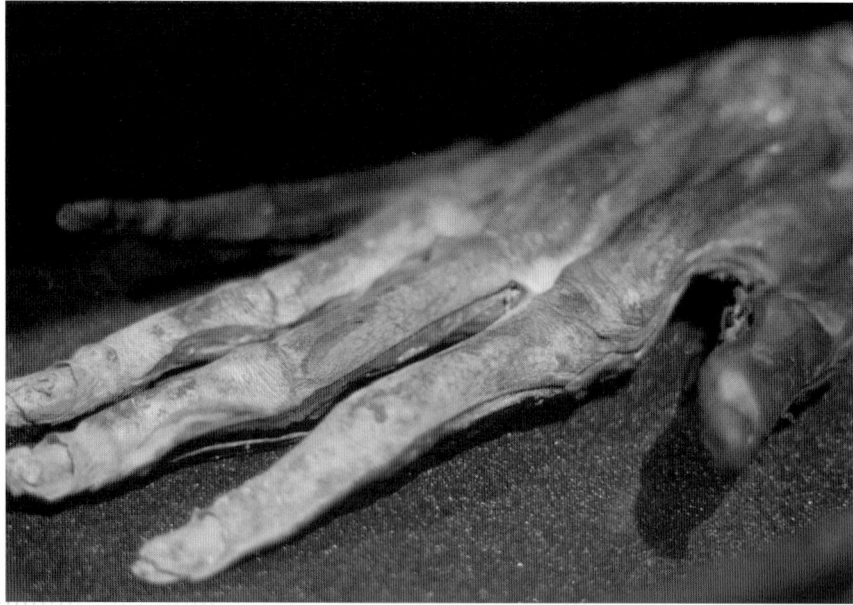

One of Bella's hands was removed from her body almost certainly by animals in Hagley Wood. In the hysteria-charged atmosphere of the 1950s and 60s, this became associated with the 'Hand of Glory', a talisman used in Black Magic ceremonies.

Above left: No one could trace the origin of Bella's shoes or the dental work she had had done. Was that because she was a spy, parachuted in to the Midlands in 1941? To some, this is Bella. Her actual name is Klara Dronkers who was a foot taller than Bella with perfect teeth!

Above right: In the tense atmosphere of wartime Britain, strangers and foreigners were regarded with suspicion; none more so than the gypsies who had lived in various parts of the Midlands since the fifteenth century.

The only foreign spy who was not caught by the authorities was Jan Willem Ter Braak. His body was found in an air raid shelter in Cambridge and he was assumed to have committed suicide. Could Bella have been another example of a spy who died out in the cold?

Aleister Crowley styled himself the 'Great Beast, the Wickedest Man in Britain'. Was he connected with a witch cult operating in the Midlands in the 1940s?

Above left: The man who made witchcraft respectable. Gerald Gardiner was a customs official most concerned with white witchcraft which led to the creation of modern Wicca. He was dismissive of Bella's supposed links to the supernatural.

Above right: The 'fantasy historian' Donald McCormick wrote widely on murder, espionage and the occult. His was the first book on the Hagley Wood murder and it has muddied the waters ever since. Full of speculation, lack of sources and downright invention, he put the cause of crime writing back for a generation.

through which women were passing frequently without the company of men'. She did not want press there, except, it transpired, Byford-Jones and a minimum police presence. Williams took along a policewoman, thin on the ground though they still were in 1953, perhaps to put Anna at her ease. Today, such an interview, without counsel and tape-recording equipment, would contravene the PACE regulations of 1994, but it was standard procedure in the 1950s.

Byford-Jones recorded the essence of what was said, without giving anything away. 'My lips are sealed,' clichéd the reporter:

> I cannot tell the dramatic story I heard one cold winter's night in an ancient habitat in the country together with Detective-Superintendent Williams and a woman detective. What I can say is that the details told were most impressive and contained names and that some details about the man concerned were verified by another person who had accompanied Anna.

This person had come out of left field, but he/she was probably there to give Anna moral support. Byford-Jones had assumed when he got Anna's letter that she was 'an educated woman of about sixty who was down on her luck'. He admitted he was wrong about that, without telling us why and that the testimony of Anna's companion was every bit as impressive as Anna's.

Williams' comment after the interview was:

> I cannot divulge who 'Anna' is or where I saw her. The matter is not by any means closed. Inquiries are now to continue through a contact in Holland to see whether there is any likelihood of a Dutch girl of that description being recognized by certain authorities. Inquiries have been made with the assistance of police forces in the Midlands, also in the London area, on the facts disclosed by 'Anna'.
>
> Persons who knew the man referred to by 'Anna' have been identified and interviewed, but none has been able to offer any useful lead to the identification of the victim. 'Anna' has been seen again, but she is not able to identify the victim and states that the story she has given was told to her by the person who died insane in 1942.

Williams' handwritten notes on Anna's story still exist in the police files. They are undated and it is not clear whether they were taken at the first meeting or subsequent ones. Bizarrely, Williams wrote in green ink (unusual in 1950s police procedure) but from this, it emerges that Anna was actually Una Ellen Hainsworth, formerly Mossop. She lived at Four Acres, Long Common, Claverley, a village near Bridgenorth nearly forty miles from Hagley. Her typewritten statement, undated, runs to two pages. She had married an engineer, Jack Mossop, in 1932 and they lived at the Bridge House, Wombourne, five miles from Claverley. Their only child, Julian, was born in the same year and was, at the time of her statement, 'somewhere in America'.[1] Although this is clearly not in the statement, Julian acquired a police record. The fact that Una had no idea where he was screams unhappy and broken home. In 1937, Jack Mossop joined the Air Service Training Corps as a pilot officer working for the Armstrong Siddeley Works in Coventry and later the Standard Aero Works at Banner Lane in the same city. The couple lived at 39, Barrow Road, Kenilworth, a small town complete with ruined castle, a few miles away in the Warwickshire countryside.

> It was in 1940 that a man named Van Ralt came to our home ... I believe this man was Dutch and as far as I know had no particular job and I have a suspicion that he was engaged on some work that he did not wish to talk about, but in my opinion it might have been that he was a spy for he had plenty of money and there were times that my husband appeared to have plenty of money after meeting him.

All this is very confusing. If Van Ralt had no job, how had he met Mossop? It could have been a casual pub situation, but this was wartime Britain. Mention 1940 and Coventry to locals even today and they will regale you with folktales of 'coventration'. In November of that year, the city was pounded in a ten-hour raid that destroyed the city centre including its fifteenth-century cathedral. The Netherlands had recently been overrun by the Wehrmacht, but nobody was naïve enough to believe that every Dutchman was an ally of Britain. In fact, as we shall see, there were two parallel and popular Dutch Nazi parties and they were indeed supplying spies as agents for the Abwehr, the German secret service (see Chapter 11). Did no one find it odd that a foreign national (people who were routinely rounded up) was wandering around the industrial Midlands heartlands, flashing his cash and teaming up with a man who worked for an aircraft production company?

'In March or April 1941,' Una went on, Jack came home 'white and agitated'. It was one o'clock in the morning and he asked Una for a drink. Reluctantly, she poured one for him and he told her that he had been to the Lyttleton Arms with Van Ralt and the 'Dutch Piece' who had got awkward. Perhaps it was Jack Mossop's style to go drinking at a pub twenty miles away, but again, this was wartime; petrol was rationed, signposts had gone, car headlights were dimmed. Were there not pubs in nearby Kenilworth?

According to Una, Jack was driving Van Ralt's Rover and the Dutch girl sat next to him, with Van Ralt in the back. Suddenly, she slumped against Mossop, presumably passed out with drink. Van Ralt told Mossop to drive to a wood 'and [he] stuck her in a hollow tree', assuring his friend that she would come to her senses the following morning.

From then until December 1941 when they left Kenilworth, Jack's mood grew worse. He drank more heavily and appeared to have more money than usual. He was also often off work and Una could not understand where the money was coming from. He had his own car, a Standard, and he would often drive off in it for days.

Una left Jack that December, with no reason given and moved to Henley-in-Arden, where she lived for ten years. 'We [presumably this refers to her second husband, Jack Hainsworth] lived there for ten years.' In 1951, they went back to Kenilworth and two years later, shortly before Una contacted Quaestor, to her present address.

Back in 1941–42, she saw Jack Mossop three times 'after I was forced to leave him'. She was trying to sort out the furniture and on the last occasion he told her that he was 'losing his mind as he kept seeing the woman in the tree and she was leering at him'. In June 1942, Una heard that Jack had been taken to the 'Mental Hospital' in Stafford. He died two months later.

Una told the police that she had no knowledge of the Hagley Wood murder until she read Quaestor's articles. She was concerned that now that she had married and had three small children, she did not want her name splashed all over the papers. She admitted that she had no proof of anything she had said.

A number of things from Una's statement should ring alarm bells. The police, no doubt heartened by *any* scrap of information relating to the murder, would have had no truck with Mossop's assertion that he and Van Ralt shoved the Dutch girl into the wych elm to sober up, but they may have put her corpse there to avoid an accusation of murder. It was possible to convict without a body – as John George Haigh found to his cost in 1949[2] – but it was considerably more difficult. Despite the misgivings they must have had, Worcestershire CID contacted the City of Coventry police in relation to the players in Una's story. Jack Mossop had been born in 1912 in Kenilworth and did a number of factory jobs before starting in the assembly shop at Banner Lane in November 1940. Before the war, he had been discharged from the RAF (why was unknown) and he had worked for two years at the Lockheed factory in Leamington Spa. There is an unexplained complaint made by him in February 1942 of a missing car and driver.

Jack Hainsworth was actually Alfred James Ainsworth and once again we are in the shady wartime world of aliases, however little removed from the truth. He was born in 1917 and worked, like Mossop, in Banner Lane from 3 September 1940 until January 1944 when he was transferred to Aircraft Production at Anstey Aero. He too had been discharged from the RAF in August 1940 (at the height of the Battle of Britain) after four months – again, no reason given. Before that he had been a garage mechanic in Berkswell, Warwickshire and had moved twice while at the Banner Lane works.

Williams also traced Bill Wilson, who lived at 45 Birches Lane, Kenilworth and he made a statement at the end of December 1953. He had known the Mossops well, lodging with them at 39 Barrow Road. He remembered Jack Mossop as a heavy drinker, becoming increasingly unstable and had a lot of absenteeism. The Standard car that he drove was a four-door black saloon model – he and Wilson shared its running expenses. Wilson knew nothing about Mossop's complaint to the police relating to the car and driver but he told police that Mossop had been invalided out of the RAF after a bad landing in a plane and that he had head injuries.

The only Rover that Wilson knew about was a write-off he and Mossop had bought from a scrap merchant and which they could never get going. He knew nothing about the Lyttleton Arms. Jack Mossop knew lots of people, but 'foreigners, I don't think'. The police had clearly given Wilson a vague description of Van Ralt with his expensive car and wads of cash. The only person Wilson could equate with this was a 20-year-old

Englishman with bad skin. He worked at Banner Lane and may have been called Vic. Jack was a flirt and would often buy girls drinks – 'I think they felt sorry for him,' Wilson remembered, 'the type of fellow that would not harm anyone … he did not have much backbone.'

Wilson tended to lose touch with the Mossops towards the end; he *had* noticed increasing moodiness but he put this down to tensions at home. He worked in Baginton, two miles away, while Jack stayed on at Banner Lane and it was from there that he was committed.

From somewhere – remember, the police archives are incomplete – comes 'Frak or Froak' – no one of that surname could be found by Coventry police. Elsewhere in the file the names are found, but no explanation is given. On the same day that Wilson was interviewed, DS Murray of Worcestershire CID was reporting on Frick and Frack, a Swiss ice-skating duo who had performed at the Hippodrome theatre in Coventry in 1938. The police had contacted theatrical agent Tom Arnold but he was hazy about them. In fact, by 1953 the pair were very well known. Frick was Werner Groebli; Frack was Hans Mauch and they had gone to the States in 1937 to join the Ice Follies Show. They performed a comedy sketch act wearing lederhosen and were so good that the term 'frick and frack' became synonymous with two people being indistinguishable from each other. Bill Wilson was clearly asked something about this because he said he had no knowledge of any 'theatrical types' in the context of the Mossops.

As time went on, the dramatic intervention of Anna of Claverley assumed an importance way beyond its bodyweight. The place 'far out in the country' was actually the Dick Whittington pub in Stourbridge and the 'waiting room which could be viewed from outside' was a snug on the premises. In the midst of all this, the mysterious Dutch girl left in the wych elm to sober up disappears. Una clearly had no idea who she was and the police were hoping that finding Van Ralt would give them some answers. They found two of them.

Bizarrely, Laura van Raalte is listed in the police files as a potential victim (i.e. Bella) but she clearly is not. On 6 January 1954, the chief constable of Nottingham contacted Worcestershire CID with the information that Laura Frances Ryllis van Raalte had been the subject of police correspondence before, in fact in the 'Spitfire Summer', August 1940. She was born in London to German parents in 1899, had a home address in Golders Green and was lodging in All Saints Street, Nottingham. She had been a teacher since 1936, employed to teach German at Mundella

Grammar School in the city. Since she had held seven teaching posts between that and May 1940, we are entitled to doubt her teaching abilities. In that month, an anonymous letter accused her of teaching the German national anthem to her charges. May 1940 was the month that Winston Churchill took over from Neville Chamberlain as prime minister. Europe was reeling from the speed of the Blitzkrieg advance of General Heinz Guderian and his panzers and a shattered British Expeditionary Force was limping back from Dunkirk; perhaps it was not the best time to get British girls singing *Deutschland Uber Alles*!

Fraulein van Raalte seemed determined to draw attention to herself. On 17 August she wrote to the chief constable of Worcestershire telling him that she was staying in Malvern for a week (the school holidays) and she wanted a guide book for walking and touring purposes.

The anonymous letter 'fingering' van Raalte is in the Archive. She is described as 'M. Van Ralty (an alien) ... I am sure you will realise that [teaching the German national anthem] is a gross insult to girls whose brothers and fathers are at the present moment faced with grave peril from our enemy.' There were threats to contact the Home Office and have her imprisoned. Since van Raalte clearly stopped the exercise and behaved without suspicion during her stay in Malvern, no further action was taken. Clearly this van Raalte has no links with Hagley Wood or the Mossops, despite the fact that she stayed briefly in Worcestershire on her holiday.

The only other van Raalt was Marius Pieter (the right gender at least!) who came to Britain in 1948. The police could find no record of employment and assumed that he was simply a tourist. His passport had been issued at Leiden in October of that year and he could not possibly be the Van Ralt that Una Mossop claimed to know.

Days after Superintendent Williams had spoken to Bill Wilson, he wrote to the police with more information. The Vic he remembered was tall and fair with a surname Draco or Drarco. He drove several cars and one of them could have been a Rover but he worked at Banner Lane throughout the war and Una Mossop would not have confused him with anyone named Van Ralt. Then again, Bill Wilson himself referred to Vic as an Englishman, when, certainly by the sound of his name, he was not.

Una Hainsworth might have been working with the best of intentions when she contacted Quaestor, but she was relying on the hearsay of a mentally ill man who drank heavily and she seemed to have met a character who did not actually exist. Una herself was of questionable integrity. She had approached Quaestor in 1953 because, via the *Express and* Star, he had offered a cash reward of £100 (around £3,000 today). According to the Kenilworth CID, when Una left Kenilworth, she owed a number of people considerable sums of money and they, in the words of the police, 'would have been delighted to have got their hands on her'. In the meantime, in 1953, while Quaestor was rekindling the horror of the woman in the wych elm and ladling it on with a trowel, Bella's murder was no nearer to being closed.

Chapter 11

The Spies Who Came in From the Cold

There is one phrase in Una Hainsworth's statement to Superintendent Williams that was music to the ears of Donald McCormick and everybody else since. When referring to the mysterious Dutchman, Van Ralt, she said, 'but in my opinion it might have been that he was a spy...'

'The first casualty of war is truth,' wrote Senator Hiram Johnson in 1917 and that can be said to apply to almost all the Hagley Wood case. Behind the lethal machinery of the Second World War, the tanks, the aircraft, the bombs, was a whole underground industry devoted to espionage. All nations used spies, agents of differing backgrounds and abilities and both sexes, to discover what they could about the enemy, to probe and exploit his weaknesses.

Little of this was known to most of the public in the Second World War. There was censorship everywhere, from actual government legislation to the limited amount of newsprint available for ordinary people to read. Had the body of Bella been found today, every national would carry long stories on it, with exclusives, photographs of the supposed murder sites and interviews with locals, if only to reassure the readership that 'such things don't happen here'. And of course, television and social media would get in on the act with a vengeance, about the vulnerability of women in the MeToo generation. As I write, the *Mail on Sunday* carries a very small article, rather lost on page 19, with the headline 'Police find "body of mother" in woodland'. The vital difference between this case and Bella's is that we know who the victim was and someone has already been charged with murder. Had that not been the case, that the remains could not be identified, it would have hit the front page by Monday with speculation drifting on for days.

In 1941, there was nothing traceable about a woman who had gone missing among the hundreds who made up such a list. In 1943, in local papers like the *Birmingham Post* and the *Wolverhampton Express and Star,* there were a few scattered columns devoted to the finding of the body. One or two nationals mentioned it briefly – the *Sunday Despatch* and the *Sunday Mercury* – but most of the newspaper coverage comes from the assertions of Dr Margaret Murray (see Chapter 14) and Quaestor in the early to mid-1950s, by which time the case was as cold as the grave.

Much of this comes from the wartime admonishment that 'careless talk costs lives' and that some things were best not discussed in public, if at all. But it was the sheer anonymity of Bella that set off alarm bells in the minds of the detectives involved in the case at the time. There were no labels in any of the dead woman's clothing. Her shoes, that looked so promising as a clue at first, had yielded nothing. Her wedding ring was anonymous and 'fake'. Even the most likely item to produce identification results – her 'snaggle' teeth – drew a firm and resounding blank. That blandness, that lack of traceability, locally or even nationally, led some to the conclusion that Bella was not a local; she was not even a British national. And that in turn led to a more bizarre suggestion. Bella might have been a refugee; after all, there were hundreds of them in England in 1941. And what about Una Hainsworth's assertion, that Van Ralt had a 'Dutch piece' in tow who had had too much to drink and had been stuffed into a tree?

The previous year, when Hitler's awesome war machine was poised to invade Britain, the SS's Walter Schellenberg drew up, as we have seen, a 'black list' of the Reich's most wanted: people who had crossed the Nazis already throughout Europe and had run for their lives to the relative safety of Britain. Many of the 2,694 names on the list were celebrities, famous, among other things, for open anti-Nazi statements or actions. The singer/actor Paul Robeson was there because he was not only a Communist, he was black; for both reasons, Schellenberg's people wanted him dead. A large number on the list were home-grown Britons; people like Robeson were just passing through, in his case having made a film in South Wales shortly before the war began. But the majority were foreigners, refugees from the various European countries that Germany had invaded by the summer of 1940.

As would perhaps be expected from a list of anti-Nazi 'subversives', the vast majority are men. But there are 231 women in the list; could Bella be among them? This list was not known in Britain at the time. It would not be discovered until the fall of the Third Reich in the spring of 1945, but we can use it as an investigative tool today. In terms of the British hierarchy at the time, there were no women in Churchill's cabinet, none in the higher echelons of business and positively none in the church. The home-grown women in the list were people like Virginia Woolf, famous on the literary scene, and Viscountess Rhondda and Eleanor Rathbone, politicians and philanthropists. Many of them were in the list because they had lost fathers, husbands, brothers and sweethearts in the First World War and were outspokenly anti-war as a result.

By and large, we can rule out conventional British women as potential Bellas because they were *so* high profile that their sudden disappearance in the summer or autumn of 1941 would have been noticed. A Dutch woman, Anita Denmer, had been writing anti-German copy for her paper in The Hague before she got out and ended up in Ventnor, Isle of Wight. She survived the war. Another female journalist who was not home-grown was Sigrid Lilian Schulz. Oddly, her name is not in the black list but it should have been. She was born in Chicago and the family moved to Berlin when she was eight. Hating all things Nazi, she steeled herself to interview both Hitler and Goering, head of the Luftwaffe. She may have been an active double agent in Berlin and telephoned journalist William Shirer on 1 September 1939 to tell him that the Germans had invaded Poland. Hurt in a later air raid, she wisely got home to Chicago and was safely there and accounted for by the time Bella died.

Moura Budberg, from Ukraine, often referred to as the 'Mata Hari of Russia' was an alcoholic and her life story is full of inconsistencies that do not add up. The widow of a Tsarist count before the Russian revolution, she had a torrid affair with the British agent Robert Bruce Lockhart and was imprisoned for a time in Moscow's notorious Lubianka prison. In London by the early 1930s, she became the lover of both the writer Maxim Gorki and the novelist H.G. Wells. She is on Schellenberg's list, but she could not possibly be Bella. She survived the Second World War too and would have been far too old for the body in the wych elm.

One of the few women in the academic section of the list, Mathilde Hertz, had a doctorate in biology and comparative physiology. Not remotely a Nazi, she was nevertheless allowed to continue working after Hitler's takeover in Germany in 1933. Two years later, however, she was in Cambridge and had stopped working by 1937, disappearing from public life. Dora Fabian was another philosopher from Berlin and, like Bella, was a murder victim. She was born Dora Heinemann and married liberal politician Walter Fabian in 1924. She obtained her doctorate in economics and political science from the University of Geissen four years later. She became an outspoken critic of the Nazis, especially in their misogynistic views, expecting women to be loyal only to the notion of *Kinder, Küche, Kirche* (children, kitchen, church) as well as the Führer, of course. She attended the colossal rallies at Nuremberg just to watch the crowds. When the Nazis took power, Dora was arrested and, after her release, travelled west to England, reaching London by September 1933. She worked as a translator but appears to have been watched by the German embassy. Her flat was burgled twice. On 4 April 1935, she and her roommate, Mathilde Wurm, were found dead in their Great Ormond Street flat. Their bedroom door was locked and the coroner decided that the cause of death was suicide by Veronal poisoning. The substance was widely used as a sleeping pill and was available over the counter in pharmacies throughout the country. Since Dora had been supplying information to an anti-Nazi agent, Roy Ganz, there is a strong suspicion that the Gestapo, free to stroll around London in what was still peacetime, had been looking for payback for some time. But Dora was long dead when the body of Bella was stashed in the wych elm.

If the corpse in Hagley Wood was not a named refugee in the black list, could she be a spy? And, straight away, we are in to the realms of fantasy. If Van Ralt was a spy, handsomely paid by the Third Reich, there was surely every chance that his drunken girlfriend was too.

'The whole point of a secret service,' wrote Compton Mackenzie in his novel *Water on the Brain*, 'is that it should be secret.' In wartime Britain, there was a need for all this, but eighty years on, and despite the Freedom of Information Act (2000) there are still files in Whitehall which are closed to the public's enquiring mind. As a result of the Second World War in particular, Britain, especially Britain's government, became a secret society where some questions cannot be asked and if they are, no answers are forthcoming. Had they pursued an espionage angle, even the police in 1943 would have met doors closed to them even more surely than they are today.

In the inter-war period, information on Britain was being collected by the German secret service (*Sicherheitsdienst* or SD) because that was what secret services did. The German embassy passed on all sorts of information and judging by the quality of information in Schellenberg's Black List it was extraordinarily accurate. Home addresses, telephone numbers, even car registration details were all typed diligently in the

Wilhelmstrasse offices of the SS in the summer of 1940. The Ausland (Outland) organization was a worldwide movement composed of Germans living outside Germany, who were expected to be loyal to the Führer and the Nazi cause. Rudolf Hess, Hitler's deputy (*stellvertreter*) was responsible for the British arm of this, collecting random information from hiking and cycling parties who took photographs of each other in dockyards and near aerodrome hangars. The outbreak of war, of course, stopped all that. From 3 September 1939, the only effective way for a German to glean intelligence was to be parachuted in or dropped on the coast. The case of Laura Van Raalte is unique, but at least it can be argued that she was British born and, as things turned out, harmless.

'Espionage' wrote Michael J. Barrett, Assistant General of the Central Intelligence Agency (CIA), with his tongue firmly in his cheek, 'is the world's second oldest profession and just as honourable as the first [prostitution].' Germany's leading spy organization, the Abwehr, had its headquarters on the Tirpitz Ufer, the embankment of the Landwehr Canal in the centre of Berlin. The word means 'defence' but the Abwehr was solely to do with 'offence', at least until the rest of the world closed in on the Third Reich by 1945. It was headed by Wilhelm Canaris, a former naval officer, who was both ambitious and competent. Unfortunately, like so many of the second rung officers of the time, he fell foul of the endless bickering and jockeying for position of Hitler's closest subordinates, men with issues as big as their egos: Himmler, Goering, Heydrich and Goebbels.

Hitler never entirely trusted Canaris or the Abwehr and put more faith in his own black-shirted SS and the SD, which was run from 1931 by Himmler and became entangled with the various police forces of the Reich, especially the secret police, the Gestapo. It was Canaris and the Abwehr, however, who bore the responsibility for planting agents in Britain. Both ways of doing this were fraught with danger for the agents concerned and the risk of detection was high. There are hundreds of bays, inlets and coves around the British coast where a U-boat could sneak close enough to land for a man to swim ashore or row a dinghy. But Coastal Command, the Home Guard, the police and the world and his wife were watching around the clock for this; not for nothing was the country called 'Fortress Britain'. There were gun-emplacements and barbed wire on the beaches and dunes and every port had an army of guards on permanent watch. When Dorothy O'Grady, a home-grown spy in the Isle of Wight was found wandering on the beach at Sandown, which was out of bounds, the authorities quickly jumped into action and arrested her. She was sentenced to death in 1941 under the Treachery Act because she had sabotaged telephone wires to impede troop movements. Her sentence was reduced to fourteen years in gaol after an appeal.

The alternative was for an agent to jump out of a plane and take his or her chances with a parachute. Thanks to the British invention of radar, which the Germans did not possess or even know about, we were able to locate aircraft coming over the Channel, unless they were virtually at sea level, in which case they were plainly visible from the ground, even at night. Assuming a plane could get through (and some did) the jump itself carried a huge risk. Paratroopers were trained long and hard to do this, but civilian agents less so. If they landed without injury, what then? They had to hide or bury the yards of silk and rope that had brought them down and find their way in an alien country where all the signposts had been removed just to make things difficult for people like them and their comrades-in-arms who were believed to be hard on their heels. In 1940 and even 1941, this was an important point. Operation Sealion had been shelved in the autumn of 1940, but there was no way of telling what project Hitler had up his sleeve. It is likely that the agents parachuted in were firmly of the opinion that they were a secret advance guard to the thousands very close behind them, rather as the Allied glider units were in D-Day, June 1944.

Joyce Coley cites just such a parachute drop in the context of Bella. 'Later,' she writes, 'the police did get a story from Mr Basterfield who, before his call-up, had been a member of the Home Guard.' According to Coley, he was patrolling in Hagley Wood Lane with a friend. Operating out of a hut in Halesowen, they 'had turned out to investigate a parachute alert'. We shall look at the Bella-related results of this later, but there is nothing in the Worcester Archive to corroborate it. And we have come across the name Basterfield before. He is likely to have been the son of the widow who lived at 408 on the Halesowen Road in Hasbury, opposite the Rose and Crown where Bella, according to one wall-writing, was supposed to live. His mother was interviewed on 1 August 1943. It is surely too much of a coincidence that he was also in Hagley Wood Lane in 1941. When did he report the incident? Was he the author of the Hasbury graffito, rather enjoying the limelight?

And without wishing to sound *too* much like the fictional Captain Mainwaring of BBC's classic sitcom *Dad's Army*, the British were ready for any agents who might descend. According to Coley, 'The harness to the parachutes was found on the [Clent] Hills but not before someone had removed the silk, as it was a favourite material to make underwear.' This defies belief. However desperate a woman may be for the luxuries of pre-war life, not reporting such a find to the authorities was just not something that would happen in wartime Britain. We know the details of everybody who tried.

Walter Schellenberg dismissed Britain's ruling class with contempt, pointing out that only 1 per cent of Englishmen attended public schools and yet these people counted for 80 per cent of leaders in all walks of the military and the government. Central to counter-espionage were the Secret Service departments MI5 and MI6, although both the RAF and the Navy had their own intelligence units. Based in Whitehall, but with outposts scattered around the country, they employed a surprising number of mavericks, men (and a few women) whose tendency was to look sideways at espionage problems and come out with often excellent results. There were mistakes, of course, but the code-breakers of Bletchley Park and John Masterman's Camp XX alone were worth their weight in gold.

Once it was obvious that Britain would have to be invaded in 1940 (this was never part of Hitler's domination plan and it was fraught with difficulties) Canaris and the Abwehr were tasked with the impossible; send agents to Britain, carry out acts of sabotage and report on the country's preparedness for war. The agents recruited worked under the codename Operation Lena, run directly by Hauptmann Hubert Wichmann. The organization was so top secret that not many in the Abwehr knew about it and for years it was assumed to be a separate organization. Agents were to be parachuted into England by the Gartenfeld Squadron; Luftwaffe planes commanded by Hauptman Karl-Edmund Gartenfeld. Under him was Nikolaus Ritter, as close to a civilian as anyone could be in a regime where *everybody* wore a uniform.

The first three agents dropped into Britain were flown in a Heinkel HeIII, painted black for night work, on 26 September 1940. The weather drove them back, but they tried again by U-boat and landed on the coast near Inverness. José Waldeburg was German, Carl Meier and Charles Kieboom were Dutch, with their delicious echoes of Van Ralt. They were caught almost immediately by troops with bayonets and placed under arrest. They were carrying a wireless for communications back to Berlin (or at least Nazi-occupied France) and a large wad of £1 notes, far more than the average man in the street would normally carry. They pretended to be refugees, like so many who had already genuinely crossed the Channel, but the subterfuge failed. Both the radio instructions and batteries were in German and their flimsy cover stories did not hold water. All three were sentenced to death by a special court. Unthinkable in peacetime, such 'kangaroo' arrangements were deemed necessary given the desperate situation at the time. Waldeburg and Meier died at Pentonville, hanged by Albert Pierrepoint, the public executioner who would end the lives of far higher profile Nazis at Nuremberg five years later. Kieboom appealed. Not only was he Dutch, not German, but he had been born in Japan and Japan at that time was neutral. He had had his family threatened by the Nazis (of which there is no record throughout the war) and this, he claimed, was sufficient for the court's leniency. He withdrew this appeal a week later and was hanged at Pentonville by Stanley Cross a week after the others.

The next pair were Robert Petter, also known as Werner Walti and Karl Drucke also known as François de Decker. They were dropped by seaplane off Scotland and came ashore in a rubber dinghy near Banff. They holed and sank the boat then split up, Drucke going one direction, Petter the opposite. Petter did not last long. He was spotted studying a railway timetable at Portgordon station and railway staff were suspicious of him. On arrest, he was found to have an automatic German pistol, a radio transmitter and a bratwurst in his suitcase. The attempts to sink the dinghy had failed thanks to Coastal Command. It was recovered, still afloat, and was found to be a two-man vessel. Drucke was found in Edinburgh, with what remained of his bratwurst in his suitcase along with £327 in sterling (over a year's wages for most people) and a torch made in Bavaria. They were both hanged at Wandsworth by Thomas Pierrepoint on 6 August 1941.

What was truly bizarre about those landings – and has the vaguest of nods to Bella – is that there was a third member of the team, Vera Chalburg. Despite the fact that she was a Russian Jewess from Kyiv, Ukraine, her brother had been killed fighting for the Waffen SS on the eastern front against Poland in the brief September War in 1940. The geopolitical alliances of 1940–41 are complicated; Russia and Germany were allies (however unlikely that seemed later on) and people like Chalburg chose their sides accordingly. It is highly unlikely she was not aware how the Nazis treated Jews, but perhaps she was able to conceal her faith. She was clearly a cut above the usual downtrodden German *frau*, being at one time the mistress of Hilmar Diêrks, head of the Abwehr marine intelligence unit.

Vera turned king's evidence against her fellow agents and after her imprisonment was released and went on to marry a British officer. Perhaps it was the famous British sense of chivalry that saved her. She told her story to MI5's interrogation centre, Camp XX (which came to be known, for obvious reasons, as the Double Cross Committee) which specialized in turning agents. There is no evidence that Vera was ever used as a double agent, nor is there any mention of her or any of her aliases in John Masterman's *The Double Cross System* written soon after the war ended.

Next came Josef Jakobs, at 43 one of the oldest agents to be sent by Lena. He was born in Luxembourg but was a nationalized German and had worked for the German army, attached to the Meteorological Office. He was parachuted in and buried his helmet and flying suit and set off in search of somewhere – perhaps anywhere – that he recognized from his weeks of poring over British maps. Again, he was carrying the tell-tale evidence that would lead to his execution – a radio transmitter, a spade and the always-incriminating sausage! He lasted for twelve hours before his arrest. Uniquely in the history of espionage in this period, he was shot in the precincts of the Tower of London on 14 August 1941.

Another agent who kept an appointment with a member of the Pierrepoint family, was Karel Richter, who used the alias Fred Snyder. He parachuted into a field near London Colney, Hertfordshire, in May 1941, hiding in a wood for two days. Unluckily for him, he was stopped by a lost lorry driver asking for directions and of course could not help. His responses were so surly and monosyllabic that the driver happened to mention it to a passing policeman on his bike, who *was* able to tell him his way. The constable overtook Richter and, not happy with the answers he gave, took him into custody. In his luggage was a wad of bank notes, a compass and a map of East Anglia. A police search of the area turned up his parachute, a pistol, a radio transmitter and a crash helmet, complete with swastika! He was hanged at Wandsworth on 10 December 1941.

The other agents dropped under the Lena operation are outside the scope of this book because they were caught after the summer of 1941 and were of the wrong sex to be Bella. Jose Key and Alphonse Tinnerman were found guilty of separate espionage offences and were hanged by Albert Pierrepoint in July 1942. Duncan Scott-Ford was a home-grown agent, as opposed to one flown in. As a merchant seaman he was potentially very valuable to the Abwehr but he was caught and executed at Wandsworth in November 1942. Franciscus Winter, posing as a steward on ocean liners, was arrested in possession of British, French, Belgian and American currency. His job, he told his interrogators, was to report on Royal Navy convoy movements. Pierrepoint met him in January 1943. Oswald Job was, at 58, the oldest man to be hanged for espionage during the war. Offering his services as a double agent, he was hanged at Pentonville in March of the same year.

What has never been fully explained is why the Lena agents were so inept. Most of them were captured within hours or days at most of their arrival and their 'covers' (refugees fleeing Nazi Germany) were easily blown. They do not seem to have been properly briefed and above all, there was no friendly infrastructure to help them once they arrived. When, later in the war, the agents of the Special Operations Executive (SOE) were parachuted into occupied France, various Resistance units were there to hide and help them. The Abwehr should have known that anyone with a foreign accent (it did not have to be German) was likely to raise suspicion in a country as paranoid as Britain had become by 1940. In June of that year, a Dane and a Swede arriving in Liverpool were each fined £15 by a magistrate 'on account of their foreign appearance'!

There was one agent, however, who requires further investigation in the context of Bella. He was Engelbertus Fukken, a Dutchman who used the alias Jan Willem ter Braak. Masterman wrote:

> The date of the man's arrival is unknown [it was 31 October/1 November 1940] but he took lodgings in Cambridge, at the beginning of November. His body was discovered on 1 April 1941, in a half-built air-raid shelter in Cambridge, where he had committed suicide. The identity card found on [him] contained five gross technical errors – a good instance of the importance of such documents for counter-espionage purposes. The rest is largely surmise, but it is more than probable that he was a parachute agent (perhaps the only agent) who succeeded in eluding capture, but who was unable to make contact with the Germans. He perished when his stock of money was exhausted. It is not altogether fanciful to speculate how much more happy and more useful his career might have been if he could have fallen into the hands of the Security Service and become a double agent.

A recent book on the subject – *Hitler's Spy Against Churchill*[1] – fills in MI5's gaps. Ter Braak, along with many other Dutchmen, joined the Nazi cause because he believed in it. His family had no idea of his work with the Lena operatives, believing that he had gone to work in occupied France. His unusually gullible landlady in Cambridge seems to have accepted his story that he was a journalist on the run from the Nazis and did not question his frequent disappearances when he claimed to be visiting London. For much of the time, alone and effectively abandoned by his masters, he seems to have spent his time riding buses in the Cambridge area and sitting about in cafes. His suicide, however, is suspicious. Information about the police enquiry and inquest is almost non-existent. The newspapers, local and national, barely mention it. One of the two surviving photographs of ter Braak's body on the floor of the air-raid shelter under Christ's Pieces, shows his head wedged underneath a bench seat. The impact of a bullet from a gun fired by the man himself would have forced his head in the opposite direction.

But the importance of ter Braak is this: MI5 pretended later that they knew all about him, but he was at large for five months with no tail by anybody before the discrepancies in his papers were noticed for the first time. Clearly, he was the one agent who had managed to elude everybody, which was what they all should have done. And if ter Braak could do it, why not someone else? Why not a 5-foot-tall woman, with brown hair and snaggle teeth? Professor Webster's estimate was that Bella was murdered in the summer or autumn of 1941, within the same time frame that ter Braak had arrived. MI5 never caught ter Braak until he was dead. Could the same be true of Bella? For all the mistakes made by the Abwehr in preparing their agents, a common-sense approach would be to remove all labels from clothing so that nothing would point back to Germany. And as for Bella's dental work, did those records lie – do they still lie? – somewhere in Berlin or Hamburg or Dusseldorf, beyond the reach of the Worcestershire CID at the time and, indeed, anyone else since?

With his usual enigmatic style, Donald McCormick claimed to have made a 'lengthy search' of Abwehr III's records which included details of a female agent being parachuted into the countryside between Kidderminster and Birmingham in March 1941. This is almost certainly Vera Chalburg and she was not parachuted in to the industrial Midlands at all. If this woman had the same luck as ter Braak, she might well have eluded the authorities potentially indefinitely. We know that European refugees littered the country in the 1940s, claiming all sorts of nationalities and horror stories and the stretched authorities could not keep tabs on them all.

But, as we shall see, the espionage connection does not end there. I have dealt at length with the Lena agents and the ease with which they were captured. If Bella *was* such an agent, and a more successful one than any of her comrades except, perhaps, ter Braak, how did her body end up in Hagley Wood? It was certainly not the policy of MI5 to murder alien agents and despite a brief tussle between Special Branch's chief constable and Karl Drucke in an Edinburgh railway station, no violence was offered to them before the hangman's rope or – in just the one case – a bullet.

Could it be, however, that somebody else wanted Bella dead? Someone closer to home.

Chapter 12

Aktion Hess

'And what exactly was the *Aktion Hess?*' Donald McCormick asks himself and his readers on page 108 of *Murder By Witchcraft*. And, more importantly, what has it got to do with the Hagley Wood murder?

> And if, my Führer, this project – which I admit has but very small chance of success – ends in failure and the fates decide against me, this can have no detrimental results either for you or for Germany: it will always be possible for you to deny any responsibility, simply say I was mad.

On the night of 10 May 1941, a lone German aircraft was spotted flying low over the coast of eastern Scotland. Although the observers from the ground and the Spitfires sent up to intercept it could not know it, the Messerschmitt 110Bf had neither bombs nor guns on board. It had been modified at Augsburg airfield to be able to make the flight to the small airstrip near Lennoxlove House. Something went wrong with the flight plan and the pilot bailed out, letting his plane crash into fields near Dungavel House. Dazed and with a damaged leg from his parachute jump, the pilot was soon arrested. He gave his name as Hauptman Alfred Horn and asked to see a serving RAF officer, the Duke of Hamilton.

It was quickly established that Horn was actually Rudolf Hess, Hitler's deputy, who was leader of the Nazi Party and before the war had run the Ausland organization which provided intelligence on Britain's military capacity in the 1930s. At the time, despite reports of the plane's crashing, details were understandably scant. And, despite the release of previously classified documents over the last few years, we still know relatively little about the extraordinary flight even today. It may count as the most bizarre single event of the Second World War, except perhaps for someone stuffing a woman's body in a wych elm.

It was left to A.P. Herbert, politician, writer and member of the Naval Auxiliary Unit, to speculate on the Hess flight:

He is insane. He is the Dove of Peace.
He is Messiah. He is Hitler's niece.
He is the one, clean, honest man they've got.
He is the worst assassin of the lot.
He has a mission to preserve mankind.
He's non-alcoholic. He's a 'blind'.
He has been dotty since the age of ten
But all the time was top of Hitler's men.
(Indeed, from all the tales he had to tell,
Joe Goebbels must be slightly touched as well)
He is to pave the way to Britain's end.
He is – as dear old Lindbergh was – a 'friend'.
He's fond of flying. He was racked with fear.
He had an itch to meet a British Peer.
He thought that Russia was a crashing bore.
He simply can't stand Hitler any more.
In such rich fancies I am not engrossed,
For this is what appears to matter most –
He came unasked, an enemy, a Hun;
And nobody was ready with a gun.

Eventually, they were; or at least, a ligature. Having escaped execution at the Nuremberg trials on the grounds of diminished responsibility, and having no direct links with the Holocaust, Rudolf Hess was imprisoned for life at Spandau prison in Berlin. For years he was its only inmate, but on 17 August 1987, he was found in a garden summerhouse in the gaol's grounds with electric flex around his neck. The cause of death was suspension by hanging, but the jury is still out on whether this was suicide or murder. As far as I am concerned, it was the latter. The old man was far too frail to hoist himself or even the cable on to the relevant window catch, but no one was charged with murder. Instead, there was an international sigh of relief – the Nazi era was at last over.

There is little doubt today that the purpose of Hess's flight to Scotland was to secure a peace deal with Churchill, the prime minister, to give Hitler a free hand in his forthcoming invasion of Russia – Operation

Barbarossa. There is no doubt in my mind that if Hess's mission had succeeded, Hitler's devastating *blitzkrieg* would have destroyed Stalin's Red Army of brainwashed conscripts in record time. But it did not succeed – and the rest is history.

Two things concern us in the context of the Hess flight. The first is the reaction to it in Germany, known as *Aktion Hess* and the second is; was the *Stellvertreter* expecting a welcoming committee at Lennoxlove – and could that committee have extended as far south as Hagley, Worcestershire? The response to the flight in Berlin was instant. Josef Goebbels' press release proclaimed:

> It seemed that party member Hess lived in a state of hallucination, as a result of which he felt he would bring about an understanding between England and Germany ... The National Socialist Party regrets that this idealist fell a victim to this hallucination. This, however, will have no effect on the continuance of the war which has been forced on Germany.

This, as usual from Goebbels, was nonsense. Hess was party leader, not merely a member and he did not suffer from hallucinations. The most egregious lie of all, of course, was that the Second World War had been 'forced' on Germany, not caused by the megalomania of Goebbels' boss. Hitler himself had flown into one of his famous rages, as usual, carefully acted out, because he must have known of Hess's plans and probably actively approved them, given the two men's long and close friendship. Hess's immediate staff and family were arrested, but all were released soon afterwards. One of the common themes in the weeks that followed 10 May is that Hess was mad. He had suggested it himself to Hitler in the letter quoted at the beginning of this chapter. It formed a 'plausible denial', a loophole which allowed Hitler to distance himself from his deputy. Germany and Russia were still nominally allies at this point and the last thing Hitler wanted was to tip Stalin off about a possible German rapprochement with the west, which would have left him free to launch Barbarossa.

And, if Hess was mad, what could have caused it? Could it have been his dabblings with the occult? Goebbels, as Hitler's mouthpiece to the German – and world – press, said, 'Recently [Hess] had sought relief [from "physical suffering"] to an increasing extent in various methods practised by mesmerists and astrologers.' There is little doubt that Hitler, Hess and above all, Himmler, head of the SS, were fascinated by the occult. When they were in prison together at Landsberg after the failed Beer Hall Putsch in Munich in 1924, Hitler said one night:

> You know, Rudi, it's only the moon I hate. For it is something dead and terrible and inhuman. And human beings are afraid of it ... It is as if in the moon a part of the terror still lives which the moon once sent down over the earth. I hate it! That pale and ghostly fellow.

Psychologists would have a field day with this bizarre comment, but he and Hess thought alike on this, as on most other things.

Admiral Godfrey, Director of Naval Intelligence during the war, believed that Hitler's astrologers had predicted that the Führer's achievements must be accomplished by the end of February 1941 and that his luck would run out after that. There is no evidence to suggest that Hitler ever visited an astrologer, but Hess and Himmler almost certainly did.

From the British point of view, black propaganda, however bizarre and unlikely, was used to destabilize the Reich's plans and spread disinformation far and wide. The men working for SO1 (part of the Political Intelligence Division of the Foreign Office) were largely laws unto themselves. Hugh Dalton ran the organization and he had mavericks like the journalists Sefton Delmer and Ellic Howe under him who came up with all sorts of ruses. From the American angle, after their entry into the war in December 1941, William 'Wild Bill' Donavan of the Office of Strategic Services, forerunner of the CIA, was another black propagandist, given to outlandish disguises and even more outlandish ideas. One of these, along with infected laundry in U-boats, was to bombard Hitler with pornography so that he became insane! This sounds like a hangover from Victorian times, when it was widely held that masturbation causes insanity/blindness/you name it.

We have to be careful about this espionage link with the occult. Much of it was nonsense, the stuff of gentleman's club jokes and a fevered press once the war was over where the Allies gloated over their victory and belittled the Axis war effort. James Hayward's *Myths and Legends of the Second World War* (2003) explodes much of this rubbish, but somewhere at its heart lies a kernel of truth. One genuine use of astrology by the Allies was to employ the double agent Louis de Wohl, a Hungarian on the run from the Nazis. As an astrologer, he lectured extensively in the United States in the months before Pearl Harbor, giving doom-laden predictions on the German war effort based on the stars. He did this for cash rather than ideology and was given a commission in the British army for services rendered.

The involvement of Aleister Crowley is more mysterious and less likely to be true. Crowley's son Amado remembered as a 9-year-old in 1940 watching a ceremony in Ashdown Forest involving robed figures and a dummy wearing a Nazi uniform, sitting on a throne. His deranged father was master of ceremonies and the idea was, perhaps, to ward off the likelihood of a German invasion.

Aleister Crowley was a neurotic fantasist who called himself 'the wickedest man in the world', a reincarnation of the Beast referred to in the ludicrous ramblings of the Book of Revelations, whose number is 666. Like many people mentioned already, he changed his name for spurious reasons. Christened Edward Alexander to Plymouth Brethren parents, Crowley turned against the cult and joined another one – the Hermetic Order of the Golden Dawn. Moving to Egypt, Italy and the United States, he set up various cults of his own, performing 'magick' with a fluctuating group of adoring female acolytes. Like many cult leaders before and since Crowley's time, sex was at the heart of most of it.

Most of the fascination with Crowley dates from the 1960s, by which time he had been dead for years. His following in the 1940s, especially in Britain, was very small and it is not known how far his reputation had spread to Germany.

What has all this mumbo-jumbo to do with the body of a woman found in Hagley Wood? The *Aktion Hess* definitely happened, a rounding up of astrologers, fortune-tellers and occultists throughout Germany. Heinrich Himmler, who had invested time and money in establishing a romantic, mystic and wholly spurious back-story for the SS, must have been seething – he *believed* that stuff. One victim of *Aktion Hess* was Hitler's own astrologer (according to him) Karl Ernst Krafft, whose fate remains unknown. Another was Ernst Schulte-Strahaus, Hitler's astrological adviser.

The link to Hagley lies, as all too often, with Donald McCormick in *Murder By Witchcraft* (see Chapter 16) but Superintendent Williams had made a step in the right direction in 1953. In the context of Anna of Claverley and the mysterious Van Ralt, he told reporters that he was in the process of contacting Dutch authorities in search of the girl stuffed into the tree to sober up.

The lack of any labelling in the dead woman's clothing and the failure to find a relevant Bella, led Williams to accept that she probably was foreign. Whether his enquiries were carried out directly or via Interpol, set up in 1923 but not called that until 1956, is not clear. There is no reference to this line of enquiry in the Archive.

Into the gaping void of the Dutch connection leaps McCormick, the intrepid researcher, with a cheerful disregard for the complexities of research abroad. 'I was able to make enquiries in Holland,' he says, and discovered that Bella was not only Dutch, but a secret agent. The Netherlands had remained neutral for as long as they could, although it was clearly in British interests to keep a careful eye on events in the Low Countries. On 9 November 1939, during the 'phoney war' when nothing seemed to be happening in western Europe, two MI6 officers, Major Richard Stevens and Captain Sigismund Payne Best, were kidnapped by an undercover agent who was actually Walter Schellenberg of the SS. They were grabbed in a slick shootout at Venlo on the Dutch/German border, having been lured there by Schellenberg's play. Ignoring all their training and contrary to the code of captured spies giving nothing away, Stevens and Best sang like canaries, destroying months of the careful creation of a spy network in the Netherlands.

McCormick gets it right when he says 'the British secret service at this time was, by the most generous assessment, in a state of flux ... controlled and run in a most amateurish fashion.' As a result – and the folly of employing men like Stevens and Best – a number of British agents were captured and top-secret files raided at The Hague. It is no exaggeration to say that in the months before Dunkirk (May 1940) British Intelligence had virtually no information of events in Europe.

We are not told by McCormick who he contacted in Holland (any more than we are by DI Williams) but he then throws up the name of Dronkers, a name that has been linked with the Hagley Wood case ever since. Johannes Marinus Dronkers was born in Utrecht in April 1896. His first post was as a seaman but he was working for the Dutch post office shortly before the war. The Netherlands at the time was a melting pot of intrigue. Most Dutch people opposed Nazism but the Germans had been their neighbours for eighty years as citizens of sovereign states and for centuries before that. There was a strong thread of support for Nazi ideals and, as we have seen, two major Dutch Nazi parties vying with each other. Johannes Dronkers had joined one of them and underwent Lena training for a mission to Britain. By the time he left Holland, in May 1942, the United States had joined the war and Dronkers' brief was to report on American and Canadian troops in Britain. He used that quaint, centuries-old technique of invisible ink (lemon juice) and had a series of undercover addresses in neutral countries as contacts.

His yacht was picked up by a British trawler risking the U-boat menace to get fish for 'fortress Britain' and he tried the usual ploy that he was a refugee on the run from the Nazis. Once on British soil, he was quizzed by the authorities and admitted that he worked for the Abwehr. He was tried at the Old Bailey, under strict security, and was hanged by Albert Pierrepoint at Wandsworth on 31 December 1942, the twelfth spy to be executed thus far during the war. According to McCormick, before he cracked, Dronkers *nearly* got away with it, even making anti-German broadcasts on Free Orange Radio run from London by the BBC. And, specifically, nowhere does McCormick say that there is a Bella link. We are left to surmise a connection because of the Dutch angle.

McCormick then changes tack, this time to the Verbindungsstab organization of Rudolf Hess. This group, roughly translated as 'liaison staff' oversaw the work of the Abwehr, the Gestapo and the SD (Security Service). Of particular importance was a group within that had gathered information from diplomatic circles since the First World War. The shadowy members of the Verbindungsstab not only had little faith in Canaris's Abwehr, they were almost certainly involved in organising Hess's mission to Scotland in May 1941.

Among the agents of the Verbindungsstab, McCormick claims, was one with the name Lehrer. There is no Christian name and it is not clear whether this is actually his surname or a code *nom de guerre* which many wartime agents on both sides of the Channel used. Lehrer was a high-ranking officer involved in recruitment, but in this particular instance, he came over himself. In the diaries of Abwehr III, McCormick maintains, is the proof of this – 'an attempt is to be made to set down the agent Lehrer with a wireless operator on the coast of South Wales in order to establish better communications'.

McCormick mentions two Operations, codenamed Green (*Fall Grun*) and Whale in this context. In fact, there were at least eight of these, all of them as precursors to Operation Sealion, the actual invasion of England,

and all of them involving the Scots and Welsh nationalists and particularly the Irish. Since 1923, Eire had been an independent nation and its hatred of the English went back centuries. This untapped source of opposition was something the Germans could exploit. None of these Operations got beyond the planning stage and without exception they had been abandoned by the summer of 1941.

We now have the names of the key figures involved in this espionage work, both the organizers and the key agents. Unless it is a *very* obscure alias, the name Lehrer occurs nowhere. Not that that deters McCormick. According to him, Lehrer had a Dutch mistress who knew Britain well and had had an affair with a man in Stourbridge, only five miles, of course, from Hagley Wood. This woman had lived in the Birmingham area in the 1930s and even spoke with a 'Brummy' accent.

McCormick's contention was that the Abwehr sent five agents from Holland between March and April 1941. Two were captured and two came by boat. The fifth was a woman, codenamed Clara, and she was dropped by plane in the Midlands between Birmingham and Kidderminster. 'If one draws a line,' McCormick wrote cryptically, 'between Kidderminster and Birmingham, it runs very close to Hagley Wood.'

The area might well have been of interest to the Lena agents – Hartlebury RAF base had vital aircraft components and Birmingham was a centre of arms production. Clara, said the Abwehr records, went missing – nothing more was heard from her by radio or any other means. This was circumstantial dynamite. But it is a lie. Jan Willem ter Braak 'went missing' too, as far as the Abwehr were concerned, because he had no means to contact anyone with any information he may have gleaned.

And unless MI5, the police, the army and vast numbers of paranoid snooping civilians had missed a number of tricks, *all* the Abwehr/Lena agents dropped in 1941 were accounted for. The only female involved was, as we have seen, Vera Chalburg, a Russian Jewess, not a Dutch girl and was picked up in the company of Karl Drucke and Werner Walti. She was not the mistress of the fictional Lehrer but of Hilmar Diêrks of Abwehr Marine Intelligence. Far from being stuffed into a tree in Hagley Wood, she was caught, imprisoned and later released to marry her British army officer.

McCormick was undeterred by any of this when writing in 1968. As far as he was concerned, Clara had been parachuted between Kidderminster and Birmingham and McCormick's task was to establish that Lehrer's mistress and Clara were the same person. Dutch police records and Nazi files made no comment on this. His researches in the papers of Abwehr III (Counter Intelligence run by Major-General von Betivegric) should have led him specifically to Abwehr IIIF involving infiltration into foreign Intelligence. He latched on to three people who might be able to identify Clara. One was Otto Behne who, McCormick says, was once reputed to be the wannabe gauleiter of Britain had Hitler's eagle landed in 1940 (in fact, it was Franz Six). Another was a Nazi named Kuhnemann who was linked with Oswald Mosley's British Union of Fascists, and the third was Franz Rathgeb. Try as I might, I could find no reference to any of these men in an extensive search of Nazi literature. Kuhnemann is probably a minor, obscure official, one of the ragtag misfits who carried on correspondence with the BUF before and just after the start of the war. Behne, however, *ought* to be high profile, if he was considered worthy to run a *gau* the size of Britain. Franz Six, nominated as the *actual* controller of Britain had it fallen in the summer of 1940, is well-chronicled, down to his membership numbers of the Nazi party and the SS.

When McCormick found the third possible link, Rathgeb, he was living under an alias in Paraguay. Rather like the ease of access to Dutch police records and Abwehr material, the casual simplicity of this piece of international detection defies belief. An unknown number of Nazis got out of the shattered Reich in the spring and summer of 1945, following the so-called 'rat lines' to South America where no questions were asked of past associations. Bearing in mind that it took Mossad, the Israeli secret service, fourteen years to find Adolf Eichmann, architect of the Holocaust, McCormick's lightning work is nothing short of miraculous. Not only that, but Rathgeb was only too happy to discuss matters with a man he did not know but had been his enemy in the Second World War (McCormick served in the Royal Navy). Rathgeb told McCormick that he had spent much time in the industrial Midlands before the war and in South Wales. He knew Lehrer and he had indeed had a Dutch mistress who had lived in Birmingham in the 1930s. So far, so pat, but it gets better:

> She was well educated, intelligent, attractive and about thirty years of age ... possibly slightly under ... I can't recall much about her except that her teeth were slightly irregular and, as she was attractive, this single blemish was perhaps rather more noticeable. She wasn't tall, probably well below average height for a woman.

Rathgeb could not remember her name, nor even her codename, but he knew she had links with the Birmingham area:

> She claimed to be Dutch and said she came from Utrecht. But I have an idea that in fact she was part German ... I do know that she had been working for Abwehr III and had helped to infiltrate Dutch Resistance right from the beginning, in the summer of 1940. She travelled between Holland and Germany regularly.

Speculating further, the ex-Nazi, living in Paraguay under an assumed name, went on:

> It is therefore quite possible that Lehrer's mistress and 'Clara' were one and the same ... the last time I saw [her] must have been about the end of 1940. I seem to remember a party at which she read horoscopes about that time. I never heard any mention of her after that ... I thought that she might have been killed in an air raid in Germany. Or even that she was rounded up in the *Aktion Hess*.

If we had any faith in McCormick's research, the case of who Bella was would be cleared up, at least circumstantially. Today, it would even be possible, if Bella's skeleton had survived, to trace her via Dutch/German relatives. But it is all too convenient. Did Herr Rathgeb actually exist? How convenient that Clara should have irregular teeth and be short – the only two characteristics available from Webster's post-mortem and which had been widely reported in the press.

McCormick speculates further. If Clara was Bella, how did she end up in the wych elm at Hagley Wood? Could she have been a double agent and was it payback time by a disgruntled fellow spy? This was simply not how it was done in the 1940s. If an agent was deemed doubtful, he was either imprisoned or watched *very* closely by MI5 and/or the police. The fate of such double agents is well known, chronicled at first by John Masterman of Camp XX and later by modern historians/biographers who have catalogued their careers. The secret services did not murder agents, except by the rope and judicial process. McCormick postulates that Clara would have been landed with few, if any, extra clothes and because she failed to contact another agent, must have bought British clothes. But that ignores the lack of labels in any of her clothing and the failure by the police to trace any of them. What stands out about the captured Lena agents is their apparent inability to disguise their German equipment; even in the case of their rations, their bratwurst!

McCormick then suggests that Clara's mission might have been to meet up with her ex-lover in Stourbridge, that he too, unlikely though he concedes it is, was a Nazi sympathizer. As we have seen, there *were* Nazi sympathizers in Britain – Mosley's Fascists, the Mitford family, Lords Brocket and Buccleuch; and even though he had been quietly shipped off to the Bahamas, the Duke of Windsor. These people were either high profile or eccentric or both, not an obscure and anonymous lover of a Dutch girl living in Stourbridge.

'In my quest for the truth about the Hagley Wood crime,' wrote McCormick, 'I had allowed myself to be lured into a blind alley and all I had to show for my pains was a sub-plot in the whole story, an interesting digression, but little more.'

He was, nevertheless, able to suppose a link between Clara and the *Aktion Hess*. She read horoscopes at parties according to Rathgeb. Was she rounded up in the witch-hunt that followed Hess's flight? Heinrich Muller of the Gestapo (one of those who escaped to Argentina as the war ended and was never caught) was on the rampage looking for occultists. In June 1941, another senior Nazi, Hess's successor Martin Bormann, banned all stage performances which involved clairvoyants.

Rathgeb had suggested to McCormick that he contact a Frau Cremer in Amsterdam. Whoever this woman was, she told McCormick that Clara was probably a code name and that she was related to Johannes Dronker, the spy executed in 1942. 'She was a very serious student of astrology,' Cremer remembered, 'and had attended conferences. She was a friend of Baron Keun von Hoogerwoerd ... who had taught Louis de Wohl astrology in Berlin long before the war.'[1]

De Wohl was utilized by SOE, the black propagandists. He made bogus, doom-laden predictions, as we have seen, for leading Germans in a tour of the United States. De Wohl was every bit as dodgy as any of his comrades in the Secret Service – or the Abwehr, come to that – Ellic Howe remembered him swaggering down Whitehall in an army officer's tunic he had no right to wear. As for the grandly named von Hoogerwoerd, he is nowhere in the Net today. This does not mean that he does not exist, but his total absence is suspicious, especially as Frau Cremer claimed that he 'was always believed to have trapped your Captain Payne Best into being kidnapped by the Gestapo early in the war'.[2]

As we have seen, the Venlo incident in which Payne Best and Stevens were kidnapped was the work of Walter Schellenberg. There were a number of others involved, many of them using aliases, but none of them was von Hoogerwoerd.

The tireless McCormick soldiers on, looking for a spy operating in the Midlands in 1940–41. He met the usual brick wall of government departments. Even now, over eighty years after the event, some of the Whitehall files on the Hess flight remain closed – of such facts are conspiracy theories made! 'During World War II,' McCormick claimed, 'a German spy, never positively identified, carried out a remarkable number of coups in Britain over a long period.' Sadly, this cross between the Scarlet Pimpernel and James Bond is a creation, like them, of fiction. He was invented to cover up the ineptitude on the part of the British establishment – a brilliant master spy being a preferable alternative to good, old-fashioned incompetence. McCormick claims that the spy produced a detailed report on docks, airfields and 'shadow factories' in the Birmingham/Coventry area. This is unprovable. Docks and airfields were common knowledge – they appeared on Ordnance Survey maps freely available before the war and in aerial photographs taken by the Luftwaffe during it. The only incident which is verifiable is the sinking of the HMS *Royal Oak* in Scapa Flow and that is a hoary old chestnut fully exposed by, among others, Simon Hayward in his *Myths and Legends of the Second World War*.

On what came to be known as Black Saturday, 14 October 1939, U-boat *U47* commanded by Lieutenant Gunther Prien took his vessel through Kirk Sound into the Royal Navy's harbour off Scotland. He had the skill and the nerve to travel on the surface and fired three torpedoes at the *Royal Oak*. He fired two more rounds and the ship sank in a mass of flames in thirteen minutes. There was a huge loss of life because the order to abandon ship was not given in time.

So smug was the navy and so confident in its defence of 'impregnable' Scapa Flow that they immediately started hunting for 'agent W', working as a watchmaker. This man was a fiction, despite various attempts to name him and ten years after he wrote *Murder By Witchcraft*, McCormick rubbished it too. Instead, he created another story which we will investigate later. The bottom line in the *Royal Oak* tale is that the navy was caught with its bell-bottomed trousers down and seized on any opportunity to evade responsibility.

McCormick's master spy was so successful that he was still lurking in Britain in 1944 (odd that he seems to have told his bosses nothing about D-Day or the build-up to it). 'One suggestion from the German side,' McCormick says, 'after the war was that he was a German-Canadian called Karl Dickenhoff, who lived in a house in Edgbaston.' The *Birmingham Post* got hold of this story in 1956 and were threatened with legal action by Dickenhoff. His real name was Hans Caesar and he was well known in the Birmingham jewellery community before the war. As *realpolitik* kicked in in 1939, he left Britain, got to Germany and enlisted in the Wehrmacht. Far from spying in the Midlands, he spent the entire war freezing on the Eastern Front, first against the Poles, then against the Russians. He returned to England in 1948 and the *Birmingham Post* was only too happy (and presumably, desperate) to offer a full written apology.

Even then, McCormick does not give up. 'It is known,' he wrote, 'that he was an associate of ... Jan Willem Ter Braak, who, according to Frau Cremer, was a friend of "Clara", alias Dronkers.' *Hitler's Spy Against Churchill*, debunks this nonsense; Ter Braak did not know Caesar/Dickenhoff. How could they have met since the Dutchman did not arrive in Britain until 1 November 1941, by which time Caesar was 'somewhere in Eastern Europe'. More relevantly, there is no one called Clara in Ter Braak's circle – he was a loner with very few friends and had no links with other agents except through his brief training.

'Edgbaston,' wrote McCormick, 'Stourbridge, Halesowen, Hagley Wood ... "Bella", "Clara" Dronkers ... a skeleton in the old wych elm ... Dickenhoff, Caesar, Willem Ter Braak. What do they all add up to?'

The answer is: an implausible load of tosh we will explore further in Chapter 16.

But there is a curious PS in the story of *Aktion Hess*. Author Andrew Sparke, in a privately printed work in 2014 (updated 2018) refers to papers found in the possession of the spy Josef Jakobs, the only agent to be executed by firing squad during the war. In Jakobs' wallet was a photograph of a young woman, smiling at the camera and curled up on an armchair. On the reverse of the photo were the words 'My Dear, I love you for ever ... Your Clara, Landau, July 1940.' MI5 were able to track her records. She was Clara Sophie Bauerle, born in Ulm in August 1905 and was 36 by 1941, which chimes well with Professor Webster's theory that 'Bella' was about that age when she died. For reasons that are not clear she came to work in England in 1930, working the Midlands Music Halls. The Register of Aliens records her leaving Warwick in June 1932. 'She spoke English with a Brummie accent,' Sparke records, 'and English audiences sometimes called her Clarabella.' All very pat and circumstantial, but Sparke's sources are not quoted.

According to the author, Clara met Jakobs in Hamburg where she was performing with Bernhard Ette's orchestra at Café Dreyer. She was popular with the Nazi elite, vaguely linked with Hermann Goering, head of the Luftwaffe (who liked a pretty face), and had had a lover in the Kriegsmarine. According to Jakobs, who seems to have been extraordinarily gobby, Clara was recruited as an agent and was supposed to be parachuted into the Midlands area to support Jakobs once he had established contact by radio. The odd thing about this is that Jakobs did not believe that Clara had any previous links with England.

Clara Bauerle seems to disappear in Germany after the spring of 1941, despite her party affiliation and apparently successful music career. The *Independent*'s Alison Vale drew the conclusion in March 2013 that this disappearance is explained by the body in the wych elm; Bella was Clara. The problem with Vale's assertion is that Clara Bauerle was nearly 6 feet tall, according to Jakobs and Karel Richter, another captured agent. The photograph shows that the singer did not have 'snaggle' teeth, eliminating her as a potential wych elm victim. Clara was in fact still performing and recording until her untimely death in Berlin on 16 December 1942. Records show that the cause of her death was veronal poisoning, the insomnia cure that had killed Mathilde Wurm.

What a pity that so many people have latched on to this piece of mischievous mythmaking and accepted it as gospel.

Chapter 13

'If I were a Blackbird' and the sillier stories

Joyce Coley came to the Hagley Wood mystery with the zeal of a local historian and was able to contact people who knew, those with an understanding of Midlands culture. The problem is that the war was a long time ago; those who lived through it still alive today were children at the time, often blissfully ignorant of events unfolding, even on their own doorstep.

Ms Coley puts flesh on some of the infuriatingly naked bones left by Donald McCormick, but, unfortunately, she raises more questions than she answers. Above all, her pamphlet *Bella: An Unsolved Murder* is a collection of stories that show how gullible the public is and how nonsense surrounds unsolved mysteries and only makes the chance of solution ever less likely. McCormick's teacher and the company executive who heard screams in Hagley Wood on 16 July 1941 become the even vaguer 'two men ... walking in the woods' without names or a date. The woman whose identity card was found near the wych elm is dismissed in a brief remark – 'There is no further work on how her card came to be placed there' – which begs all sorts of questions.

Coley reports another story to which we have already alluded and which is most unlikely, given the national paranoia in Britain in 1941. The Mr Basterfield who lived opposite the Rose and Crown in Hasbury, waiting for his call-up, joined the local Home Guard and found himself in a scout hut in Halesowen. Word came through that a parachute drop had been made in the area (again, we have no date) and the supposed target was the Clent Hills, to the south of Hagley Wood. Basterfield and a comrade were searching the area and noticed a car parked in a lay-by opposite a gate that led into the wood. There are no details of the car, colour or registration but there was an airman at the wheel, easily identifiable by his powder blue uniform. Next to him was a woman lying under a greatcoat (presumably also RAF blue). Basterfield tapped on the driver's window and the airman held up a card (presumably his identity card) and the Home Guardsman told him to move on. When they returned (we are not told how much later) the car, driver and passenger had gone.

It is difficult to know where to start with this snippet. It is conceivable that the airman and his girlfriend had stopped for a bit of 'nooky' in the lay-by. There were airmen at Hartlebury not far away and although journeys were always suspect, short distances were possible even with petrol rationing. The Home Guardsmen seem to have been easily fobbed off with an identity card they could only have seen for seconds and do not seem to have engaged with the car's occupants at all. How much of the woman could they see under the greatcoat? Presumably, her face betrayed no sign of fear, panic or anything untoward other than possibly embarrassment at being caught 'in flagrante' in the car. I have had to use the word 'presumably' simply because so much hard evidence is missing.

And how does this probably innocuous sighting fit with the parachute harness? We have already seen the meticulous attention paid to aliens by locals, civilian, police and the military in the period, which is why almost all the Abwehr/Lena agents were caught. What has any of this to do with Bella? Was she the woman in the car and did the airman, having already been seen by the Home Guardsmen, kill her and stuff her in the tree? We do not know from Coley what, if any, follow-up there was from the police, but the whole thing smells very strongly of red herring!

Then, we have the version of the oddly named Warwick Aston Plant; the story of the impoverished singer alluded to in Chapter 5. Joyce Coley interviewed this man when writing her book. His family kept the Crown, a genteel pub in the High Street, Brierley Hill, but Plant himself went into a career in accountancy, his company having offices in Bromsgrove and Dudley. He was still living at home with his parents in 1941 and one day, having gone home for lunch, noticed a little woman in scruffy clothes sitting alone in the pub. She had asked Plant's mother, the landlady, if she could play the piano and sing. She had a beautiful voice and came twice a week to entertain the lunchtime guests. Her favourite song was 'If I were a blackbird', a haunting love song from Scotland. The woman also sang in the Mitre in Stourbridge and Plant once saw her working with a man in fields near Hagley Wood. He remembered that 'Bella' was the nickname her father had given her because of her beautiful voice. She lived in rented accommodation in Birmingham Street, Stourbridge and her landlord was a drunk.

'Bella's' back-story is as implausible as the parachute harness. She had joined a concert party touring Europe and the party had come to England, unable to find work once war had broken out. 'Bella's' shoes were very worn and Mrs Plant gave her a pair of hers, crepe-soled. One day, the singer turned up with a black eye, the work, she told the Plants, of her landlord.

Then 'Bella' stopped coming to the Crown. At his mother's insistence, Warwick Plant looked for her in the Mitre, but had no luck.

In 1944, he was home on leave from the RAF and his sister showed him a copy of the *Daily Sketch*. There was an article in which Professor Webster, the Home Office pathologist, was asking for aid in identifying the shoes found with the body in the wych elm. With it was a photograph of the shoes, which Plant immediately recognized as the pair given to 'Bella' by their mother. The sister contacted the paper and the police but to no avail. Interestingly, Joyce Coley's search for the Webster article in the *Daily Sketch* turned up nothing.

Once again, we have vague memories without hard facts that always bedevil unsolved murder cases. Whoever the singer in the Crown was, she did not end up in a wych elm in Hagley Wood. And the shoes that the Plant children remembered so vividly, the ones that were brown and cream, could not have been found with the body. Webster's report is quite clear that they were blue.

When the shoe factor Mr Cogzell contacted the Forensics Department of Birmingham University he got nowhere. Cogzell was faced with a wall of red tape. Letters were unanswered; phone calls were not returned. Eventually, in some desperation, he went unannounced to the department and was given short shrift. Professor Webster was dead and his successor, Dr Griffiths, told Cogzell there was no skeleton and no shoes, even though both were regarded by Webster as prize exhibits, still capable, at least in theory, of producing answers. Joyce Coley has her own theory about this unhelpful volte-face on the part of officialdom. Someone she met had always found Griffiths polite and sociable so his attitude made no sense. 'Had he been told not to talk?' Coley wonders, opening the door to conspiracy theories in a case that is already infuriating in its vagueness. A more plausible explanation is that an over-officious or lackadaisical underling had failed to pass Cogzell's requests on and his suddenly turning up at Griffiths' door out of the blue would have annoyed anybody.

The Hagley Wood case generated a host of letters from all over the world. One of the most bizarre came from Toronto, Canada, posing a series of questions – 'Hasn't the answer been known to those who matter for many years?' Unfortunately, Ms Coley provides no details here. When was the letter written? To whom was it written? And in which newspaper, if any, did it appear?

Yet again, we are in the realms of conspiracy theories, the notion that there is a secret society – or societies – who operate under the radar. They are powerful people who manipulate others and only surface occasionally to cover up mistakes – probably the finding of Bella's body.

'Didn't he die a year before she was found?'

This presumably refers to Bella's killer and is perhaps a nod in the direction of Jack Mossop who died in an asylum in 1942.

'When the answer was found, wasn't it allowed to rest out of kindness to those, dead and alive, who were involved for the most part unwillingly in a situation that was not of their making? Aren't these the questions you should ask?'

Certainly, this is the attitude of the British government in the context of 'sensitive' material. When I wrote to Scotland Yard several years ago in connection with the Craig and Bentley murder case of 1952, I was told that the Metropolitan police could not provide any information. Neither could the curator of the Black Museum, who remained suspicious of me throughout our brief and unhelpful interview. 'A lot of shit's been written about this case and most of it has come our way,' was his bottom line. Fifty-year rules, seventy-five-year rules, hundred-year rules may make life easier for those who would rather forget the past, but unfortunately that includes thieves, rapists and murderers, all of whom can rest easy in the certain knowledge that they are protected by obsolete and arcane thinking.

'What was the connection,' continued the Canadian contact, 'between Hagley Wood, Germany, Canada and Holland?' And now we are back in Donald McCormick country, a hint, a rumour, a suspicious Nazi too easily found and too ready to talk. Joyce Coley may believe she has solved the Canadian connection, and she links the two elements in her pamphlet. One of the two men who guarded the wych elm on the night of 19/20 April 1943 was Peter Douglas-Osborne. At the end of the war, he found himself stationed briefly in Holland (the Dutch connection that will never go away!) and met a group of Canadian soldiers who 'had been inspecting the records of the German Secret Service. They were trying to find out what happened to some of our SOE personnel.'[1]

The Special Operations Executive was the brainchild of Winston Churchill and was divided into two sections. SO1 were the black propagandists we have met already, concocting all kinds of nonsense to confuse the Reich. SO2 were the agents, female as well as male, who were parachuted behind enemy lines to carry out espionage and sabotage, usually working with various Resistance units. The Canadians (not part of SOE) had looted a house in The Hague and were taking the documents they had found back to Canada. There is no doubt that documentation relating to the German secret service was found in those hectic and confused months following actual fighting, but a vast amount had been destroyed. All over the Reich and its occupied territories, filing cabinets were smashed and papers burned. Of the estimated 20,000 copies of the Special Search List GB (the Black Book) only two could be found in 1945. Osborne would have us believe that he and the Canadians swapped war stories on the boat crossing the Channel. He mentioned the body in the wych elm and they told him of 'the many spies who had worked in the area'.[2]

What they told him, however, chimes exactly with the McCormick version we know to be false, about the agent called Clara dropped by parachute between Kidderminster and Birmingham. The whole business is as disappointing as it is suspicious.

Ms Coley has a cutting from an anonymous national newspaper referring to the Hagley Wood case of 'more than 50 years' ago, so it must date from the 1990s. Alongside a photograph of Douglas-Osborne, the article by John Simpson attempts to put flesh on Bella's bones. Douglas-Osborne's father was a special constable in the Stourbridge area in the 1940s (which might explain why Peter volunteered to guard the wych elm) and was annoyed in the 1960s when a new outbreak of graffiti prompted a conversation in the Douglas-Osborne household in which the ex-special refused not only to contribute but to allow any further mention of the subject. The implication of Simpson's article is that Douglas-Osborne senior had somehow obtained dental records from the Luftwaffe which match the unusual dentition of the body in Hagley Wood:

[She was] a highly educated member of Hitler and Goering's occult practices. We can suspect that she was a spy because Goering ... was interested in any information concerning aircraft production.

And with Longbridge works, Rolls Royce at Derby and the RAF storage at Hartlebury, Hagley was the perfect place for all round access to the aircraft production business. The records also revealed the woman had been to Heidelburg and Cambridge Universities to learn perfect English and there were no further records about her after 1940 ... the mystery is certain to baffle detectives and Hagley people for years to come.[3]

About the only thing that makes some sense in this article is the last sentence! The Luftwaffe report surely *might* have come from Douglas-Osborne junior (via his Canadian buddies) not his father. The mention of Goering has echoes of Clara Bauerle, but of all the Nazi elite, the Renaissance man Goering had no interest in the occult, any more than Clara did. It is quite bizarre to believe that dental records of agents could be found in the ruins of the Reich – once again, we are in the neat situation of referring to the only really distinctive thing about the body in the wych elm – her teeth.

'Who were the pro-Nazi sympathizers in Birmingham, Wolverhampton and Stourbridge before and during the war? Who knew the Dutch girl's man friend in Stourbridge?' the newspaper article asks.

The Fifth Column of Nazi sympathizers which worried the authorities so much in 1939–45 was largely a myth born of paranoia. At the top of society, a number of aristocrats, including the ex-king, Edward VIII, quietly approved of Hitler without really grasping what National Socialism was all about. Hitler opposed Communism in the 1930s and that was music to the ears of the British aristocracy and gentry who saw, in Karl Marx's insane dogma, the end of civilization. Then there were those who admired Germany's bounce back from defeat in the First World War, making the German economy stronger than that of Britain or France. Still others applauded Hitler's anti-Semitism. For centuries, Jews had been excluded from Britain and when they returned, they lived in ghettoes. Their sudden arrival from Eastern Europe in the 1880s for example, drove the Irish out of East London. The Right Club published books extolling Nazism – and Mussolini's Fascisti – and urged ever-closer cooperation with Germany.

Once the war began, however, things changed. There were still Fascists like Oswald Mosley, but he was interned under the swingeing regulations of 18B. The Mitford family, with Unity as the 'Storm Troop Maiden', were regarded as embarrassing freaks it was best to avoid. In the face of a German invasion, a genuine reality until well into 1942, people of all social classes rallied round Churchill and the flag. Suspicious behaviour was observed and reported. Action was taken. Even John Amery, the son of a cabinet minister, was hanged for making propaganda broadcasts for the enemy – but that was in Germany and Italy, not the industrial Midlands near Hagley Wood.

In the summer of 1940, the Ministry of Information set up the Silent Column, a propaganda outfit designed to scotch rumour and defeatism. Most of the so-called Fifth Columnists were actually stupid and careless people who would no more help the Nazi cause than fly. Mr Knowall, Miss Leaky Mouth, Mr Pride in Prophecy, Miss Teacup Whisperer and Mr Glumpot sound like spoof characters made up by the Puritan John Bunyan in the seventeenth century; in fact, they were the fictional names given to the unthinking by Duff Cooper's Ministry of Information.

Yet the Canadian correspondent to the *Bugle* would have us believe that there was an entire *gau* operating in the Birmingham/Stourbridge area, spearheaded perhaps by Bella's British boyfriend. This brings us back, as always, to Donald McCormick and the testimony of the almost certainly fictional agent Lehrer whom Herr Rathgeb had told McCormick had a lover called Clara who had a lover in Stourbridge.

The Canadian in the letter which Joyce Coley quotes then gets to details:

Who was the Dutch girl known as Clara?
    She was not Dutch, she was German. There were no female Dutch agents dropped in Britain or anywhere else during the war.

Did Clara work for the Abwehr?
    According to Josef Jakobs, yes, she did, but who knows how much we can rely on his testimony? He had after all been caught and was being interrogated by MI6 (never a rosy prospect).

Did Clara drop in on her old friends in 1941?
    We have no way of answering this because we do not know who Clara was supposed by the writer to be. If Clara is Jakobs' girlfriend, then the answer is no. He told MI6 that the parachute drop never happened and we know that she was still working with a number of orchestras in Germany in 1941 and 1942.

Did Clara visit anyone in Stourbridge?
See above.

Who died insane in 1942?
According to Anna of Claverley, this was her husband Jack Mossop and we have seen already how shaky his story was and her re-telling of it.

Was Karl Dickenoff [*sic*] really a Canadian?
This is McCormick's version. Hans Caesar appears to have been German and even McCormick does not suggest any connection between him and Bella.

What did he do while he was living in Edgbaston?
He carried on his trade as a jeweller as he had before the war.

What happened to the dead woman's child and who was the father?
This is impossible to answer. Professor Webster believed that Bella had given birth at least once but clearly could tell no more from her skeleton.

There are those on both sides of the Atlantic and in both hemispheres who you could ask these questions but why?
And we are back in the land of international conspiracies.

There is an eternal justice beyond earthly laws.
Perhaps, but writing garbled rubbish like this is not going to get us any nearer to any kind of justice for Bella.

The silly stories actually began long before Joyce Coley began collecting them. In the Worcester Archive is a letter from Alfred Armistead of Bath, Somerset, dated 26 November 1953 and addressed to the Chief Constable CID, Worcestershire Police. It referred to an article a year earlier in the *Sunday Pictorial* asking the public's help in connection with a variety of unsolved murders and missing persons. The letter writer remembered 'a case of some woman being stuck into a tree' and he had a vivid picture in his mind of a man who had travelled for miles and could get no rest (the last two words were underlined in the original). Armstrong made a sketch of the man he pictured, with one leg raised on a bank or a stone wall and looking at the tree in question. The sketch is still in the Archive and is so vague and badly drawn as to be useless. Armistead had clearly come across the name Anna somewhere and wondered whether she was the sister of the man in the sketch. She 'feels there's an unwritten chapter still to be unfolded'.

There is no reference to any police follow-up to this and I suspect it was stashed into the 'time-wasters' folder at Worcester CID's headquarters.

Another letter was sent to the chief constable, the long-suffering Captain J.E. Lloyd Williams on the same day as the one quoted above, which can only be a coincidence. This one was from a clairvoyant, Mrs Zita Boyden of Compton Road, Wolverhampton. She had visited Quaestor and was absolutely convinced that she had discovered the truth about Bella. She cited Scotland Yard, Carmarthen police, Richmond police and Halifax police in the context of recent murders, such as the Towpath murder and the Harries murder, both of which were headline-grabbing at the time, if only because the government was seriously toying with the abolition of the death penalty (not actually removed until 1965). Alfred Whiteway raped and murdered two teenaged girls, Barbara Songhurst and Christine Reed on the Thames towpath near Richmond. He withdrew a confession to the police and claimed that the axe which was the murder weapon had been planted on him by them. Albert Pierrepoint did not believe that any more than the jury did and he hanged Whiteway at Wandsworth on 22 December. The trial had only ended three weeks before Boyden wrote to the chief constable. Thomas Harries killed his relatives John and Phoebe for money at their farmhouse in Pendine, Carmarthenshire in October 1953. He was charged with the crime only a fortnight before Boyden wrote and did not meet Pierrepoint until 1954.

Did Zita Boyden pester the chief constables of London and Carmarthen in these cases as she did at Worcester? It seems likely, although what convicted both Whiteway and Harries was good old-fashioned police work and hard evidence. It was the era, however, of the psychic detective. Such people offered their advice, which was rarely taken, in the Meon Hill murder of Charles Walton in 1945, but the most celebrated was Dutchman Peter Hurkos who located the symbolic Stone of Scone stolen from Westminster Abbey by Scottish nationalists in 1950 and helped Boston police with their enquiries into Albert de Salvo who strangled a number of the city's elderly female residents in the late 1950s and early 1960s.

Zita Boyden's visionary ability – 'call it what you will'[4] – told her that Lou Bella, as she called her, was 'a country type, slow-spoken, fresh coloured' with brown hair. She worked as a domestic in some sort of Catholic institution. The man who put her body in the tree was 'tall, blond, tanned, fresh skin'. He wore a leather jacket with a sheepskin collar. 'He was, I believe, a Dutch Canadian with a name such as Franz or Franc (short for Francis).' The surname could be Christener or Kristener. Boyden saw him as a motor-cycle '"cop"', dressed in dark uniform and riding a motorbike. Bella's dress denoted 'Institute clothes' and the place she worked had polished oak floors. She probably had a child aged about 12, who looked like her father. The ring she wore was worn on 'the middle finger of her right hand and it may have had a depiction of a saint on it'.

The actual ring had appeared in umpteen newspaper photographs by this time and bore no relation to this. It was assumed to be a wedding ring worn on the *left* hand. 'She had small, fat fingers with pointed ends.' By this time, the fact that the dead woman's right hand was found separated from her body was front-page news and being linked to the 'hand of glory' in the sensational witchcraft connection (see Chapter 14). Bella had 'something wrong with her throat, maybe strangulation'. She was hauled into the tree using a rope 'with a loop so that it could be removed'. No rope had been found in the wych elm but Boyden had to have an escape clause to explain this fact. She believed the name Hipkins might be relevant, but could not be certain. As for the Christian name, a popular song was *Bella Bambina* or it might have been 'a joke that stuck to her that she was a daft loob, Ella'. *Bella Bambina* had been an Al Bowly number some years before but I can find no slang usage of loob meaning stupid anywhere.

Boyden was nearly as interested in Bella's child as she was in the woman herself. It (she does not specify gender) was 'solid, plump, with straight hair … broad, flattish nose, blue eyes'. She assumed that the murder had a domestic motive – a quarrel with a man in her life – 'perhaps the man was already married?' And, as if the police did not have enough to do, Boyden suggested that they should try all the institutions (what we would call care homes) in the Midlands.

Armistead and Boyden pale, however, beside what one journalist at the time called 'the ramblings of Mr Elwell'. John Wilcox of the *Birmingham Gazette* forwarded a tape from George Elwell of Merriden Avenue,

Wolleston which the reporter had made with him on 10 January 1954. Elwell was able to put himself into a trance to solve the case for the police. A railway clerk, Elwell, like many locals, was fascinated by the case and took to wandering Hagley Wood late at night, to pick up what today we would call 'vibes'. After ten minutes near the site of the wych elm, he went home and using a mirror and light bulb to create a 'strobe' effect, hypnotized himself and was able to pick up messages.

He had set an alarm clock to wake himself up and whatever entity he believed he was talking to gave him the name of the dead woman and of the man who killed her:

> Cold ... it is very cold. I hear a horse neighing somewhere ... it is cold, very cold ... rain dropping on the trees, on the leaves ... dark, very dark ... horse neighing again. A tree, yes, a tree ... what has he got on his shoulder? Oh, God! Untying string ... Oh, my God! Blood down her face on to her hair. Oh, she is dead ... she is dead.
>
> Name, name, name. What is her name? Bradman, no, no. Bradley – yes, that's it. Annie Bradley, of Leeds. Yes, the man. Tall ... moustache ... five buttons down his jacket ... narrow trousers ... light blouse ... funny sleeves ... John Connor ... John Connor ... C-O-N-N-O-R. Tying it up. Got to get away.

The recording lasted about fifteen minutes. What are we to make of it? It reads like a bad B movie script; good lighting and tolerable acting *might* make it acceptable to a cinema-going audience. A tree was hardly remarkable – Bella had been found in one. It was safe to assume that the disposal of the body happened at night, which explains the darkness. The implication is that Bella was killed elsewhere and her body brought to the wood in a bag. Blood on her head, which would imply blunt force trauma and probable damage to the skull, is not reported by Professor Webster, who assumed that the cause of death was suffocation. The names Bradman, Bradley and Connor led nowhere; neither did Leeds. According to McCormick, who had not seen this file but quotes Elwell extensively (presumably from the John Wilcox article), the police followed up Elwell's suggestions, but there is nothing in the Worcester Archive to suggest that they did. Another cold trail; another waste of police time.

By 1953, the papers, especially local ones, were full of the Bella story. Quaestor was particularly good at keeping the story alive. In the *Express and Star* 16 January 1958, he not only repeated the Anna of Claverley story but seems to have added his own embellishments. An officer had come to see her late one night 'in fact, on a day which was consistent with the expert assessment of the day of Bella's death – and told her that something terrible had happened to him'. Here, we have a wilful misconstruing of Webster's suggestion – he gave a six-month window for the murder, which contains an awful lot of 'consistent' days. Here, too, we have George Elwell's five-buttoned jacket, the usual pattern of an officer's full-dress khaki at the time. 'He confessed to her under secrecy,' Quaestor went on, 'that he had a friend, a male trapeze artist then appearing at the Coventry Hippodrome and a Dutchman, in a car.' Here was a garbled version of the ice-skaters, not trapeze artists, Frick and Frack.

> The officer was driving it. Between the other two men in the back was Bella. Suddenly, as the car was descending Mucklow Hill, Halesowen, something happened. The girl seemed to have collapsed. The officers stopped the car. The two men then told him to drive on. "She's dead" they told him curtly.
>
> The car was driven through the blacked-out town of Halesowen, then Hasbury. Finally, after several tentative halts, he was told to turn right off the main Bromsgrove road. He found himself in Hagley Wood. Here the body of the girl now known as Bella, was carried out and the officer was called on to help stuff it into the hollow trunk of the Wych Elm.

Quaestor claimed to have been present at the mysterious rendezvous with DI Williams and Anna, yet this is so far removed from the statement she made to that same police officer as to defy belief. The anonymous 'officer' was her own husband, Jack Mossop. There was only one man in the back seat, not two and nobody there was a trapeze artist. Bella was in the front passenger seat, not the back and she did not die; she passed out. If Anna was lying to DI Williams when she made her statement, why, how and when did she give Quaestor the 'real' version?

But by now the journalist was in full flight. The terrified officer returned to Hagley Wood the next night and told Anna 'There's no mistake. The body is there all right, just as we left it.' And it was Anna who told her husband this story 'long ago'.

Concerned that such a murder remained motiveless, Quaestor then came up, via Anna of course, with the idea that the Dutchman in the car was a German spy, often dripping with cash, who asked questions about aircraft factories in the area. Bella 'or "Lubella" had entered the country illegally "after Dunkirk"' and was a spy who had fallen foul of her fellow agents and was killed by them. The officer was so unnerved that he had a nervous breakdown and was 'taken to a mental home' where he died.

All of this brings us back to the vicious circle concocted by Donald McCormick; it has virtually no bearing on Una Mossop/Hainsworth's statement to the police. In true journalistic style, Quaestor concludes that MI5 were brought into the case and the trapeze artist was probably never discovered. Because, of course, he did not exist.

Quaestor saves his best piece of nonsense for the end of his article, supposedly quoting 'the pathologist' (presumably Webster) on ITV as saying 'But after extensive inquiries by the superintendent [Williams] he was able to identify [Bella]. It was a classic piece of detection.'

And the Quaestor article is a classic piece of misinformation. There are a number of items in the police Archive which seem out of place, but they clearly all had relevance at the time of the investigation and had to be followed up. There is a black and white snapshot of a woman who may be Ethel Prosser, standing with two men. She is wearing a bright summer frock and is squinting into the sun. she is clearly not Bella – her teeth are too regular and she is too tall. The Archive contents give us her name, but no other information and her significance is now lost.

Then there is the letter from Lieutenant Colonel O. Gibson of GHQ (India), New Delhi, dated 24 January 1943. This was written to a Leonard Hughes, c/o Stewarts and Lloyds Coombs Wood Tube Works of Halesowen. This is simply a 'hello' letter, reminiscing on rabbit-hunting in Britain and lamenting the fact that Gibson does not have time to take pot shots (actually, with a tommy-gun!) at the Indian wildlife. There is no reference to Bella or Hagley Wood, largely because it was written four months before the body was found!

This India connection *may* have links with another photograph in the Archive, that of Billy Gibson. Despite the spelling of the Christian name, Billy was a woman. The photograph shows an attractive girl, with blonde hair and shorts, standing between two men. A separate sheet tells us that she was the wife of Gerald Gibson and they lived at the Manor House, Hagley. However, since the couple moved to India in 1938, neither the photograph nor the letter can have any relevance to the Hagley Wood murder at all.

Among several letters offering solutions to the Hagley Wood murder in the *Express and Star*, some point to gypsies, others claim that local foxhounds would have smelt the decomposing body long before it was found. Then there was this one of 23 November 1953:

> Is it not possible that the adherents of the cult of witchcraft, who, it would appear, were responsible for the death of Bella, adopt some form of commemoration of the date of her death which would be of significance to members of the group, but to no one else? By coincidence, there appeared in the *Express and Star* on the day [Quaestor's] second article was published, an "In Memoriam" notice referring to a woman named Bella. Obviously, this notice did not refer to the woman in the wych elm, but might not a study of "In Memoriam" notices possibly provide a slender clue?

And was there anybody out there who could carry out such a study into cults and the occult? In fact, there was. Her name was Dr Margaret Murray.

Chapter 14

Lord of the Gallows

Something very odd happened soon after the end of the Second World War. Today we have seen another outbreak of it in response to the Covid pandemic. In the recent case, the mass stupidity of whole nations has been manifest by a panic, a blind belief in 'the science', all of it fanned by the hysteria of social media. The result has been serious damage to economies, children's education and increasing mental health problems. It has brought the oddballs out from under their rocks, giving ammunition to Quanon, for example, a group that believes that the pandemic was yet another example of the American government's cabal of cannibalistic child-killers intent on ruling the world. Anti-vaxxers appeared from nowhere, stepping back into a Medieval hell where there was no science that actually worked. A definitive book on all this has yet to appear, but the responses are not unique. Wherever there is upheaval to the normal, the routine, elements of society go haywire and this is certainly true of the immediate post-war period.

On 24 June 1947, experienced pilot Kenneth Arnold was flying over the Cascade Mountains in Washington State. He was looking for the wreckage of a plane that had crashed there earlier, when he saw nine objects flying in formation. He estimated their air speed at over 1,000 miles an hour, faster than any known aircraft at the time. 'They flew like a saucer would if you skipped it across the water,' he told reporters, and the concept of the flying saucer was born. Governments across the world have invested millions into projects to prove or disprove the existence of alien life on other planets and in other galaxies. In 1952, even a realist like Winston Churchill could write to the Air Ministry, 'What does all this stuff about flying saucers amount to? What can it mean? What is the truth?'

We have all been lulled into a broad acceptance that there must be something else 'out there', not just mankind on planet earth – the whole existence of a 'science fiction' genre in literature and the media is proof of that. But the same question, slightly adapted, can be raised in connection with the body in Hagley Wood – what is the truth?

It was not flying saucers that provided a potential answer, but an older, more fundamental bogeyman – witchcraft. It is difficult to find the beginnings of this in connection with the murder of Bella, but certainly even by the end of the 1940s, sporadic letters to local newspapers hinted that witchcraft may be involved. According to Quaestor, Anna of Claverley's letter to him said, 'The affair is now closed and involves no witches, black magic or moon night rites.' But who had said it did? In the public mind, witches lived in woods. They cavorted under the moon in woodland clearings at their sabbats, having sex with the Devil. The very name – *Hag*ley – had a sinister sound and although the Saxon word wych had nothing to do with a devil's disciple (as we have seen, it meant pliant or bendable), it sounded as if it did. From such ignorant and simplistic beginnings, a whole industry can spring up – witness Kenneth Arnold's flying saucers.

The only 'evidence' that witchcraft was involved came from Bella's hand, which was found by police thirteen paces from the wych elm. According to Professor Webster, these were a disarticulated jumble of bones, just like others found in the bole of the tree itself, but to the journalists of the sensation-seeking Fifties, it became a whole hand. Indeed, one of them refers to it as an entire arm. This became equated with the *main de gloire*, the French term for the hand of glory, from which the magic (and poisonous) plant Mandragora (mandrake) may take its name. In certain witchcraft traditions, the severed hand of a corpse had supernatural powers, especially if it was removed from a victim dangling on the gallows; the phrase 'Lord of the Gallows' was synonymous, some said, with the Devil. It had to be preserved carefully, using certain herbs and could then be used to open locks, discover buried treasure and render enemies powerless. If the fingers were set alight, anyone in the vicinity would fall into a trance-like sleep. So far, so much nonsense. In one of the worst examples of anti-witch hysteria, in 1591, a number of women were put on trial for the attempted murder (by spells) of James VI of Scotland, who believed in witches to the point of obsession. During the trial, one of the accused, John Fane, admitted to breaking into a church at night by using a hand of glory to force the locks. This ignores the fact that churches were supposed to be open night and day for the Godly to pray and the fact that Fane, along with his fellow accusees, had been tortured for days before they made their confessions, which was often the case in trials during the 'witch-craze' of the time.

The disarticulated hand found in the leaf mould of Hagley Wood belonged to Bella. She was not a felon hanged on the gallows and the hand had almost certainly been bitten off by an animal, probably a badger, before the body was dumped into the wych elm. Badgers are omnivorous and have powerful jaws. The only other woodland predator, a fox, would have been agile enough to climb the elm if it had to, but its jaws would not be strong enough to dissect a human arm in this way. In another example of a woman's body found hidden in the wild, Joan Wolfe in Houndown Wood, her fingers had been gnawed away by rats. It is a common situation.

But the lunatic lobby would not accept the natural. Bella's fate had to involve the supernatural. Why? To begin with, witchcraft was still a crime in Britain during the war, one of the many examples of obsolete legislation then still on the statute books. And there was still, for all the advent of science, technology and cold reason, a fascination with the macabre that was centuries old and still grips us today. Recent research, carried out by psychologists at the University of Hertfordshire, suggests that a third of us have brains that are hard-wired to accept the supernatural as natural; to them, ghosts, for example, are real. The case of Helen Duncan is one in point. The woman already had two convictions against her for obtaining money for fortune-telling and in 1944 she was charged with fraud. The case was actually tricky legally because Helen asked for payment for claiming to be able to contact the dead, as spiritualists have done for decades. In the end, how could this work if her client believed in her powers? The solution, unsatisfactory as it was, was to charge her and two others under the Witchcraft Act of 1735. This was not repealed until 1951. The queues at the Old Bailey stretched around the block and Hannen Swaffer, one of the most revered journalists of the day, spoke in her defence. She was found guilty, however, and gaoled for nine months. Nor was she alone. In July 1944, as the Allies were fighting their way towards the Rhine, 72-year-old Jane Yorke of Forest Gate, London was tried at the Old Bailey on four charges of 'pretending to exercise or use a kind of conjuration contrary to the Witchcraft Act'. As was more usual in such cases, Yorke was fined without gaol time.

But Helen Duncan and Jane Yorke were only the tip of the 'diabolical' iceberg. The war poet Rupert Brooke was only one of the Edwardian literati who referred to themselves as neo-Pagans. Jehovah's Witnesses, fortune-tellers, clairvoyants and spiritualists all came to the fore during the Second World War, sometimes because they 'doorstepped' people, or because what they did was to profit by the war; spiritualists like Helen Duncan were preying on a country gripped by grief and fear. As one magistrate put it – 'to pretend to conjure up [the spirits of the dead] when it is false and a hollow lie is nothing less than a public mischief'. There was nothing like the round-up engendered in Germany by the *Aktion Hess* simply because no one in the corridors of British power was obsessed by the occult. As a young man before the First World War, Winston Churchill apparently visited fortune-tellers, but he had long outgrown all that by 1940.

In the public mind, there was a blurred distinction, if there was one at all, between the worlds of spiritualism and witchcraft. Between the wars, characters like Montague Summers were writing a plethora of books on witches, vampires, Satanism and black magic. Summers was a Catholic priest with an unlikely list of Christian names – Alfonsus Joseph-Mary Augustus Montague – and he earned his living as a theatre critic, especially knowledgeable on Restoration drama. He revelled in the gory and his works on witchcraft in 1926 and 1927, were not well researched, but read brilliantly and he captured the dark world of Bohemian London where hundreds of bored socialites flocked to buy his books. The bibliography for his *History of Witchcraft and Demonology* runs to thirty pages and looks very scholarly. He neglects to tell us, however, that most of his sources were unprovable nonsense. 'There were some unbridled imaginations,' Summers wrote about these sources, 'there was deception; there was legerdemain [sleight of hand]; there was phantasy; there was fraud.' But his readership either ignored this line or could not distinguish which was which.

In fact, Summers was backed up from an unlikely source: the hard-bitten detective Robert Fabian. He has a chapter in his *London After Dark* (1954) called 'And so to the Devil ...'. It is unfortunate that he believed that witches used to be burned on Tower Hill. Burning as a punishment for witchcraft was confined to Scotland and Europe; in England, witches were hanged, but Fabian was in no doubt that in London at any rate, diabolical rites were being practised as never before. He knew of pagan temples in South Kensington, Paddington and Bloomsbury where naked ceremonies were held on a regular basis. What worried Fabian was the use of narcotics at these ceremonies, especially the influence of the newly arrived West Indian communities with their drums and voodoo.

'The door to black magic,' Fabian wrote, 'is through the back offices of two or three dusty little London bookshops that specialise in volumes on the occult, diabolism, alchemy.' There was a house in Lancaster Gate that the Met knew well, because beyond the dingy little flats at the front was a temple to Satan, complete with high altar, black candles and magical symbols painted on the walls and ceiling. Pan, Abramelin, Saint Sécaire – these were the deities worshipped during the ceremonies which involved sex (often with minors) and flagellation. All this sounds like a film set from the Hammer studios, the physical reality of one of Dennis Wheatley's novels, but it was real and it was happening in London in the middle of the twentieth century.

Enter Dr Margaret Murray. More than anyone else, this brilliant but eccentric academic gave credence to links between the occult and Bella. An anthropologist and archaeologist, Margaret had had a long and colourful career by the time the body was found in the wych elm and she was by then 80 years old. She had worked under the archaeologist William Flinders Petrie on digs in Syria and the Valley of the Kings in Egypt years before Howard Carter put Egyptology centre stage by finding the fabulous tomb of Tutankhamun in 1922. She lectured at University College London and was a tireless defender of women's rights, immersed as she was in what was almost entirely a man's world. A Suffragette, she had volunteered as a nurse in the First World War and suffered a minor breakdown as a result.

In the world of academe, however, she was never fully accepted. The degrees she had were acquired later, almost in a pseudo-honorary capacity, and her views were always outside the conventional. As well as works on ancient Egyptian linguistics, which had little interest for the general public, she wrote a definitive book on witchcraft, *The Witch Cult in Western Europe* (1921), at the same time that Montague Summers was putting pen to paper and writing articles for *The Bystander* on black magic in fashionable London. *The God of the Witches* followed ten years later and the quite bizarre *The Divine King in England* in 1954 when interest in Bella was being revived. In contrast with Summers' slavering accounts of sabbats and orgies, Murray concentrated on the sociological and anthropological origins of the witch cult. She claimed, in a theory still held to be likely, that witchcraft was simply the Old Religion before the arrival of Christianity. The gods of prehistory, she argued, were linked to fertility and survival – the weather, the harvest, even the phases of the moon. Central to survival and fertility was the male animal – the horned god (which ran a little counter to her espousal of the feminist cause). Paintings in the Lascaux caves in France show such animals, with stags' horns, standing upright on their hind legs. In the Roman period, such a figure is often called Cernunnos, depicted in mosaics and murals all over Europe. In time, he would metamorphose into the legendary Herne the Hunter, riding with his spectral hounds in Windsor Great Park. He was last reported as a 'genuine' sighting in 1962.

Because Christianity wanted to oust the Old Religion, the horned god became the Devil, complete with cloven hoofs and tail, the epitome of evil. And witchcraft, originally a mix of folklore, superstition and early attempts at medicine, became inextricably linked with the occult. Later writers had to differentiate between black magic (evil, once referred to as *malifici*) and white magic (good). They even invented the middle ground of grey magic, obviously a mixture of the two.

In English social history, the white witch or 'cunning woman' was a real character, not a Disney nightmare to scare small children watching *Snow White* in a spookily darkened cinema. Such people were midwives and nurses in their local village communities (perhaps, even, a village like Hagley) and they invariably helped to lay out the dead for burial. There were still white witches dotted around the country in the 1930s because real medicine was expensive before the creation of the National Health Service. Older inhabitants of Bubbenhall in Warwickshire, for example, remember 'Friday' Watts (actually a man) who acted in this capacity between the wars.

Margaret Murray's *The Divine King* went further, claiming that all the kings of England who died bloody deaths, from William Rufus in the New Forest in 1100 to Richard III at Bosworth in 1485, were all acts of ritual sacrifice in which the king in question was murdered to appease the vengeful gods of the Old Religion.

It was the murder of the labourer Charles Walton in February 1945 that intrigued Dr Murray. She gave her opinion that this was 'probably' to do with witchcraft and that of Bella 'possibly' so. The Walton murder, in the Warwickshire village of Lower Quinton, has been linked with Bella and Hagley Wood ever since and it has effectively stifled any serious investigation of either crime. The pernicious effects of Walton's death will be dealt with in another chapter, but to understand the way in which Margaret Murray's views were distorted, we have to discuss the involvement of another man with a chapter to himself, Donald McCormick.

'[Dr Murray] was no crank,' McCormick wrote, 'no credulous romanticist, but a sober, even sceptical analyst of the occult.' As he says, she went on to write much more after the Hagley Wood case (which she typed herself) including her autobiography in 1963, *My First Hundred Years*. Despite handling a number of ancient bodies, she had never had the sense of being haunted by any of them. She relates the story of a fellow-archaeologist, Arthur Mace, who woke up in his tent in Egypt one morning with a mummy's hand around his throat. His terrified screams brought the rest of the team running, only to discover that a recently exposed mummy had been left on a shelf over Mace's bed and had crumbled in the night, the entire arm landing on his chest with the fingers under his chin. The younger members of the team, not to mention the general public, had been brought up with Boris Karloff's *The Mummy* (1931) and various spinoffs. They almost expected something of the kind to happen.

Margaret Murray dismissed the story of the curse on the tomb of Tutankhamen (although she does not specify the pharaoh) as mass hysteria, which is precisely what it was. What McCormick does not tell us about the Egyptologist is that she had a wicked sense of humour, implying that a particular 'haunted' mummy caused both the sinking of the *Titanic* and the *Empress of Ireland* and, when sold to the Kaiser, caused the First World War! Was she, a little cynically perhaps, mocking the hysteria surrounding Bella's corpse?

In discussing ghosts, Dr Murray makes an observation which fits the Hagley case perfectly. 'It has long been the fashion to deride what you cannot understand, or to misinterpret the evidence, or even to believe evidence which is clearly false.'

According to McCormick, Dr Murray believed that witches still existed in England in the 1940s and 1950s. 'I wouldn't say that some of my best friends are witches, but, on the other hand, some of my casual acquaintances are.'[1] In November 1951, she wrote an article on witchcraft for the *Sunday Dispatch*. 'That [by having others believe in them] is how witches are made and maybe always have been made, though with the growth of motor travel and the steady penetration of remote rural areas by the outside world, there are fewer with each decade.'

McCormick claims that Dr Murray visited Hagley (when is not recorded) and got a hostile reaction from locals concerning witchcraft links with Bella. One newspaper had suggested that Hagley was 'a village of devil worshippers' even though Margaret had made no such claim. McCormick claimed that the occultist had compiled a detailed account of both the Hagley Wood and Meon Hill murders, but if she did, they have not survived. She died in 1963, so any comments on Hagley Wood come through the prism of McCormick; not, as we have seen, the most impeccable source.

She dispelled the notion that the public was fascinated by the case of Bella because of newspaper misprints referring to the 'witch elm' by mistake. 'In all those chalk writings,' she told McCormick, 'the word was "wych elm" spelt perfectly correctly.' This, of course, is not true. The writer who jokingly referred to the killer as Jack the Ripper spelt it 'witch elm'. J.H. Jones wrote 'Wyce' before he corrected it and Raymond Boffey managed 'Wic Hlm' before DI Williams told him how to spell it. These are the only three examples of handwriting in the police files (which of course, Margaret Murray had not seen). All the others are typewritten and who knows how many unconscious spelling changes happened during that process.

Margaret Murray wrote to Professor Webster 'but he offered no encouragement in my theory'. What was the theory? The Egyptologist contended that placing a body in the hollow of a tree was associated with witchcraft. The cult of tree worship was ancient and linked with sacrifices. We have discussed this already, in Chapter 1. Dr Murray believed that witchcraft, however much it had become watered down and bastardized by the twentieth century, was a legacy of the Old Religion before Christianity. In other words, it was the polytheistic faith of the Celts. But, as we know, the Celts worshipped the oak and the mistletoe, not the elm. The Celtic priests, the Druids, held their ceremonies in sacred groves, not near single trees, and there is no record of bodies being sacrificed in this way. Afficionados of cult cinema will be familiar with Robin Hardy's *The Wicker Man* (1973) in which a human virgin (the unlikely Edward Woodward) is burnt alive inside a huge wicker cage to appease the gods of the harvest. Julius Caesar, the geographer Strabo and a handful of others refer to this horrific custom, but no one seems to have witnessed it. And the whole point about such sacrifices, be they human or animal, is that the victim is still alive when caged, not dead. 'The wych elm,' says Murray/McCormick, 'is also significant in terms of witchcraft lore.' No, it is not. Then, interestingly, 'Whoever committed this murder must have known about the hollow in the tree.' Perhaps ... or was it Bella herself who knew about it?

Having dismissed the graffiti as so many hoaxes, Dr Murray asserts that Bella and Luebella are witches' names. She had compiled lists of attendees of covens and sabbats over several centuries and had come to the conclusion that the eight most common (with variants) were: Ann, Alice, Christian, Elizabeth, Ellen, Joan, Margaret, Marion. If we add in the variants, we have twenty-two more. They are simply common female names, many of them belonging to saints. Where do Bella and Luebella come from? Variants of Elizabeth, along with Eliza, Isobel, Isabella and Betty. In her book *The Witch Cult in Western Europe* written in 1921, Dr Murray cites the names of 646 witches from the trials of the sixteenth and seventeenth centuries. There are seventy-eight Elizabeths with a number of variants and forty Isobels with a number of variants. Neither Bella nor Luebella occurs at all. This is a classic example of misinterpreting the evidence which Dr Murray warns us against in connection with ghosts.

Warming to her theme, the Egyptologist tells us that Halesowen is particularly associated with witchcraft:

On the golf course at Mucklow Hill ... there is supposed to be a particular patch of ground that has the reputation of being haunted. Many people over the years have reported having had a feeling of something peculiar happening to them when they walk over it, a feeling that someone or something else is present invisibly.

Quaestor reports that, according to Anna of Claverley, the officer, the Dutch spy and the trapeze artist drove Bella down Mucklow Hill on the way to her death or burial in Hagley Wood. That said, the notion of a haunted golf course is completely at odds with Dr Murray's contempt for the existence of ghosts in her autobiography.

Margaret Murray was not an expert in murder and I believe her interpretation of Bella's last resting place is wrong. She was clearly of the opinion that witchcraft was alive and well in the England of 1950 as, presumably, it had been for generations. That, in itself, is a highly debatable contention, as were many of the theories in the various books that she had written.

In terms of folklore, Worcestershire seems surprisingly devoid of supernatural memories. The standing stones on the Hagley estate are not some forgotten henge, but a folly erected in the 1750s at a time when the Druids and Celts were experiencing a revival. If haunted Mucklow is widely believed locally, it has not reached the level of compendium books on the subject. Bromsgrove has the tale of Sir Ryalas who killed a huge, vicious boar nearby and he was, it is true, prompted to do so by a woman in a tree (very much alive) who turned out to be a witch. And sacrifice of a sort was once carried out in the county's hopfields when a couple were 'buried' annually under hops in a crib before being ritually resurrected, symbolizing the cycle of growth. At Kidderminster, a white witch called Becky Swan was visited by a black cat at some vague point in the mid-nineteenth century. After three days, she was found burned to death in her house, the cat vanishing up the chimney as neighbours arrived.

It is difficult to find in any of this any serious folklore which might have its echoes in Hagley Wood in the 1940s.

The heyday of the witch fever was the late sixteenth and early seventeenth centuries. The Reformation which began with Martin Luther in 1517 had unleashed the monster of Puritanism, creating two armed camps, Catholic and Protestant, who literally fought each other all over Europe until at least 1648. With a loss of faith and competing bias from both sides spewing forth ever-increasing bile from the pulpits, congregations became lost, confused and frightened. God was no longer in His Heaven. Frantically trying to defend itself, the Catholic church created the Inquisition and the fanatical torturers of the Jesuits, accusing innocent people of worshipping the Devil rather than God, evil rather than good. The various Protestant churches did the same.

In England, legislation began in earnest in the early reign of Elizabeth and the rest of the sixteenth century was littered with printed pamphlets, most of which carried the title 'A true record of …' whereas in fact almost all of it was nonsense. The law against witchcraft became ever harsher. In 1604, using witchcraft to search for treasure or lost property was punishable by death. So was injuring a person by the same means. Taking bodies out of graves and conjuring evil spirits led to the gallows too, as did 'provoking a woman to unlawful love' by means of potions. All this was sanctioned by a Puritan parliament obsessed with the evils of 'popery' and presided over by a religious bigot (James I) who *knew* that witches existed and were trying to kill him. The line from the new translation of the Bible which James commissioned in 1611 that probably pleased him most was 'Thou shalt not suffer a witch to live' (Exodus 22:18).

Years before this, two sexually repressed monks, Jacob Sprenger and Heinrich Kramer, had written *Malleus Maleficarum* (the Hammer of the Witches) for Pope Innocent VIII. It contained all kinds of lurid and juicy stories about *incubi* and *succubae* and is one of the most misogynistic works ever written. As woman had brought about man's fall through the weakness of Eve in the Garden of Eden, so women were most likely, in the fifteenth–seventeenth centuries, to worship the Devil and practise blood sacrifice.

Because the accusations of witchcraft could be made so easily and because they were so difficult to deny, we are left with the sense that nobody survived. It has echoes in the 'witch-craze' of the McCarthy era in post-war America and today's cancel culture. Pointing a finger is easy and infectious. In fact, if we examine the legal cases of Essex, the most witch-haunted county of all in the sixteenth and seventeenth centuries, of the 291 people accused of witchcraft, 151 were found not guilty. Of those found guilty, 55 were imprisoned and 74 were executed.

Wood of various trees was indeed used in witch rituals, as often for good by white witches as evil by their black sisters. This is the element of witchcraft which is linked with holistic and herbal medicine and lies vaguely on the fringes of science and genuine medicine.

Certainly, the witches of the sixteenth and seventeenth centuries were accused of murdering people with magic, but the notion of using them as part of a sacrifice in the sense that Margaret Murray used it is almost entirely missing. There are a number of ancient texts that refer to animal sacrifice, which we know was practised regularly by most ancient civilizations. The Roman poet Seneca wrote, 'He pours a libation of blood on the altars and burns the sacrifices entire and soaks the trench in pools of blood.' Human sacrifices were associated with the Sabbat, the Black Mass which was an inverted parody of the Christian service. People, naked in woodlands away from the prying eyes of local villagers, danced 'widdershins' (in an anti-clockwise circle) or back to back. They kissed the Devil's arse rather than the face of Christ, smeared their limbs with the hallucinogen hemlock and took part in wild orgies – Dennis Wheatley would have fitted right in! In virtually all cases, however, the sacrifice was a child, not an adult like Bella. In eighteenth-century France, a report on one such gathering read 'Astaroth, Asmodeus [demons] I beg you to accept the sacrifice of this child which we now offer to you, so that we may receive the things we ask.'

In another account by Frenchman Nicholas Rémy from the 1590s, the witches brought their own children to be sacrificed, as though it were the most natural thing in the world.

Harry Wedeck, in *A Treasury of Witchcraft* (1961) wrote:

> The Black Mass has not entirely disappeared. To this very day it is reputed to be administered among Satanic circles, in the highly cosmopolitan locales of two continents: in New York and London, in Paris and in lesser provincial cities. In the metropolitan areas the cult has its own adherents, its own carefully guarded chambers, its own secret communications. At such rituals the atmospheric aura of purposeful maleficence is heightened, among the celebrants, by the subtle use of black: black wine and black candles, while the sense of impalpable yet potent evil is intensified by the clamorous demoniac falsifications, by the acknowledgment of alien allegiance, Satanic loyalties.

As we have seen, Montague Summers and Robert Fabian claimed that such cults did exist in London in the 1920s, 1930s and 1940s. Be that as it may, by the time Margaret Murray was giving her views to various newspapers and to Donald McCormick, a seismic change was happening in British witchcraft; it was turning into Wicca, which had a 'feel-good' factor wholly missing from the horror stories of earlier centuries.

The 'high-point' of this movement was a retired customs officer, Gerald Brosseau Gardner, who had been a devotee of Aleister Crowley and was very impressed by the scholarship of Margaret Murray. Gardner was into flagellation and regarded sex as a central part of ritual (as did Crowley). His book *Witchcraft Today* and *The Meaning of Witchcraft*, although probably only intended for his own disciples, became the benchmark of the occult that continued in the post-war world. Interestingly, Gardner's rituals became watered down in later covens and that element of Wicca, as opposed to holistic medicine, was the work of Mancunian Alex Sanders who came to dominate the London occult scene in 1967.

Gardner waited until the laws against witchcraft were fully repealed in 1951 before he set up his covens, but there is considerable evidence that he was involved in witchcraft as early as 1940. In that context, he had indirect links with whatever happened in Hagley Wood the following year. Was there a coven operating in the area in wartime? We have no idea, but, contrary to Margaret Murray's belief that covens were a survival of a wide-spaced movement found among ordinary people in rural village communities, twentieth-century witchcraft, if it exists at all in the conventional sense, is an urban, middle-class sophisticated movement. Birmingham would have been the most likely centre for anything of this sort in the 1940s, the strictures of wartime notwithstanding.

Undeterred by the realities of history and the existence of an Enlightenment and scientific revolution that has destroyed the notion of 'things that go bump in the night', McCormick takes one of his famous leaps of logic. He is certain that the screams heard in Hagley Wood in 'late July or early August' were the last sound that Bella made and that this would coincide with the 'witches' festival of Lughnasadh in the Celtic calendar'. This of course is from the ear-witness accounts of two unnamed men whose evidence is not in the record.

Lughnasadh had nothing to do with witchcraft. It was one of four festivals that heralded the change of seasons, but McCormick was influenced by the fact that neo-Pagan groups, by the 1960s, had taken it over as an unofficial holiday. Lughnasadh was linked to the harvest, with its concept of growth and fertility.

The feast of Lughnasadh (stolen by the Christians as Lammastide) falls on 1 August, which misses the screams heard in Hagley Wood by two weeks. The phases of the ceremony are well attested from Welsh and Irish records and folklore. It was all about happiness, dancing and music, with (as usual) a little bit of copulation. The only thing that was buried (in the ground, not in a tree) was flowers, representing the end of summer.

The links between the murder in Hagley Wood and witchcraft are non-existent. Yet, today, if you check the plethora of websites on the subject, virtually all of them focus on this aspect. Why? Because witchcraft, with its nonsense of worship of the Dark Lord, the Lord of the Gallows, with a liberal sprinkling of nudity and sex, has a universal appeal that will not allow little things like facts get in the way.

Chapter 15

The Shadow of Meon Hill

'The modern world,' wrote the editor of Marshall Cavendish's *Murder Casebook* in 1991, 'baulks at the idea of the supernatural, of unseen forces playing havoc with our lives but ... people can still fall under the spell of the occult.'[1]

On the evening of 14 February 1945, the body of Charles Walton, a 74-year-old labourer, was found near a hedge in fields near Lower Quinton, Warwickshire, below the high ground called Meon Hill.

In international affairs, the war ground on. From the east, Stalin's Red Army pushed through Pomerania, forcing the Wehrmacht back on itself, trying to hold the most vital areas. In the west, British and Canadian troops reached Emmerich on the Rhine while the Americans to the south were re-grouping for a new push. The Indian Divisions from IV Corps crossed the Irrawaddy river as the Japanese fell back to protect Mandalay. It would be days before any of this news would reach Lower Quinton, once it had been assessed by the censors and the continued shortage of newsprint meant that only the basics got to the public.

Charles Walton was not a popular man. Cantankerous and bigoted, he had largely kept to himself, living in Lower Quinton with his niece, Edith, in what, after gentrification, would be an idyllic thatched cottage. The winter had been grim, with deep snow and biting winds, but St Valentine's Day that year was crisp and sunny and Walton had been out in the fields all day with his pitchfork and his long-handled slash-hook. Both of these weapons had been used to kill him, the pitchfork pinning him to the ground and the slash-hook still lying in the wound to his throat. His killer had carved the rough shape of a cross in his chest.

Except that he had not. Read any account of the Meon Hill murder today and the pitchfork and the cross are essential to the story, and from them, stories of witchcraft grew. Walton was certainly mutilated, but there was no cross on his chest, merely a series of cuts.

We have already quoted Graham Greene in *The Ministry of Fear* about single murders disappearing in the greater slaughter of war, but in fact the Meon Hill case was a sort of escapism. The generation who lived through the war, adults and children, became immured not only to the privations of rationing and the horrors of the Blitz, they accepted death in a more immediate and personal way than their fathers who had fought the First World War. With the exception of a handful of bombing raids, mostly on the coast, 1914–18 had been a war confined to France and Gallipoli. Returning soldiers were horribly wounded, damaged irreparably by gas and traumatized by shell-shock, but that was as bad as it got. The Second World War, however, had made Britain the Home Front – instant, impersonal death rained from the skies.

If the Blitz proper was over, there was now a new terror – the 'doodlebugs'. The first V1 flying bombs were fired from the German-occupied Channel Islands on 13 June 1944. Only one reached London, killing six people, but it was the fact that the V1s had no pilots that made them so sinister. They made a whining sound, but when that stopped, suddenly, they fell, exploding as they hit the ground. V2s, widely used by the time Charles Walton died, were even more deadly.

Against that, a grisly 'home-grown' murder using weapons prosaically used as tools by the average country labourer, was a distraction and it fed the deep-rooted fascination that most of us have for murder. While the Warwickshire police began their enquiries, Professor James Webster, still no further forward in the Hagley Wood case, was called in to conduct a post-mortem on Walton.

Unlike Bella's case, where the Worcestershire CID decided to go it alone, the Warwickshire force called in the Yard. This was standard procedure; the Met had wide experience of murders of all kinds, with more examples than any other city. Their fingerprint section was the most comprehensive in the world. And they sent a detective who was already a legend to the criminal fraternity – Chief Inspector Robert Fabian. His later books – *Fabian of the Yard* and *London After Dark* – were a goldmine of police procedure and thinking and he became the first real television detective, with a series of half-hour programmes, in grainy black and white, in which he prefigured virtually every British cop-show that followed. Everything from *Dixon of Dock Green* to *Midsomer Murders* owes a great deal to Bob Fabian.

But in the end, not even Scotland Yard could solve the Meon Hill murder and the killing of Charles Walton remains unsolved. The same romantic prurience which has become attached to Bella has smothered Meon Hill too. Charles Walton was a witch; he spoke to toads, the Devil's familiars. Lower Quinton was in the heart of haunted Warwickshire. The hill called Alcock's Arbour near Temple Grafton was called the Devil's Bag of Nuts. The battlefield of Edge Hill, where the forces of parliament and king clashed in the first engagement of the Civil War (1642) still echoed to the tramp of marching feet. Guy's Cliffe near Warwick was the home of the celebrated knight who had killed the monstrous Dun Cow that had ravaged the neighbourhood for years. Above all, there were the Rollright Stones, an ancient stone circle believed to be a king and his knights who were calcified by a witch's spell. Then, there was the old saying, 'There are enough witches in Long Compton to draw a load of hay up Long Compton Hill.' This reflected a nineteenth-century murder in which a man had killed a woman because she had bewitched him.

'A man'. 'A woman'. Folklore is full of such vagueness. It is permissible in light-hearted guidebooks for tourists, but it is of no use at all in trying to solve real-life murder cases.

The *Murder Casebook* volume quoted above contains three murders – Charles Walton's in Lower Quinton, Bella's in Hagley Wood and the French case of Denise Labbé, one half of the 'demon lovers' convicted of the sacrificial murder of Denise's daughter Cathy, aged 2 in 1954. The volume, typical of the series, throws all sorts of irrelevance into the mix: Saxon witchcraft; the madman artist Richard Dadd who axed his father to death in 1843; witches' sabbats; Margaret Murray; 'the master satanist' Aleister Crowley; psychic detectives; and the Jonestown massacre, a mass suicide of a cult in 1978.

Such salaciousness sells. And that is precisely the problem; it does not solve crimes. Why is the Meon Hill murder so often lumped together with that in Hagley Wood? Both happened during the war, only thirty-five miles apart. Both remain unsolved. Both have undercurrents of witchcraft and the supernatural. But there the similarities end. Charles Walton was male, elderly and well known in his local community. Bella was female, young and seemingly not known to anybody. Walton's body was left in the open, easily found; someone had gone to extraordinary lengths to hide Bella. The murder methods were totally different – bladed weapons in the case of Walton; probably suffocation for Bella. The sole reason for the cases being lumped together can be attributed to one man – Donald McCormick.

'Charles Walton has been pinned to the ground by his own hay-fork. Across his throat a rough but unmistakeable sign of the Cross had been savagely slashed. "Witchcraft" whispered the villagers.'[2]

Gripping stuff. Except that it is not true. And of course, 'Dusk was creeping slowly and mistily across the Warwickshire fields' when the old man's body was found. But it was not. Those who found his body were working by torchlight; it was pitch black.

By page 17 of *Murder by Witchcraft*, we already have the sinister Rollrights:

Rise up stick and stand still stone,
King of England thou shalt be none!
Thou and they men hoar stones shall be,
And I myself an eldern tree.

McCormick does not give the source of this creepy rhyme. Neither does he mention Bella in the context of the elder tree, but is it not there, lurking in the dark, playing with our minds? And the author rather disingenuously quotes the 'father' of modern Wicca, Gerald Gardner. 'I think we must say goodbye to the witch. The cult is doomed, I am afraid, partly because of modern conditions, housing shortage, the smallness of modern families and chiefly by education. The modern child is not interested. He knows witches are all bunk.' McCormick utterly rejects witchcraft as a motive in the case of Bella in favour of espionage (his real passion) but by quoting Gardner, he is actually keeping the nonsense alive.

I mention earlier the cartoon witch of *Snow White* which terrified children in the 1930s. Unaccountably, the hand-held camerawork in *The Blair Witch Project* (1991) had the same effect, but this time it terrified adults too. Film-makers know – and Donald McCormick knew – that audiences and readers *love* to be frightened. And what better way to frighten them than by lumping together two totally unconnected murders in a single volume?

Bella does not kick in in *Murder By Witchcraft* until Chapter 4 on page 53. As we have seen, the very first line has two mistakes. It was not 'Sunday evening' but midday and there were not 'three boys' but four. It does not exactly fill us with confidence. Neither does McCormick's discussion of the evidence. In the middle of a chapter entitled 'The Puzzle of Charles Walton's Watch', he suddenly plunges us back into the Hagley Wood case, on the grounds that his enquiries at Long Marston (a former Prisoner of War camp near Lower Quinton) had thrown up a woman (unnamed, of course) who was making her own enquiries into a Hungarian astrologer who may have been a prisoner there. This of course takes us back to *Aktion Hess* and again, a primeval link is made in our minds. Did a clairvoyant who knew the agent Clara end up in a camp only two and a half miles from the place where Charles Walton was killed?

With the full-blown cynicism for which McCormick became famous, he ends *Murder By Witchcraft* with 'As to the crime at Lower Quinton, I am convinced that witchcraft was a motive, although the murderer was neither a witch, nor a warlock. I do not pretend to have solved the crime [!] but I think I know who did it.'

If the whole sorry muddled story had ended there, we could write it off as a book for its time. For some, the 1960s was the end of civilization as we knew it. McCormick cites a tenuous link between Medieval witchcraft and 'the LSD cult of today'. By 1968, Hammer horror films were in their heyday and they have been superseded by a whole industry devoted to hapless teenagers from America's west coast who will persist in going unarmed and unprepared into lonely (usually haunted) cabins in the wilderness where they encounter (Shock! Horror!) a homicidal maniac with a machete. In these schlockers, nobody goes to a motel unless it is run by Norman Bates of *Psycho* fame. Nobody carries a gun for self-defence, despite the huge number of Americans who own them. Nobody even switches on a light in a darkened building they do not know at all.

This is, of course, good old-fashioned 'entertainment' and the human mind is notorious for being able to separate fact from fiction. Teenaged slasher movies are not real; the blood is fake; the victims get up again once the director yells 'Cut!' The reality, of course, is horrendous. Recently in the tragic shooting of a cinematographer on the set of a B-feature Western, the shock and grief is unimaginable. This time, the blood was not fake. And nobody got up just because it was a 'wrap'.

In 2009, author Paul Newman trod McCormick's road with his *Under the Shadow on Meon Hill*, again linking the Lower Quinton and Hagley Wood murders. He is absolutely right when he says:

Those drawn to the supernatural have poured a great deal of what they know into both murders and, as a result, they are now part of the Gothic-Nightmare heritage of the British Isles: half fact, half fable, standing beside films like *The Wicker Man* and the legends of Springheel Jack, Sawney Beane and Jack the Ripper. This disconcerting underworld has its roots deep in the national identity, the underbelly of empire, where shadows of violence, torture and oppression lurk ...

As with McCormick, Newman tackles the Lower Quinton crime first, with some first-rate observations wholly missing in *Murder By Witchcraft*, then, on page 77 comes 'Who Killed Bella?' Unlike McCormick, Newman gives a credit to the infamous Bella sketch with its labels and unlikely hairstyle. He says it is a 'police reconstruction of Bella'. This I doubt. It seems to have appeared first in an edition of the *Birmingham Mail* in 1968, which of course was the year of McCormick's book. Who actually commissioned this work is unclear, but it is a wholly misleading piece of art in terms of identification and is still trotted out today by almost everybody (see Chapter 16).

In Newman's version, we have the dialogue used by McCormick, for instance, in the police visit to the woman with the lost identity card which I demolished in Chapter 5. And we have the often-reproduced photograph of the hand of glory which of course is not Bella's and comes from a different (usually uncredited) source altogether.

What Newman does well, apart from criticising McCormick, is to plot the direction that the Hagley Wood case has taken since the 1960s. He quotes composer Simon Holt who has written an opera *Who Put Bella in the Wych Elm?* which premiered at Aldeburgh, Suffolk, in June 2003, 'Bella's macabre story has become part of local mythology in South West Birmingham. Everybody has their own angle on who or what she was.'[3] The composer saw a group of lads adding to the graffiti on the base of an obelisk on Wychbury Hill. It was probably they who changed the spelling from 'wych' to 'witch', making or missing the point, depending on one's point of view. In his opera, Holt calls one of the skeleton-finders Matty after one of these lads but immediately falls into a McCormickesque trap of misinformation. '... a name I would use for the boy who had been the first to discover "Bella's" body down the tree: he would soon die after from the shock and birds'-nesting would never be the same again for the other two boys.' The boy who died, later in the 1940s, was Frederick Payne and the cause was not shock but kidney disease. Nor was he the first to find the body; Bob Hart was. And there were not two other boys, but three. Minor points, perhaps, but important when it comes to research into murder.

In *The Children's Crusade* (Palgrave Macmillan 2010) author Gary Dickson makes a distinction between history and what he calls mythistory. History is based on evidence and facts and draws conclusions from that. Mythistory is based on anecdotes, folklore and supposition. It is usually more satisfying, rather like a crime novel, in which loose ends are tied up by the final chapter and the perpetrator brought to book. This is what has happened with Bella, except that we still have no answers. She was a witch, wasn't she? Wasn't there something about spying? A Dutchman? A trapeze artist? The myths swirl around us partly because well-meaning, honest and talented people like Simon Holt use their fertile imaginations to weave something new out of the tangle of the old. And most members of the public do not know the difference. Because of that, I am sure that Simon Holt was right when he says, 'Poor Bella, whoever and wherever you are – rest in peace. You have become more vivid to us in death than you possibly ever could have done in life.'[4]

And, in the 'sillier stories' folder, the shadow of haunted Meon Hill spreads further. Paul Newman quotes David Taylor, head of Parasearch, a paranormal research unit who visited the Badgers Sett pub in Hagley (called the Gypsy's Tent in the 1940s) as a boy. In the 1970s, the 'full monty' of paranormal activity occurred there – cold spots, telekinesis, doors opening and closing by themselves. This was a manifestation by 'Bella', a former barmaid who may have ended up in a wych elm nearby. What the staff did not tell Taylor was that such manifestations long pre-dated the body in Hagley Wood and were linked to the second Civil War, in the vague proximity of the Battle of Worcester, 1651.

Towards the end of *Under the Shadow of Meon Hill*, Newman wanders into supernatural irrelevance such as the occultist Cecil Williamson, Elizabeth I's 'mage' Dr John Dee, ritual sacrifice and the ramblings of the opium addict Thomas de Quincy, who wrote 'On Murder Considered One of the Fine Arts', with his tongue firmly in his cheek, in 1827. After all Newman's common sense and shrewd observations on the Hagley Wood murder, in the end, he plumps for mythistory, continuing our international obsession with 'things that go bump in the night'.

That insane playground of misinformation, the Internet, has only made matters worse. In the past, as is clear from Bella's case, such casual mishandling of the truth was the domain of 'red-top' journalists, intent on a good story to boost sales. With the Net, everybody and his wife is at it. Scores of websites devoted to Bella regurgitate the witchcraft/espionage elements as if they are proven fact. One American website has Bella's bones being distributed by a possum, an animal that has never existed in Britain. Another refers to the notorious tree as the wyke elm. In some, there is a lot of dry ice in gloomy glades, absolutely nowhere near Hagley Wood. People chat together in an amateur studio, cracking feeble jokes; they make 'documentaries' for Halloween. The podcasts have titles like *The Monsters Under Our Bed, Dark Histories, Dark Curiosities* and *Haunted History*. Some presenters wear witch makeup; others carry selfie-sticks. The worst have swathes of bad poetry and excruciating music. I counted nearly a hundred of them. There is at least one film, a 36-minute 'short' directed by Thomas Lee Ruther, an 'enchanting piece of film-making, bound to delight fans of hauntology' according to one review. Unfortunately, it cannot delight devotees of true crime. Neither could the BBC's flimsy Radio 4 programme in August 2014, narrated by comedian Steve Punt, which simply regurgitated the paid and conflicted testimony of Una Mossop. Even the much trumpeted 10-minuter fronted by John Stalker, everybody's favourite senior policeman in the 1980s, was filmed in the wrong wood!

Meon Hill and the spurious nonsense that emanated from the murder of Charles Walton is still casting its shadow, longer and darker than ever. Bella is lost in that darkness.

Chapter 16

The Fantasy Historian

I met Donald McCormick years ago in connection with a project that never came off. Despite his deafness, he was charming company, as was his wife. They were sparkling conversationalists and generous hosts, but McCormick had a tendency, I knew, to make things up. This is fine for a novelist, working long before the idea of 'faction' became an established literary convention, but it does not reach the bar necessary for an historian. And, despite the title of this chapter, used by a reviewer of one of his books, McCormick was not an historian; his background lies in journalism, which, as we have seen from various papers commenting on the Hagley Wood case, is a very different animal.

McCormick gave the impression of having been involved in espionage in the Second World War, which he was not. Undeterred, using the penname Richard Deacon, he wrote a number of books on the subject. In the preface to one of these, *Spy!*, written with his long-suffering researcher Nigel West, he says:

> It is not without significance that in the jargon of the world of espionage, a spy, Intelligence agent, or even a spy-catcher, is referred to as a 'spook' ... Their lives are, to some extent, ghostlike. Even if they themselves can be seen, their real purpose must remain unseen. And, like ghosts, they often inhabit a kind of twilight world of their own.

And no one more so, he might have added, than Donald McCormick himself.

His generation of intelligent men, often with a public school and 'Oxbridge' background, dominated the corridors of power in the 1940s and 1950s, as the SS's Walter Schellenberg had noted in his Black Book – 1 per cent of British society controlling 80 per cent of it. McCormick was not *quite* of that breed. He attended Shrewsbury, a minor public school that had produced the First World War poet Wilfred Owen, but did not go on to university, let alone 'Oxbridge'. Whether this gave him a chip on his shoulder, I do not know, but he mixed with the elite whenever he could. One of his closest friends was genuinely involved in espionage – Ian Fleming of Naval Intelligence and creator of the most successful spy franchise of all time, James Bond. Another was Dennis Wheatley, tasked by the Secret Service in Whitehall to write a blueprint for a successful invasion of Britain in 1940 from the Nazi viewpoint. He went on to write ever-more-lurid tales of the occult, many of which were turned into films.

I first came across McCormick's work in *The Identity of Jack the Ripper* (1959) when several of the Whitechapel murderer's crime scenes were still (just about) standing. The man knew what sold books and the Ripper crimes have spawned an entire industry proffering solutions to the world's most famous unsolved murders. In one of the better books to emerge from this, Stewart Evans and Keith Skinner produced *Jack the Ripper: Letters from Hell* in 2001. They include a chapter called 'The Mysteries of McCormick' which is written by Evans alone because he and Skinner could not agree on the extent to which McCormick made his research up. I know both authors personally and have the highest regard for them both, but in this instance, I have to side with Stewart!

To be fair to McCormick, he was writing at a time when sources were not deemed that important and a certain amount of licence was acceptable. His real problem, though, was lack of training. He did not have the rigorous discipline of an historian and most people were happy to take journalese with a pinch of salt as long as it was not actually libellous. *The Identity of Jack the Ripper* was acclaimed at the time but has since been totally discredited. It includes dialogue, which is a highly debatable literary form in true crime and the rhyme that begins 'Eight little whores with no hope of Heaven, Gladstone may save one; then there'll be seven' has been found nowhere other than in McCormick's book.

And it was not just in the world of Ripperology that the man went overboard. In *Hayek: a Collaborative Biography Part III* (Palgrave MacMillan 2014), editor Robert Leeson describes McCormick as a fraud. He cites a (very short) list of McCormick's admirers – Terence Hutchinson, Professor of Economics from the University of Birmingham and Hugh Trevor-Roper, Regius Professor of Modern History at Oxford. Trevor-Roper's own legacy lies in tatters today because he believed the clearly fraudulent *Hitler Diaries* to be genuine. The list of detractors

(Leeson calls them McCormick's 'victims') is much longer. Arthur Pigou was president of the Economic Society and founder of the 'modern market failure school' with a Cambridge background. John Maynard Keynes was also a Cambridge man, a neo-classical economist who was *the* government's go-to adviser in the 1920s and 1930s. Rudolf Peierls, John Habbakuk, Wilfred Noyce and Raymond Carr were all academics with impeccable records; McCormick had a pop at them all. Among many other detractors was the historian E.P. Thompson, who described McCormick's *The British Constitution* as 'warmed-up fourth-rate crap'.

Leeson sums up McCormick's skills brilliantly – he was 'a failed fiction writer; his prose is both flowery and plodding. Yet when disguised as non-fiction it is sensational.' He was a full-time journalist on *The Times* and also wrote regularly for the *Spectator* and *Encounter*. His output was prodigious, ranging from *The Talkative Muse* in 1934 to *The Life of Ian Fleming*, 1993. He wrote *Erotic Literature: a Connoisseur's Guide* in 1992 and, perhaps most tellingly of all, *Taken For a Ride: the History of Cons and Con-men* in 1976.

In the 1950s, he was focusing largely on murder, including a load of tosh on the con-man Maundy Gregory as an unlikely killer and the pre-Victorian pot-boiler the Red Barn Mystery where he claimed to have found new evidence. The 1960s were largely dominated by books on espionage. A right-wing Conservative, many of his sources originated with *The News of the World*, a now defunct newspaper that specialized in shock horror tales of sex scandals, 'orrible murder and UFOs. Shortly before his death, he sold his private papers, at auction, to Ian Sayer; it would be fascinating to know what, if anything, he has to say on the Hagley Wood case.

Why is all this important? Why have I spent the last three pages devoted to just one of the writers on Bella? Because some books are important and assume an influence far beyond their actual worth. When Peter Benchley's *Jaws* first hit the bookshops (and even more so when the film came out) seaside towns were seriously hit by the timidity of American bathers. The cause of the great white shark was put back decades. On a more serious note, Harriet Becher Stowe's *Uncle Tom's Cabin* is revered today as a blow struck against the evils of slavery. In fact, Mrs Becher Stowe had never seen a slave nor set foot on a plantation. The work was fiction. When the president, Abraham Lincoln, met her, he said, 'So you're the little woman who has caused this great war of ours.' He was not wrong.

Because Donald McCormick was the first writer to produce a full book (or rather, less than half a book) on the Hagley Wood case, he has assumed a central role which has done considerable damage to the researches of those of us who have followed. Paul Newman (*Under the Shadow of Meon Hill*) is wise to him, but other writers – and, more importantly, readers – are not. Throughout this book I have tried to point out the areas where McCormick is clearly sailing by the seat of his pants, but he is a clever writer and would have us believe that he is making various assertions more in sorrow than in factual accuracy. He is plain wrong on the number of boys who found the bones and the time of day that this took place. He claims that one of the lads died from shock at the find; this is not true. He invents dialogue between the boys. In reality, we have no idea what was said. He claims that Professor Webster set up Sheffield's first forensic science laboratory in 1929 although there is nothing about this in the man's record. McCormick claims that a mannequin was produced, complete with wig and clothes with the correct height. If so, there is nothing of this in the Worcester Archive and, as ever, McCormick does not give his sources.

We have the story of the anonymous woman's identity card and that she was interviewed by police in an equally anonymous Midlands town. We even have dialogue from the police interview with her, though none of this exists in the police files. There is the story of the anonymous teacher and industrial executive hearing screams in Hagley Wood in July 1941 which had been reported to the police. If it had, the report is not there any longer and the original files make no reference to it – 'Eight little whores ...'

McCormick claims to have insight into the police mindset. They rejected, he says, the idea that Bella was a 'street walker ... lured by car to her death'. He does not explain why. They dismissed the idea, too, that the woman was a gypsy, largely because gypsies expel troublesome women rather than kill them. This predisposes that Bella was the victim of some sort of Romany judicial process, not that a psychopath had met her. The police warmed to the notion, McCormick said, that Bella may have been a temporary refugee from the bombing of nearby Birmingham and perhaps her killer was too. This *may* have been discussed at the various CID conferences referred to in the Archive, but if so, such a discussion was not entered into the minutes.

'But why was it?' McCormick asks, 'that shortly after the murder of Charles Walton, the police took another look at the files of the Hagley

Wood case?' The answer is that they did not, as McCormick probably knew full well. There was a flurry of activity in 1944 because of the wall writings and again in 1953/4 because of the emergence of Anna's story. Claiming disingenuously that 'to this extent the murder of Bella had a slight resemblance to that of Charles Walton' is good old-fashioned McCormick wishful thinking.

Hagley Wood, McCormick contends, 'had the reputation of being the haunt of witches' covens and also there was an ancient tradition that the spirit of a dead witch could be imprisoned in the hollow of a tree and thus prevented from wreaking any harm in the world'. There is no evidence of covens in Hagley Wood. All writers on the occult in the twentieth century claim that the new witchcraft movement which would morph into Wicca was urban, not rural and the hollow tree is the kind of detail that McCormick relished. In various Iron Age burials, including the 'bog people' of Denmark, branches of trees have clearly been laid criss-crossed over corpses, presumably to pin their souls to the earth. But this is only an informed assumption, and it never consists of an entire tree.

It is in the context of Dr Margaret Murray that I find McCormick's behaviour most reprehensible. He wrote *Murder By Witchcraft* five years after the Egyptologist's death and we only have his word for her views on Hagley Wood, Meon Hill and the conversations between them. We can accept Dr Murray's articles in various newspapers because they are a matter of public record, but the casual chats he had with her may never have happened at all. Certainly, she makes no mention of either McCormick or Hagley Wood in her autobiography *My First Hundred Years*. She went to Hagley, he says, but there is nothing about her in the police files. McCormick's quotations from her are extensive, reading either like a written report or perhaps a telephone conversation taken down in shorthand. Either way, McCormick, as ever, does not give his sources. Instead, he wanders off for four pages into child sacrifice, citing the Moors murderers Ian Brady and Myra Hindley, the Marquis de Sade and the alleged[1] child-killer Gilles de Rais, none of whom has any connection with Bella; but they sell books!

McCormick then focuses on the Hagley Wood victim's right hand, claiming that Dr Murray probably believed that its burial away from the tree was proof of a witchcraft connection. He waxes lyrical about the magic hand featuring in West Indian voodoo and African cultures as often as it does in Britain. He quotes, inevitably, the 'hand of glory' and a 200-year-old murder case he had read in that tome of scholarship and authenticity *Lord Halifax's Ghost Book* (1936) 'Dr Murray had insisted that there was evidence that ghoulish rites were performed in secrecy on dark nights in remote parts of the Midlands and that they included devil-worship.' This does not sound like the same sensible, sceptical academic who said that the Hagley Wood murder had 'possible' occult connotations.

When it comes to fantasists like George Elwell, McCormick is again less than honest. He says that, in his self-imposed trance, the railway clerk names Bella's killer, but there is no such name in the police files. In the case of Anna of Claverly, we have already noted the mysterious 'far out in the country' meeting place between her, her friend, Quaestor and a policeman. Clearly, McCormick had no idea where this was and he is happy to go along with Quaestor's overblown journalese because that was the sort of style he himself used. On the question of Bella's shoes, we only have McCormick's word that all but four pairs were traced, even though the enquiries are covered at length in the Worcester Archive. Similarly, of the 200 or so missing women in 1943, all but twelve were traced, alive and well; again, no hint of these in the police files.

We then come to the most ludicrous part of McCormick's research – the ease with which he traces wartime records in both the Netherlands and Germany. He glosses over this with five pages describing the espionage situation as it was in 1939–41, throwing in Rudolf Hess and his flight to Scotland and establishing an agent – Lehrer – who appears in no one else's account ('eight little whores ...') and whose name is obtained from a Nazi in hiding in Paraguay. And he is disingenuous in the extreme when he says 'In my quest for the truth about the Hagley Wood crime, I had allowed myself to be lured into a blind alley and all I had to show for my pains was a sub-plot in the whole story, an interesting digression, but little more.' In fact, it is clear that McCormick, having rejected witchcraft as a motive, is making espionage the *plot*, not the sub-plot – and he has just spent nine pages delineating it. And the next line does not sound like Donald McCormick at all – 'I was no professional detective and where professionals had failed, how could I hope to succeed?' How indeed!

McCormick admits that he did not link Hagley Wood with the murder of Charles Walton, yet by placing them together in the same book and discussing the witchcraft angle in both cases, he is doing just that. He concedes at one point:

The problem when an author tries to be an amateur detective is that he is apt to become too interested in playing with ideas and in the purely literary aspects of what he discovers. Shrewd as he may flatter himself to be, the subconscious mind will too often draw him from facts to fantasy.

And despite that, in the middle of the chapter on Charles Walton's watch, he plunges into *Aktion Hess*, Fraulein Dronkers and Jan Willem Ter Braak which I believe had nothing whatever to do with Bella.

His conclusion, limp and wrong though it is, is that Bella 'probably was Clara, alias Fraulein Dronkers' and that 'only Fraulein Dronkers' dentist could prove that.'

McCormick's evidence does not add up in *Murder By Witchcraft* any more than, according to others, it did in any of his books. As to Bella's killer, he merely falls back on the inquest verdict – 'murder by person or persons unknown'.

Chapter 17

Case Closed

By July 2005, the anonymous murder victim known as Bella had been dead for approximately sixty-four years. In all probability, most of her contemporaries were gone by then. Professor Webster, who had performed the post-mortem on her, died in 1973. Donald McCormick, who wrote the first ever book on her, in 1998. The others are just names on faded documents, typed out on battered typewriters and consigned to brown cardboard boxes. And by that time, with no realistic hope of confirming Bella's identity or finding her killer, the West Mercia police, as the Worcestershire force had become, decided that enough was enough and shut operations down.

In reality there had been nothing new for years. The odd wall writing would reappear, mostly on the monument on Wychbury Hill, from time to time and journalists, historians and paranormal researchers would produce the occasional article before the creative world of poetry and music took over and Bella became a wandering wraith indistinguishable from the Arthurian Morgana Le Fay or Titania of the Faeries. We need to get back to reality.

The 2005 closure report was written by Detective Chief Inspector I. Nicholls and had been commissioned by his boss, Detective Chief Superintendent T. Abbutt. They were the successors to Williams and Inight who had handled the original case from April 1943:

> The purpose of this document is to record the review of the ... file which pertains to the investigation surrounding the recovery of the remains of a female from within the naturally hollowed-out trunk of an elm tree located within Hagley Wood adjacent to the main Birmingham to Kidderminster Road ... now designated ... the A456.[1]

Nicholls makes an important point in the second paragraph. 'The nature of the bones missing would induce a presumption that the absence was as a result of wildlife intervention rather than being removed at the time of or immediately after death.' In other words, there was no ritual dismemberment, no 'hand of glory' and, by definition, no witchcraft. To be clear, this had never been part of the original investigation. The first mention of the occult that I have come across is in Quaestor's version of what Anna/Una Mossop said in 1953 – 'The affair is closed and involves no witches, black magic or moon night rites' – and this came about as a result of the new obsession with witchcraft prevalent in the 1950s and the fact that Quaestor had just paid Anna one hundred pounds.

Because of the way the body had been stuffed feet first, Nicholls reminds us, this was certainly a case of murder, echoing the police view of the time that it was neither accidental nor suicide. Oddly, he then seems to backtrack, claiming that because there was no discernible cause of death (Webster, of course, had suggested suffocation) 'to make the leap to a murder is questionable'. It is a marvellous piece of police double-speak and legalese to claim that 'in line with the current standards contained within the National Crime Recording Standards (Revised April 2004), specifically the "Balance of Probability" test, the balance is that the individual was subjected to unlawful actions, which led directly or indirectly to death.' This hedging of bets was clearly designed to allow a verdict of manslaughter rather than murder, as it was impossible, without a bona fide suspect, to confirm motive. Murder has to mean pre-planning – 'with malice aforethought' – and since nothing was known about Bella or her last moments, this was not definite.

The 'Executive Summary' section noted that the death occurred at the height of the Axis bombing in the area and that the deceased had still not been identified. Her final resting place is unknown. By the 1970s when the shoe factor Mr Cogzell made enquiries at Professor Webster's laboratory at Birmingham University, the bones had gone. So had Bella's clothing in that the shoes he was shown were not those retrieved from the wych elm. Nicholls goes on to say that the 'investigation was skewed by false reports' which is probably true of any murder enquiry given the unreliable nature of witnesses and some people's compulsion to get in on the act. These would include Anna of Claverly's assertions and the rash of wall writing hinting at some arcane knowledge. No more witnesses had come forward after 1953 and the forensic evidence, though at first promising in terms of Bella's shoes and teeth, had led nowhere. 'Two potential suspects were identified as a result of information in 1953, one of whom was dead, the other remains unknown.' This has to refer to Jack Mossop, who died insane in 1942, and the enigmatic and probably non-existent Van Ralt.

Nicholls points up the bizarre background to the case. In the people's war, 'death without record' was far more frequent than in peacetime and the movement of people, especially in the Blitzed industrial Midlands, made police progress difficult.

Particularly galling were the chalk graffiti that appeared over a wide area and Nicholls is gently reproving of the time wasted in this. Although he does not say so, what could the police have hoped to prove by finding the culprit(s)? Anyone can copy a line for any number of reasons and they may well have no actual links to a crime at all.

In terms of missing persons, the 2005 report lists: Mary Lee, aka Wenham, aka Beaver; Bella Tonks; Ann Forrest; Bella Beech; Bella Luer; and Violet Goode. I could find no mention of Goode in the police Archive. Nicholls reports that she was the 'other woman' in a domestic breakdown between Thomas (Harry) Truman and his wife Gladys. Truman got back with his wife but there was a suggestion that he had killed Violet (his mistress) to make this rapprochement possible. In fact, Violet Goode was found alive and well in Stourbridge. There is no mention in the report of Billy Gibson, a short woman whose photograph is in the file; this is perhaps because she did not come to light until 1951 and did not feature in the original investigation.

In the section called 'Line of enquiry not finished'. DI Nicholls includes the tortuous tales of Dinah Curley aka O'Grady (see Chapter 7) and adds the curious addendum: 'There are on file a number of connections which it would seem prudent not to follow as the basis for the content is at best questionable.' This presumably refers to the 'ramblings' of George Elwell and the offer to meet from A. Wood.

Under 'Suspects', Nicholls summarizes the case against Jack Mossop and Van Ralt as outlined by Una Hainsworth. Even though the police file contains an entire folder on Julian Mossop, Nicholls quite rightly discounts him as a suspect; he was only 11 when the body was found. He also makes the comment that 'Mrs Hainsworth seemingly had some history, as it would appear that the removal from the Kenilworth address left behind considerable debts.' The inspector was absolutely right that the whole nonsense regarding an espionage connection comes from Anna of Claverly; before that, it did not exist.

Reviewing 'status of crime', DI Nicholls makes the point that forensic science has moved on considerably since Professor Webster's day (although, I contend, not necessarily in the right direction) and today perhaps different conclusions would be reached about the cause of Bella's death. As Nicholls says, this, without the body in question, gets us nowhere.

The inspector analyses the effectiveness of media appeals and communication strategy. The problem is, and was even in 1953, that such appeals usually bring out what Nicholls euphemistically describes as 'obsessional theorists', the oddballs who long to be involved and who seriously hamper police enquiries. We all see ourselves as armchair detectives and some of us are not very good at it. Nicholls applauded the rational, factual documentary approach of the television programme fronted by John Stalker in 1994 and laments that that led to no new leads. In fact, the odds were stacked against it. The Stalker programme was only ten minutes long and it was broadcast over fifty years after the body was found.

Nicholls identifies a number of strategies relating to the case. In the 'arrest strategy', the death of Jack Mossop and the inability to find anyone called Van Ralt mean that there are no leads to follow and 'an arrest is not envisioned'. The 'search strategy' would fail too, because any potential offender would probably himself be dead. Without such a person, the 'interview strategy' could not happen. In terms of 'identification strategy', the obvious development of DNA has effectively revolutionized the search for missing persons and identification of the deceased. Today it would be possible to fix Bella's identity exactly, as that of Richard III was in 2013; existing members of the Plantagenet family gave samples that could be categorically linked with the bones in the Leicester car park. Without Bella's body, however, such a line of enquiry cannot happen. Nor can we trace existing members of her family, because we do not know who they are. 'Extensive enquiries' to find Bella's bones have failed, although, as is also true of the murder itself, someone knows, or at least knew. At some point between 1943 and 1978, Bella's bones disappeared. They did not, of course. Someone in the corridors of science in Birmingham University either threw them away or gave them a decent burial in a pauper's grave under what is known in police jargon as 'disposal of evidence'. And that person is not talking.

DI Nicholls lists the formidable array of experts who could today be wheeled in to resolve who Bella was and how she died. Forensic archaeologists, anthropologists, environmentalists, palaeontologists and odontologists all have a role to play. Particularly annoying is the lack of photographic evidence from the crime scene itself. If Superintendent Inight and his team had begun earlier in the day on 19 April 1943 or taken photographs the next day, we might know more. The Worcester Archive has a photograph of the wych elm, showing how low the bole was in connection with the ground. The pollarded branches radiate out from it like the rays of the sun, as one journalist at the time put it, and the early leaves of spring are sprouting from it. The photograph in almost all newspapers and books that followed shows the wrong tree; because Constable Pound had to hack at the wood to get the bones out, it had gone for all practicable purposes by the end of April. This was a pity, because even in 1943, the bark of the wych elm would potentially have had recoverable fingerprints of Bella's killer.

The photographs of the body are of little help in comparison with the actual bones themselves, although of course they were all that craniofacial expert Professor Caroline Wilkinson of FaceLab had to work with. The first photograph shows Bella's skull from the left side, which is presumably how Bob Hart had left it that April Sunday eighty years ago. From a different angle, we see the skull, some vertebrae, clothing debris and one shoe. It is not clear where the full-frontal photograph and the right side were taken, but since the bones have not been cleaned and the background suggests undergrowth, this was probably in Hagley Wood itself. We have no idea who took these photographs. Was it Webster himself? His assistant, Dr Lund? One of the police personnel present? There is simply no record.

Another photograph shows Bella's shoes, of which the original investigation was so hopeful. The laces have gone and they are damaged and bent out of shape, as we might expect from over a year of decay in the wych elm.

Nothing is made in the 2005 report of Bella's clothes. Bizarrely, the slip and skirt are mocked up using material of approximately the right colour, but the wrong medium. The slip is certainly not taffeta. The cardigan and knickers are drawings, done in coloured crayon and there are two versions of the cardigan, markedly different from each other. Contrary to Professor Webster's description, both are shown with sleeves.

The conclusion that DI Nicholls reached in 2005 was inevitable:

> At this stage with the passage of time, there are no clear investigative leads. If the location of the remains were established, development of the DNA processes has not afforded investigative opportunities. Any person involved, if surviving, would be in excess of eighty years of age [today, of course, mid-90s] and the prospect of a prosecution would be at best remote. I therefore make the following recommendations:
> - The case is identified as being closed
> - Consideration should be afforded to placing the documentation in the Worcestershire Records Office as an historic document

That duly happened and they lie there, warts and all, in duplicate and triplicate, raising as many questions as they answer. As an Addendum, on 28 July, Nicholls adds: 'this file has now been declared closed and is not henceforward to be regarded as a live investigation.'

But, for some of us, the investigation is very much alive.

Chapter 18

The Raggedy Rawney

For eighty years, we have been haunted by Bella in the wych elm. That is because we do not know who she was and without that basic information, we cannot hope to find her killer.

What do we know? For all DI Nicholls' careful approach in 2005, not wishing to jump off the fence between murder and manslaughter, there is no doubt in my mind that Bella was murdered 'with malice aforethought'. The fact that no one came forward to report her missing, even in the disjointed, nightmare world of the Second World War, is very telling. So is the fact that her clothing had no labels other than a code number in her shoes. The shoes were relatively expensive; the rest of her clothing was not. Despite the poor sketches in the police file, her cardigan had no sleeves; her skirt was too long for her. And that, surely leads to an obvious conclusion; Bella was wearing somebody else's clothes. They were not the product of some European tailor/haberdasher under the yoke of Nazi oppression, the clothes worn by a spy. They were home-grown; home-made. Only the shoes told a different story.

Bella was indeed, as Superintendent Inight had said back in 1944, 'a victim from another world'. But it was not the world of witchcraft. Or the world of wartime espionage. She was not known in the area or *someone*, surely, would have come forward as a relative or friend. She must have been born somewhere, been to school, held down a job. Born, yes, obviously. But school, I doubt it, at least on a regular basis. And I believe she did have a job, but it was one that was not considered respectable and was fraught with danger. When journalist Simon Askwith was working on a Bella-related article for *The Independent* in 2003, he met two octogenarians 'out for a stroll, who told me that they thought she had probably been "on the game" as they put it. They laughed uneasily when I asked them if they had known her personally.'[1] If Askwith was right about the ages of the couple, they would have been in their twenties during the war and might, indeed, have remembered Bella. The police, of course, considered the idea that

Bella was a prostitute. The night job (although it is carried on in broad daylight too) is arguably the most dangerous in the world. The victims of Jack the Ripper and nearly all the victims of the 'Blackout Killer' Gordon Cummings and the creepy landlord John Christie, were prostitutes. But the police files offer little in the way of evidence in the pursuance of this line of enquiry. There are vague references to a woman who plied her trade on the Hagley Road and a letter discussing 'women of this sort' but there is no information on any interviews and no names or addresses. For that, and to find out who Bella really was, we have to go south from the Midlands, to the capital of prostitution as it was of the country; we have to go to London.

In 1954, when Bella had been dead for thirteen years, ex-superintendent Robert Fabian went into print with *London After Dark*, a fascinating glimpse of vice in the world's second largest city. Fabian had been in charge of Scotland Yard's Vice Squad – 'the dirty mob' – for years and knew all the ins and outs of the trade. At the centre of the 'game' was Soho, then, and for years afterwards, the heart of street prostitution and grubby little shops that flashed 'Strip-Tease', 'Girls' and 'Books'. 'Soho,' wrote Fabian, 'is not so much an area you could work out as an atmosphere that pervades part of the West End.'[2] The Vice Squad had a ledger that contained the names of every known prostitute in the capital:

> Their phony names and genuine names, ages, photos, descriptions, habits, weaknesses, regular cronies and haunts – even the names of their sorrowing, respectable relatives ... We did a fairly sound job of checking upon the movements of the 'regulars' and noted when they left Town for a week-end or a brief holiday abroad. This we did in case they never came back. Being murdered is one of the risks that a prostitute takes in her trade.

I believe that one of these was Bella, but she had not gone to Hagley Wood for a weekend or a holiday. She was going home. And she was trying to escape.

In April 1936, the banner headline in the *News of the World* asked 'Is There a "Jack the Strangler" At Large?' There had been two murders of prostitutes, described coyly in the paper as of 'uncertain virtue', both in Soho, between 4 November 1935 and 16 March 1936. Before that, on 8/9 May 1935, the body of Dutch Leah (actually a British woman) was found in her Old Compton Street flat with her tongue slashed, perhaps, the media speculated, because 'she knew too much'. The November murder had been of 'French Fifi' (actually a Russian woman).

The women were linked with the 'Brigade of Iron', an underworld gang of pimps and prostitutes headed by Latvian Max Kassel from Riga, whose people included charmers with the street names Coco the Animal, Mariot of the Big Eyes, Albert the Arab, Bibi the Bitter and Titi the Big-Footed. Although this group sounds like characters from a radio comedy show, like the much-later *Beyond Our Ken* or *Round the Horne*, they were real-life gangsters and their molls that make television's *Peaky Blinders* look like the fiction it is. It is likely that these names were in the Vice Squad's ledger, as well as the personal notebook that Bob Fabian carried in his pocket.

In its 23 May 1936 edition, the journal *John Bull* read:

Soho is the place, for its area has a worse record for blood or violence and for darker forms of vice than any other in Great Britain ... Decent, hard-working, clean-living foreigners ... living cheek by jowl with the scum of continental gutters ... And now the mixture is getting too strong for anybody's taste.

Kassel himself was shot dead in Little Newport Street, Soho in January but that did nothing to stamp out the increasing vice in London. Chief Inspector Frederick Sharpe, who was leading the Kassel murder case, described him as 'a very small-time ponce who lived on the earnings of one woman'. Kassel was found in a ditch near St Albans with six bullets in his body and, at the time of his inquest, two people were awaiting trial in France over his death. Kassel had died in a fight in the London flat, but his body had been taken by car to St Albans in an attempt to distance the crime from the people involved. Another hard-bitten detective, Fabian, had nothing but contempt for pimps like Kassel:

Many men in London live upon the immoral earnings of prostitutes. The name for such men is 'Ponces' or 'Johnsons' and they are the lowest form of animal life on the criminal scale, although you might not think so to look at them, for they can – when business is good – dress quite expensively and are often surly, determined-looking types ... well able to look after themselves in a fight.

He speculates on the background of the pimps, 'Some are army deserters [especially in wartime] but more often they are born into the underworld of London and know its warrens and its devices and its strange language, as a skilled gamekeeper knows the secrets of copse and hedgerow.'

What is interesting about the murder of Kassel, Dutch Leah and the others is the press's xenophobia. Blithely ignoring the fact that prostitution in London was centuries old, they blamed it all on foreigners, like Kassel and Dutch Leah, despite the homeliness of her birth. The Association for Moral and Social Hygiene attributed the growing problem to Europeans on London's streets. The police themselves, charged with coping with it all, pointed to 'marriages of convenience' by which British men could marry foreign brides, often years younger than they were, for a simple cash transaction. Such women were then farmed out to work the streets and there were headlines that screamed about white slavery.

There was something dark, ancient and, of course, racist about all this. One of the most successful 'illicit' books in the pre-Victorian era was *The Lustful Turk* (1827) in which a series of innocent white women were ravished by the potentate of the title. They were wholly victims, the Turk the disgusting perpetrator. As both Sharpe and Fabian knew, vice was a two-way street; without willing girls, there would be no 'white slavery' and no Soho sex trade. When William Booth, founder of the Salvation Army, had been brave enough to break every taboo of the Victorian era and actually write about prostitution,[3] a surprisingly high percentage of the working girls he spoke to admitted that they offered their services because they enjoyed it as well as for the money. That was something the do-gooders of the 1930s did not want to hear; neither does the 'sex-worker' lobby of today.

The Yard's Vice Squad dossier lists only 102 prostitutes of foreign extraction, out of an estimated 3,000 in C Division (the West End) alone. Stefan Slater in *The London Journal* March 2007, discusses what amounts to a 'moral panic' over this European human traffic and in doing so he highlights the shady world of London's prostitution and the fact that powerful and eminent men effectively got away with using prostitutes' services simply because of who they were. In 1922, Sir Almeric Fitzroy, Clerk to the Privy Council, was arrested for accosting women in Hyde Park, a crime as old as Hyde Park itself. Found guilty, he appealed and unsurprisingly, the verdict was overturned. The press-reading public was outraged, not, as they would be today, by perverts in high places, but by the fact that the Met had been too heavy-handed in arresting Fitzroy in the first place. As a result, arrest rates involving prostitutes dropped from 2,291 in 1922 to a mere 650 a year later.

The writer Alec Waugh was as fascinated by Soho as Fabian and the editor of *John Bull*: 'There is a glamour about the word [allegedly originally an eighteenth-century hunting cry to call foxhounds],' he wrote in the first volume of *Wonderful London* in 1926. 'It is crude and rough. It suggests mystery and squalor and romance ... It has a dusky swarthiness and oriental flavour, a cringing savagery that waits its hour.'

'Why go to Paris for a good time?' Stephen Graham asked in 1925 in *London Nights*. 'It can be arranged in London just as well.' An estimated 87 per cent of French prostitutes (whether they were actually French or not) operated not in sleazy Soho but the 'swanky' apartments of Piccadilly, Mayfair and Bayswater. By the outbreak of war, local property owners were working with the police to clear them out.

On 4 November 1935, by coincidence or design the day on which French Fifi (Josephine Martin) was murdered, police arrested Fernand Modena, known as 'Little Pascalle of Marseilles' in the Charing Cross Road. He was charged with making a false statement to an immigration officer, but at Vine Street police station, he was found to have nine house keys in his pocket. They were to the flats of prostitutes that he ran as a professional pimp. One of them was his own wife, Martha Pirie; two others were Marie Andrews and Germaine McEvoy, whose surnames may refer to the fact that they were involved in the marriage of convenience trade. Two other women are not named, but the sixth is and unlike the others, she was British. Her name was Lavonia Stratford, she was 21 and she was from Birmingham.

I believe that Lavonia Stratford was Bella.

It would be fascinating to know Lavonia's physical details. Was she dark haired, with snaggle teeth? Did she stand 5 feet tall in her stockinged feet? Was a photograph taken of her? Was she included in Scotland Yard's dossier? It seems unlikely, in that the discovery of Modena's harem had clearly come as a surprise to the Met. Would they include her in their files now? Was her name added to Bob Fabian's little pocket book?

What stood out for me was the fact that Lavonia is singled out as being from Birmingham, whereas the others were probably brought over by Modena from France. He and they were deported once the case for procuring and soliciting was heard, but because Lavonia was British, she stayed here. The moral indignation of the public over white slavery and prostitution generally was not matched by the punishment meted out by the law. The fines for prostitution were ridiculously light in comparison with their earnings. If a prostitute solicited in the street, she could only be charged with the same penalty as a public obstruction by a barrow boy or a pavement artist. Lavonia Stratford may have paid as little as £2 which was far less than she paid Modena for his 'protection'; it was an occupational hazard. But there would, ultimately, be a far heavier price to pay.

When I first came across Lavonia Stratford, I was struck by the name. Lavonia could, of course, be a typo or a mishearing of Lavinia, but both are highly unusual names, far more so than Bella. I looked up Stratford in the *Journal* of the Romany and Traveller Family History Society and there it is, listed as a fairly common 'gypsy' name. As for Lavonia, it too is a gypsy name and the Romany word *luvvani* means prostitute.

When I read the views of Churchwarden Hodgetts of Hagley on the gypsies of the 1940s, I wrote them off at first as a typical Englishman's take on all things foreign and different. Bella, he believed, was a gypsy who had fallen foul of her tribe and had been punished by them, according to traditions that Hodgetts did not understand and her body had been buried in some arcane rite in the wych elm. I did not accept that, but in one respect, I believe Hodgetts was right – Bella was indeed from another world, the world of the travelling people. Interestingly, when Professor Caroline Wilkinson examined Professor Webster's photographs of the Hagley Wood skull, she came to the conclusion that the dead woman was Caucasian, but with a suggestion of Indian sub-structure. And where do Roma people *actually* originate? India.

Let us look again at her clothes. A skirt that was too big for her – it belonged to someone else in the tribe. A slip that showed beneath it without the belt to hold it up – belonging to that same larger person. The sleeveless hand-me-down cardigan and the non-matching blue belt – not only somebody else's but very much what a gypsy of the 1930s and 1940s would wear. There are online today a number of photographs from the period showing gypsy camps. Horses and vardo wagons are still very much in evidence and a whole range of multi-coloured, rather outlandish clothes are worn, especially by the women. Constable Pound, who had chopped down the wych elm to retrieve Bella's body and had made enquiries into the 'Smith' family of gypsies in the Hagley area in 1942, also reported the stash of clothes that they left behind when they moved on. It was found 115 yards from the site of the wych elm at Christmas time 1942 (before the body was found) and included a pair of red-painted shoes and a knife. It was all filthy and ragged, as of course were Bella's clothes in the wych elm.

But Bella's shoes were different. They were her own, costing 13/11d and more than any traveller could afford, reflecting her very different life in London. Perhaps she could not bear to part with them.

The police report on Fernand Modena gives Lavonia's age as twenty-one. This was in 1935, so she would have been born in 1914 and at the time of her death would have been 27, within Professor Webster's age range for the body in the tree. It is true that he personally veered to the slightly older likelihood of 35, but that was not his first conclusion and, on his own admission, such estimates were largely informed guesswork. Can we find a Lavonia Stratford, born in 1914, in any records? Nearly. A Lavinia F. Stratford was born in London on 17 October 1914. It may be that Lavonia *was* a misprint when the police arrested her along with Modena and that this is the same person. If that is so, how can she be called a Birmingham woman and how can I believe she came from a gypsy community?

Because we know nothing about her parents, we cannot be sure, but I believe they hailed from the great gypsy centre of Black Patch, on the outskirts of Birmingham. This is only twelve miles from Hagley and we know it was closed down by local authorities in 1905. We also know that many families refused to move, while others left and drifted back. I believe that the Stratfords were one example of this. Like countless people before and since, they perhaps hoped that the streets of London were paved with gold, as legend said, and they drifted to the capital to make a living any way they could. They may even, as large numbers did, became sedentary for a while, adopting a more or less conventional lifestyle. Then, for whatever reason, they may have drifted back to the Midlands, if not to Black Patch Park as it was by now, then to the Hagley area generally.

A little girl like Lavonia was now effectively under the radar. She may have attended school from time to time as the family moved around, but never for long enough for any teacher or classmate to remember her and report her missing in 1941. This would also explain why there is no record of Lavonia Stratford in the 1921 census; she was 7 by this time, on the road and invisible to the authorities. Note that whenever in the Worcester Archives we have references to locals seeing gypsy camps, like that of the 'Smiths' at the Nimmings, children are never mentioned. The travellers kept them hidden in case the authorities came nosing around, asking too many questions. By 1931, Lavonia may still have been living with her people. She was 17 by now and would have left school, had she attended with any kind of regularity, three years earlier. Unfortunately, the figures for the 1931 census were destroyed by fire, so even when they become due in another eight years from now, we will still have no idea if she was registered then or not.

Was it now that she gave birth? Professor Webster believed that the woman in the wych elm had produced at least one child, but of course he could not be certain when. In view of what happened later, I believe that Lavonia left this baby with her tribe to be raised by them. There is no record of a birth to anyone called Lavonia Stratford, but that should not surprise us, given the 'outsider' status of the travelling community. Neither, more ominously, is there any record of her death.

Four years later, she was arrested for prostitution in London. Once again, was the lure of the bright lights too much to resist? We know that Marthe Watts, a French prostitute who got to London in 1937, described the grim conditions of the brothels she had worked in, in France and Spain, and they were regulated by the government! J.B. Sandbach, a Metropolitan magistrate, was talking about French prostitutes, but the lifestyle for many would have been the same and Lavonia had been arrested with a troupe of French girls. 'Instead of lying in bed and at about midnight,' wrote Sandbach, 'going out for a drink before having a meal in a café, they get up early, do their own shopping and cook at home. This is not only healthier but a cheaper mode of life.'[4]

If Lavonia moved to London in her late teens, she might have caught the disapproving eye of Bob Fabian:

> Not one of them had any more morals than a hen. What makes a girl become a prostitute? I think I can tell you – it is sheer laziness and vanity ... Her love gestures are as automatic and insincere as the wide smile on the face of a tired chorus-girl. A whore is a bad apple. There is a big brown bruise on her soul, of self-indulgence and selfishness. I do not think that there exists in London any such person as an honest prostitute. They taint any flesh they touch.

This is tough reading but it is the honest opinion of an old-school copper who has seen too much of what organized vice does to people – and what it would do to Bella. How Lavonia met Fernand Modena and how she became part of his stable is unknown, but trying to go it alone in a strange city were danger lurked on every corner was never really an option. The girls who haunted Piccadilly, Curzon Street, Half Moon Street in Mayfair, or Gerard Street, Old Compton Street and Lisle Street in Soho had their designated pitches – and God help the wide-eyed, snaggle-toothed Romany girl who tried to muscle in. Lavonia's relationship with Modena, potentially lethal as it may have been, was symbiotic – they needed each other.

But that relationship came to an abrupt end in November 1935 and Lavonia was suddenly on her own. If Lavonia wanted to maintain her lifestyle – and it was certainly more lucrative than selling pegs from a painted wagon – that meant one thing in 1937; the Messinas.

Despite the title of Dick Kirby's excellent book *Mayfair Mafia* (Pen and Sword, 2019), the Messina family were not actually Mafia. In fact, they left their native Sicily to avoid that family obsessed gangsterhood, drifting to Malta in 1896 and arriving in London by 1934. As Kirby says, 'the Messinas were unable to lie straight in bed' and the culture of corruption around them spread to witnesses, lawyers and of course the girls they ran. Because the Messinas were, above all, pimps. Most of them were pretty handy with a razor, but open violence was not their stock in trade – they left that to the racecourse gangs like the Sabinis, Billy Hill and Jack 'Spot' Comer – they probably stayed wide of Fernand Modena in Soho because the place was already spoken for and moved their girls out to the west, Mayfair, Hyde Park, Holland Park and Bayswater.

The father was Giuseppe, a peasant with some carpentry skills. He and his wife produced five sons who were chips off the old block and a daughter, the white sheep of the family who may have embarrassed the others. The oldest son was Salvatore, who married a French prostitute with an Italian name, Maria Burratti. He adopted the name Arthur Evans, to blend in better with London society. If the *real* Arthur Evans, the famous archaeologist, had found out about this, he would have been *very* annoyed! Next came Alfredo in 1901, who married Andrée Astier, known as Colette, who had well over a dozen convictions for prostitution in her first year in the country. Alfredo called himself Alfred Martin.

After him, in 1908, came Eugenio, who did a little gun-running and drug smuggling on the side. Probably a genuine psychopath, he styled himself Edward Marshall. Two years later, Attilio arrived, the only member of the family whose photograph I can find, taken as a young man. He is darkly handsome, with the tall Homburg and sharp suit fashionable among inter-war gangsters. Canelo was the youngest boy, born a year after Lavonia in 1915. He married prostitute Ida Pomirou from France and used the moniker Charles Maitland. Margherita, the youngest, was the white sheep.

Giuseppe's wife, Maltese-born Virginia, could claim British citizenship by virtue of her place of birth and that would come in handy later. In the meantime, the Messinas with their growing brood moved to Egypt in 1904 and set up a number of brothels, made legal there in that year. They trafficked girls as young as four. With the International Civil Police Organization (later Interpol) breathing down their necks, the Messinas were kicked out of Egypt in 1932 and obtained British passports for the entire family by leaning on and/or bribing customs officials.

The law relating to prostitution was chaotic. Keeping a 'disorderly house' (brothel) had been illegal since 1751, but the last legislation relating to prostitution dated from 1912; even the fine of £2 for soliciting had been set in 1839 and had not changed by the time Lavonia paid hers. It was not even an offence to procure a woman for sex if she was already a working girl. The definition of a brothel was equally confusing; only if two or more women lived under the same roof could the police act – a girl on her own got away with it. The penalty for keeping a brothel, however, was steeper – £100 or a three-month prison sentence for a first offence; £250 or six months for a second. Even these sums, however, did not deter the Messinas, whose large team of girls earned them thousands in three years, especially when the war started and the Americans arrived. 'We Messinas,' Attilio bragged, 'are more powerful than the British government. We do as we like in England.'

Violence between pimps was commonplace, with the girls getting in the way. Charles Balalla was shot dead in London in 1926 by 'Mad Emile' Berthier. Casimir Micheletti, known as 'The Assassin' had his club and dancing school firebombed three years later.

The Messinas tended to avoid trouble when they could, claiming to be diamond merchants and operating in the areas from Park Lane through Oxford Street to Regent Street. Under their aegis came hotels with high reputations in polite society – the Ritz, Claridge's and the Berkeley. Robert Fabian knew the clubs well, on first-name terms (although he was always 'Mr Fabian') with doormen, cab-drivers, maitres d' and hoteliers themselves. He made a point of introducing himself to new girls on his patch. 'This is Ursula,' one barman did the honours in a club in Frith Street. 'She's a Polack. Ursula, this is Mr Fabian, Chief of the Manor – you don't give him any nonsense and he'll treat you fair.'

Kate Meyrick was the formidable hostess of the 43 Club in Gerrard Street, as used to handling peers of the realm as the lowlife who occasionally tried to gatecrash her premises. The Big Apple was an up-and-coming black venue that would burgeon in the 1950s, with jazz and the cloying scent of 'reefers' (marijuana). Hell was run by Geoffrey Daybell and in Wardour Street was the Shim-Sham Club. The laws against the sale of liquor, almost as silly as the Volstead Act which brought prohibition to America, cramped the style of these clubs and barmen had to be careful with men like Fabian on the prowl. The Studio in Knightsbridge, the Esquire in Piccadilly, the Unity in Jermyn Street and the Strangers in St James, the Messinas and their girls were probably known in all of them.

Some of the Messinas' girls merely had the job of getting themselves invited into a club where the 'house' would fleece the punters accordingly. There were 295 registered clubs within a mile of the Eros statue in Piccadilly Circus and fifteen unregistered that the police knew about – 'a total' computes Fabian, 'of 310 places, ablaze with lights and activity into London's dawn, where music, dancing, drinks and companions await the well-filled wallet.' That wallet got there by courtesy of Messinas' girls, who 'for £2 would cuddle a baboon'.

It was, in the end, all about money for girls like Lavonia Stratford; money to survive. Rates varied, especially when the 'Mug' (punter) wanted a special service, perhaps involving bondage or what today we might call 'cosplay'; but the usual in the late 1930s and early 1940s was £5 a session. The session was brief – the ten-minute rule that the Messinas insisted on became widespread and was reduced still further for the benefit of the Americans after 1942 (who also paid double or triple for the privilege). On average, girls like Lavonia earned £4 an hour, far above the rate of a shop girl or factory worker. Remember, too, that employment like factory work or farming only came on the market as a result of the war itself, because of the sudden shortage of manpower. Before that, girls were employed as shop assistants, secretaries, telephonists and maids. If Lavonia's education was as patchy as I believe it was, at least some of that work would have been beyond her.

We next come across Lavonia, still listed as Lavinia Stratford, in 1939. By now she was 25, still using her maiden name, so had not officially married. And she was still in London; her address is given as 120 Princess Court, Bayswater. This was a fashionable apartment block built eight years earlier, in the art deco style that the Thirties loved. Tellingly, she is listed as having 'private means'. This could be that she had the private income of a respectable lady, a legacy from the family so that 'trade' and similar inconveniences would not bother her. Or it could mean that her income was literally a private matter, the cash she received from the 'Mugs', 80 per cent of which she had to give to her 'protectors', the Messinas. Bayswater in those days was not the upmarket part of London it is today. 'Ladies of the night' with their faux furs, cheap jewellery (perhaps even wedding rings) and Gibson shoes lived in the Bayswater Road.

The reason that Lavonia Stratford is listed at all in 1939 is that by now there was a war on. The government realized that with such chaotic upheaval going on, there could not be a conventional census in 1941, so they opted for a register two years earlier instead.

As it happened, Lavonia Stratford would not have appeared on a 1941 census even if it had gone ahead.

Because Lavonia Stratford would be dead.

Chapter 19

The Last Days of Bella

At the time, the press attributed the murder of three prostitutes in London between August 1935 and May of the following year to a single killer, the 'Soho strangler'. No one had forgotten the media frenzy that surrounded the Whitechapel murders of 1888, when newspaper sales had rocketed out of all proportion. There were certainly similarities in the 1930s cases – all the victims were prostitutes, with accompanying 'street' names. Paulette Estelle was 'French Marie'; Josephine Martin was 'French Fifi'; Constance Hinds was 'Dutch Leah'. And the MO was similar too – strangulation, even if hands, a silk scarf, a silk handkerchief and piano wire were the actual weapons involved.

'Dutch Leah', also known as 'Stilts' because of her love of high heels, was found dead in bed by her husband, Stanley King, on 9 May 1936. She had been garrotted with wire and her head smashed in, probably by an iron. She was lying with her clothes disarranged, as though ready for sex. But pathology determined that no sex had taken place, any more than it had for Bella, whose slip was not torn, whose knickers were complete.

In the case of 'French Fifi', the Russian girl was found in her flat in Archer Street, Piccadilly by her maid, the elegantly named Felicité Plaisant. Like 'Leah', 'Fifi' was heavily in debt. She was found to owe 40 guineas to one person (over £3,000 today), £20 to someone else. But the fact that she had a maid spoke volumes. These women were not domestics in the conventional sense; they worked for pimps and reported on the girls to ensure that they were not keeping their earnings dark. I believe that Bella would have had one too, hovering around the Princess Court address. The maid would have noticed everything – the regulars who liked the girl with the Birmingham Roma accent and the funny teeth that made her look cute and fresh-faced as opposed to the usual Soho drabs. Mary McLeod, a prostitute murdered in Stepney in 1952 was 50, but years of alcoholism made her look much older; and without wishing to be unkind to the dead, was far from an oil painting. Bella's maid would have seen the 'one-offs' come and go, men given the slang term 'Steamers'. Robert Fabian knew these men too. As head of the Met's Vice Squad, he met many of them, caught literally with their trousers down in raids all over the West End. 'The great majority,' Fabian wrote, 'are soft-hearted men. Nine out of ten ... are looking for romance. They have a few drinks, and wander out into the streets, hoping to discover under some lamp post a young creature who has been driven by hunger or despair into proffering her body.'

Stefan Slater, a professional criminal psychologist writing many years after the hard-bitten London copper, comes to much the same conclusion. The average prostitute (although he concedes that there is really no such thing) hails 'from a poor background', a background like that of a gypsy girl, living hand to mouth in a community regarded as outcasts by the rest of society. 'She is probably in her mid-to-late twenties' – Bella was 26 or 27. She 'has a criminal record'. Bella/Lavonia did; she was arrested for soliciting along with her French oppos and Fernand Modena.

And her maid would have reported it all to the next Fernand Modena, the next pimp, the lowest of the low who offered his girls 'protection' at a price and took a huge cut of their income. Bob Fabian said there were two 'highly experienced' institutions scouring the London streets looking for likely lasses. One was the Met itself, especially the 'Zombies', the women police officers who drove the 'Children's Waggon' that parked outside a different central park every night. The other group was made up of the pimps, the 'Johnsons', who picked up girls lost, on the run, looking for romance and adventure just as their future 'Steamers' were. Lavonia Stratford had been one of these at some time in the early to mid-1930s. Her circumstances after 1935 cut her adrift again. And the *only* organized people-trafficking gang in London then were the newly arrived Messinas. She was hired – still a fresh-looking country girl. Perhaps she did use the name Bella, continuing the exotic-sounding, chic ambience of the French connection. And if she was now working for the Italians, who was to know?

But the rates had gone up. While she probably paid Fernand half her wages, she had to pay the Messinas 80 per cent. They secured the flat for her in Princess Court and they collected the money she earned on a regular basis. Fifteen years after Bella died and when the power of the

Messinas was broken, it was still going on. Conservative MP Arthur Baxter wrote in 1956:

> I have some friends living in Bayswater, just off Hyde Park and they tell me that practically every night – and I have seen it myself – up comes a car with a couple of men who take money from the prostitutes in that area ... These women are drawn up like a guard of honour – or dishonour – three yards apart. We love London, but its streets are the most disgraceful in the world.[1]

What happened in the case of Lavonia? I believe that her particular pimp was Eugenio Messina, known as Gino, who styled himself Edward Marshall. The last 'client' seen in the company of 'Dutch Leah' was described as 'tall, slim, clean shaven, long hair, slouching gait, foreign'. Was that Gino too? Was 'Dutch Lena' one of his girls and was she short-changing him, as I believe Bella was? Fabian knew these pimps, the riff-raff the Victorians had called 'bullies' for a good reason. A 'pimp's only pride,' Fabian wrote, 'is in his ability to intimidate a woman. He will shred her face unforgettably. A slender phial of acid dropped inside her clothing and then shattered with a blow from his fist. Or he can set fire to her hair ...'

Or he can take out her teeth one by one. *That* is why a tooth had been extracted from Bella within a year before she died. *That* was why no dentist could be found who had done the work. The travelling community, especially in the days before a national health service, never went within a country mile of a dentist's surgery. Bella was keeping money back; her maid had a quiet word in Gino's ear and Gino went to work on her, taking out a tooth this time, as a warning. But next time ...

She was terrified. Caught out in a lie, her pimp had worked her over already. Back in the Hagley area were her people and probably her child. She ran. She caught the next train to Birmingham, fighting her way through the crowded platform, jostling in the corridor with servicemen with kitbags and gas masks. She would have been carrying one too and an identity card; you could not be too careful.

If she caught the GWR's train from Paddington, she would have got off at Birmingham Snow Hill, and made her way on the stopping service to Worcester to Hagley, into the country, passing through Halesowen and Bromsgrove, past the buildings where the haunting question would appear about her three years later – 'Who put Bella in the wych elm?' She found her people, perhaps on the Nimmings, but more probably elsewhere and she told them she was on the run. Perhaps she found her child again and cuddled him or her on the steps of a Vardo wagon in some country clearing as the night sky glowed red with the bombing raids over Birmingham. She ditched her clothes. She gave away the smart, fashionable 'uniform' of the London prostitute and took whatever people gave her in return; a shapeless slip made from a coat lining, an old khaki skirt stitched together in panels. Even her frilly lace panties went, exchanged for a plain blue pair, like respectable women wore. Her top was stitched together with old wool that a gypsy woman had knitted together by the firelight. She had got rid of her bra – travellers did not use them. And anything else that betrayed her past vanished too – her handbag, her identity card, even the gas mask. She tried to lose herself again in the anonymity of the travelling people, people whose names were unknown but who called themselves 'Smith' and kept their heads down.

Outside that tight-knit community, which had probably not seen her for ten years, no one knew who she was. The name Lavonia, the possible nickname Bella – it meant nothing to anybody. She was safe here.

Perhaps she lived like this for days or weeks; it cannot have been longer. It was the summer of 1941 and the papers she never read carried brief, cryptic stories about the arrival of a mysterious German airman calling himself Hauptman Horn. But all that was eclipsed by news from the east – Hitler had turned on his former ally Stalin and had invaded Russia. So it was true – the man *was* mad, after all.

Then, Gino found her. It was probably not difficult. She may have told him months before about her people, the great settlement of Black Patch which was still a vibrant folk memory for her. And Gino was not a stupid man. He sniffed out likely girls in London, grooming them for work. He knew what Lavonia looked like and where her haunts were. He may have driven from hotel to hotel for a couple of days, eking out his petrol allowance so that no one asked too many questions. He signed himself in as Edward Marshall and had a ready identity card to match. He had a story ready too – explaining what he was doing in the Midlands in the first place, should any nosy copper ask awkward questions.

When he found her, why did she go with him? Why not scream, run, bring her menfolk to her defence? We have no idea. Perhaps she had no menfolk to hand. If her father was dead or had never been on the scene, if she had no brothers, that would have left her isolated. And then there was Gino. Yes, she was afraid of him. And, yes, he had hurt her. But he could be charming, kind even and they may have had a certain rapport. He was in his mid-thirties, perhaps mercurial, perhaps dazzling; the Heathcliff to his Cathy.

She kissed her child, promising to come back soon. Yes, Gino would have said, that would be fine, but he needed her in London. Then they drove away, south perhaps, towards the capital, making for the bright lights. Except that they never got there. Somewhere along Hagley Wood Lane, he stopped the car. She was not afraid. She knew this road well, had told him all about the wood she had known as a child, where she had picked bluebells and danced around that funny old tree, the one she could just make out from the road, the dying one with its curious hollow trunk.

He may have suggested they have one last look at it, one last glimpsed memory of childhood before going back to the Blitz and the Steamers, the life she hated but which made money. Lavonia never quite got to the tree because Gino stopped her. He grabbed her from behind, pulling her striped cardigan up over her face and ramming it into her mouth, pressing her nostrils closed with her hand. There was a razor in his pocket, and he would fall back on its use if he had to. It was dark now, the car silent on the road with its headlights off. She struggled because she could not scream, the shoes she could not bear to be parted from scraping in the undergrowth as her breath ran out and her heaving lungs gave up. He felt her slump in his iron grip and let her fall. He checked her pulse. Nothing.

And he looked around him. Night in the middle of nowhere. He had known the slums of Cairo and every dark corner of Fabian's London. But here, he was all but lost and in wartime, a car in darkness caused suspicion. He would find a hotel, sign in as Edward Marshall and decide what to do in the morning.

Where did he stay? The Lyttleton Arms perhaps or the Gypsy's Tent, if either of them took paying guests at the time. Travellers in wartime were not as common as they had been before 1939, but a man with nerve and a plausible story could get away with it. Still, the body bothered him. He had left it lying in the open, the woman he had had to shut up. Nobody walked away from Gino Messina, trying to take his money. Nobody. Perhaps the finding of her body would leave the necessary message to other girls in his stable, as it might have done already in the case of 'Dutch Leah'. But that had been a risk and he had a feeling he had been seen with her in the hour or two before he killed her. What if someone had seen him with Lavonia? What if one of the gypsies talked? That was not likely; the travelling people kept to themselves and they did not like policemen any more than Gino did. No, this body would have to be hidden and he knew just the place.

He had seen corpses before and had created a couple too, but even so, he had to steel himself to the task in hand. He did not know that Constable Jack Pound walked his beat along Hagley Wood Lane, that Sergeant Richard Skerratt might have been watching him from the Clent Hills. He did not know that the Home Guard patrolled the area regularly and that terrified people from Birmingham drove out this far to find shelter from the bombs. Still less did he know that gypsies camped at the Nimmings, yards from where he had left Lavonia and that courting couples might trip over the body. So the next day, he went back.

Mechanically, he checked the corpse. The stiffness of rigor mortis had all but gone. She was not carrying a handbag, a purse or a wallet. She had no identification on her at all. He hauled her up and felt his heart thump. Some animal had ripped off her right hand and he could not see it anywhere. A badger? A fox? He knew nothing about English woodlands, but he knew exactly where to hide the evidence. The old wych elm that Lavonia had talked about, with its gnarled bark and writhing roots, its branches stretching to the sky like the rays of the sun. She was only 5 feet tall and not heavy, for all her dead weight, to a man like him. He lifted her, balanced her awkwardly on the opening of the trunk and let her fall, her own weight pulling her down, her knees buckling as her feet hit the internal base of the trunk. Her head lolled back and she looked at him through sightless eyes, her arms thrust upwards, wedged in the wych elm, like a parachutist suddenly cut from her harness and her silk.

Gino looked around. There was no sign she had ever been there. Nor had he. He wandered back through the bracken to his car. Then, he was gone.

Is this – or something like it – what happened to Bella? Was she really Lavonia Stratford, the little gypsy girl who had got in with the wrong crowd and had she paid the ultimate price? I cannot prove it; not any of it. The men who could, the men who had that job back in 1943, the police and the pathologists, signally failed her. There are reasons why and, with the passage of time perhaps we should be tolerant.

In 1988, Bob Hoskins, himself of Romany descent, made a film called *The Raggedy Rawney*. Rawney is often spelt Rani, Roma for woman. Bella was most assuredly a ragged woman as she was found in the wych elm. But that is not how she started out. She was a flesh and blood human being, like the rest of us. And she deserved an altogether better end.

Bibliography

BEGG, Paul, BENNETT, John, *Jack the Ripper CSI: Whitechapel*, Andre Deutsch, 2012
BEGG, Paul, FIDO, Martin, SKINNER, Keith, *The Complete Jack the Ripper A to Z*, John Blake, 2010
CALDER, Angus, *The People's War*, Pimlico, 1969
CAVE BROWN, Anthony, *Bodyguard of Lies*, Star, 1977
CAVE BROWN, Anthony, *The Secret Servant*, Sphere Books, 1988
COLEY, Joyce, *Bella: An Unsolved Murder*, History into Print, 2007
FABIAN, Robert, *Fabian of the Yard*, Heirloom Library, 1955
FABIAN, Robert, *London After Dark*, Naldrett Press, 1954
FLEMING, Peter, *Invasion 1940*, Rupert Hart-Davis, 1957
Folklore, Myths and Legends of Britain, Readers Digest, 1973
GARDINER, Juliet, *'Over Here': the GIs in Wartime Britain*, Collis and Brown, 1992
GOODALL, Felicity, *Voices from the Home Front*, David and Charles, 2008
GREEN, Miranda J., *The World of the Druids*, Thames and Hudson, 1997
GRESSY, David, *Gypsies in English History*, OUP, 2020
HARRIS, John and TROW, M.J., *Hess: the British Conspiracy*, Andre Deutsch, 1999
HATHERILL, George, *A Detective's Story*, Andre Deutsch, 1971
HAYWARD, James, *Myths and Legends of the Second World War*, Sutton, 2003
HIGGINS, Robert, *In the Name of the Law*, John Long, 1958
HILL, Douglas et al, *Witchcraft, Magic and the Supernatural*, Octopus, 1974
KENNEDY, Ludovic, *Thirty-Six Murders and Two Immoral Earnings*, Profile Books, 2002
KONDRATIEV, Alexei, *Celtic Rituals*, New Celtic Publishing, 1998
LEFEBURE, Molly, *Murder on the Home Front*, Grafton, 1990

LEFEBURE, Molly, *Murder With a Difference*, William Heinemann, 1958
LINNANE, Fergus, *London's Underground*, Robson Books, 2004
MASTERMAN, J.C., *The Double Cross System*, Yale University Press, 1972
McCORMICK, Donald, *Murder By Witchcraft*, John Long, 1968
McFARLANE, Alan, *Witchcraft in Tudor and Stuart England*, Routledge and Kegan Paul, 1970
MERRILL, Pete and WILKINSON, Caroline, *Bella in the Wych Elm: Bella's Facial Reconstruction*, APS Publications, 2020
Murder Casebook (issue 71), Marshall Cavendish, 1992
MURRAY, Dr Margaret, *My First Hundred Years*, William Kimber, 1963
MURRAY, Dr Margaret, *The Witch Cult in Western Europe*, Clarendon Press, 1921
NEWMAN, Paul, *Under the Shadow of Meon Hill*, Abraxas and DGR, 2009
PADFIELD, Peter, *Hess*, Cassell and Co, 1991
PICKNETT, Lynn, PRICE, Clive, PRIOR, Stephen, *Double Standards*, Time Warner, 2001
RANKIN, Nicholas, *Churchill's Wizards*, Faber and Faber, 2008
ROSS, Anne, *Pagan Celtic Britain*, Constable, 1992
SALGADO, Gamini, *The Elizabethan Underworld*, BCA, 1977
SMITHIES, Edward, *Crime in Wartime*, George Allen and Unwin, 1982
SUMMERS, Montague, *History of Witchcraft and Demonology*, Kegan Paul, 1926
THOMAS, Donald, *An Underworld at War*, John Murray, 2003
TROW, M.J., *War Crimes*, Pen and Sword, 2008
WEDECK, Harry E., *A Treasury of Witchcraft*, Garaway Books, 1961
WHEATLEY, Dennis, *The Devil and All His Works*, BCA, 1971
WILSON, Colin, *Murder in the 1940s*, Carroll and Graf, NY, 1993
WINDER, Robert, *Bloody Foreigners*, Abacus (Time Warner), 2004
ZIEGLER, Philip, *London at War*, BCA, 1995

Articles, journals and periodicals
Birmingham Gazette
Birmingham Post
Empire News
Evening Dispatch

Reynolds News
SLATER, Stefan, 'Pimps, Police and Filles de Joie: Foreign Prostitutes in London', *The London Journal*
Sunday Dispatch
Sunday Mercury
Wolverhampton Express and Star

Notes

Chapter 1
1. *Wolverhampton Express and Star* November 1953.
2. Lady Celia Congreve, *The Firewood Poem* 1930.
3. Joyce M. Coley, *Bella: An Unsolved Murder*, History into Print, 2007.

Chapter 3
1. Quoted in H.M. Howgrove-Graham, *The Metropolitan Police at War*, HMSO, 1947.
2. Molly Lefebure, *Murder on the Home Front*, Grafton 1990.
3. Robert Higgins, *In the Name of the Law*, 1958.
4. John Du Rose, *Murder Was My Business*, W.H. Allen, 1971.
5. Iain Anderson, *The Great Detective*, Frederick Muller, 1966.
6. Jack Henry, *What Price Crime?* Hutchinson, 1945.

Chapter 4
1. Robert Higgins, *In the Name of the Law* op.cit.
2. Keith Simpson, *Forty Years of Murder*, Granada 1978.
3. Professor Webster's report at Regional Conference, Birmingham, 3 May 1943.
4. All quotations in this section are from Webster's report of 23 April 1943.
5. National Crime Police Report May 1943.
6. Caroline Wilkinson, *Bella in the Wych Elm; Bella's Facial Reconstruction*, Merrill and Wilkinson 2020.

Chapter 5
1. Keith Simpson, *Forty Years of Murder*, 1978.
2. All quotations in this section are from the Worcester CID files, Worcester Record Office.

3. Quoted in Coley 2007.
4. Donald McCormick, *Murder By Witchcraft* John Long, 1968.

Chapter 6

1. Most Ripper writers make the victim count five after the 'canonical five' listed by Melville McNaghten, Assistant Commissioner CID at Scotland Yard at the time. This was an assumption on his part and I believe he was wrong. See M.J. Trow, *Quest For a Killer*, Pen and Sword, 2009.

Chapter 10

1. Worcester Archive.
2. Haigh believed that without physical remains, a charge of murder could not be bought. His attempts to dissolve Olive Durand-Deacon in a vat of acid failed, however, and he was hanged for her murder.

Chapter 11

1. Jan-Willem van den Braak, *Hitler's Spy Against Churchill*, Pen & Sword, 2022.

Chapter 12

1. McCormick p. 139.
2. Ibid p. 140.

Chapter 13

1. Coley p. 16.
2. Ibid.
3. Cited in Coley p. 17.
4. Worcester Archive.

Chapter 14

1. Unless otherwise specified, quotations in this chapter are from McCormick 1968.

Chapter 15

1. Murder Casebook Vol 71 1991.
2. Unless otherwise specified, quotations in this chapter come from McCormick 1968.

3. Simon Askwith, *The Independent*, quoted in Newman p. 104.
4. Ibid.

Chapter 16

1. Alleged because the Catholic Church has now formally acquitted de Rais, Marshal of France, of any wrongdoing. He was a victim of the politics of his day.

Chapter 17

1. All quotations in this chapter are from the West Mercia Police Case Closure Report unless otherwise stated.

Chapter 18

1. Askwith, quoted in Paul Newman, *Under the Shadow of Meon Hill*, p. 104.
2. All quotes, unless otherwise stated, are from Robert Fabian, *London After Dark*.
3. William Booth, *In Darkest England or the Way Out* (1891).
4. Quoted in Slater p. 63.

Chapter 19

1. Quoted in Dick Kirby, *Mayfair Mafia*.

Index

Aktion Hess, see Hess, Rudolf
Anna of Claverley, *see* Mossop, Una
Armistead, Alfred 127-9

Bauerle, Clara 113-16, 118-19, 124-7, 151, 161
Bella viii, ix-x, 50, 52-6, 58, 60-2, 65, 67, 72-7, 82-5, 91, 94-7, 99, 101-105, 111-12, 115, 119, 121-4, 126, 128-33, 135-6, 138-9, 141-2, 144, 146, 149-50, 152-4, 157-63, 165-6, 168-9, 172-4, 176, 180-2, 185-6
  Beech, Bella 63, 164
  Luer, Bella 63, 66-7, 164
  Tonks, Bella 62-3, 164
  Wall writing viii, 48-60, 183
Birmingham Gazette 51-2, 55, 129
Birmingham 2, 8, 12-13, 15, 25, 27, 32, 39, 41-4, 49-53, 55, 57, 63, 66, 71, 75, 80-2, 104, 113-15, 117-18, 124-6, 146, 152, 158, 162, 172, 174, 180, 182-3, 185
Black Country Bugle 43-4, 126
Black Patch Park 82, 174, 183

Boffey, Raymond 50, 141
Boyden, Zita 128-9
Bradley, Mrs 15, 45
Burns, Rev Robert 13, 77
Byford-Jones, Wilfred 1-2, 4, 19, 86-7, 89, 92-3, 95, 128, 131-3, 135, 142, 160, 163

Clent 3, 18-19, 46, 53, 63, 83, 100, 120, 185
Cogzell (shoemaker) 43-4, 122, 163
Coventry 7, 88, 90-1, 117, 131
Crowley, Aleister ix, 110, 145, 149
Curley, Dinah 65-6, 164

Deacon, Richard, *see* McCormick, Donald
Douglas-Osborne, PC Eric 19, 123-5
Dronkers, Clara, *see* Bauerle, Clara
Dronkers, Johannes 111-12

Elwell, George 129-31, 160, 164

Fabian, DCI Robert 137-8, 145, 148, 169-72, 175, 178, 181-2, 184
Farmer, Robert 3-4, 10, 13

194 The Hagley Wood Murder

Fifth Column 45, 57, 125-6
Frack (Groebli, Werner) 91, 131
Frick (Mauch, Hans) 91, 131

Gardner, Gerald ix, 145, 150
Gibson, Billy 132, 164

Hagley Hall 2, 5-6, 64, 142
Hagley Wood vii, viii, 2-3, 5-6,
  8, 17, 19-20, 22, 25-7, 30,
  33-5, 45-6, 49, 51-7, 64, 67,
  71, 73-4, 82-4, 92, 97, 99,
  105, 110, 113, 116, 120-2,
  124, 126, 130-3, 135-6, 139,
  141-2, 145, 153-4, 158-9,
  162, 166, 169, 184-5
Hagley 2-3, 12-15, 18-19, 32,
  45-8, 53, 61-4, 73, 75-7, 80,
  82, 84, 108, 110, 125, 133,
  135, 139-41, 153, 159, 169,
  173-4, 182
Halesowen 2, 51-4, 82-3, 99, 118,
  120, 131-2, 142, 182
Hart, Robert 3-6, 10, 13, 18-9,
  26, 28, 40, 153, 166
Hess, Rudolf 98, 106-19, 151,
  160-1
Hodgetts, A.H. 77, 80-1, 85, 173

Inight, Supt Sidney 22, 41, 44,
  47, 83, 162, 166, 168

Jakobs, Josef 102, 118-19, 126
James I (VI) 5, 77, 135, 141
Jones, John 31-2, 55-6, 72, 141

Kassel, Max 170-1

Lambourn, PC Charles 16-19
Lee, Mary 65, 82, 164
Lehrer, Agent 112-15, 126, 160
Lyttleton Arms 2, 89-90, 184

McCormick, Donald ix, 39-40,
  45-7, 61, 67, 84, 86, 94,
  104, 106, 110-18, 120,
  123-4, 126-7, 130, 132,
  140-41, 145-6, 150-2, 154-62
Messina Family 176-82
Modena, Fernand 172-4,
  176, 181
Mossop, Jack 88-92, 123, 127,
  131, 164-5
Mossop, Una 88, 110, 127, 131-2,
  135, 142, 154, 159-60, 163-4
Murray, Dr Margaret 95, 113-46,
  149, 159-60

Operation Lena 100, 102-105,
  112-13, 116, 121

Payne, Frederick 3, 10, 13, 153
Pierrepoint, Albert 60, 71-2,
  101-103, 112, 128
Pound, PC Arthur 18-19, 26, 46,
  83, 156, 175, 185

Quaestor, *see* Byford-Jones,
  Wilfred

Rathgeb, Franz 114-16, 126

Skerratt, Sgt Richard 18-19, 53, 83, 185
Stourbridge viii, 3, 39, 50, 63-4, 74, 91, 113, 116, 118, 121, 124-7, 164
Stratford, Lavonia 172-9, 181-5
Summers, Montague 137-8, 145

Van Raalt, Marius 92, 95
Van Raalte, Laura 91-2, 98
Van Ralt 88-92, 94-5, 97, 100, 110, 164-5

Walton, Charles 45, 128, 139, 147-54, 158-61

Webster, Professor James x, 19, 23, 25-33, 38-41, 43-5, 54-5, 63, 72-3, 84, 104, 115, 119, 122, 127, 130-2, 135, 141, 148, 158, 162-3, 165-6, 173-5
Wilkinson, Professor Caroline 26-7, 32-3, 39, 166, 173
Willetts, Thomas 3, 16, 18-19, 53
Williams, DI Thomas 22, 39, 41-2, 44, 50-5, 83, 86-8, 90, 92, 94, 110-11, 131-2, 141, 162
Wolfe, Joan 35-8, 41, 45, 58, 61-2, 83, 136
Wolverhampton Express and Star 1, 4, 19, 54-5, 77, 86, 93-4, 131, 133